"Here is a fulsome celebration of Paul's central conviction that in Christ, God's love is all in all. Wide-ranging and accessible, written with scholars, pastors, and laypeople in mind, Gupta's study insistently reminds us that Paul was not a dry logician but a passionate emissary of the in-breaking love of God in every aspect of human life. This is a welcome gift indeed!"

—**Susan Eastman,** Duke Divinity School

"Love is an emotional knot. Nijay Gupta disentangles love by using Scripture and other resources to tease out its beautiful strands. When we discover the quality of love that is at the heart of the gospel, not only is Paul's theology clarified, but our affections are changed. Disciples who yearn for a greater love for God and neighbor will rejoice over *The Affections of Christ Jesus*."

—**Matthew W. Bates,** Northern Seminary

"Inviting readers to consider an idea that may have suffered from lack of attention due to its pervasiveness, Gupta provides a revitalizing analysis of love. Situating Paul in a variety of conversations modern and ancient, from the testament Old and New, *The Affections of Christ Jesus* provides research and admonition for the scholar and lay reader alike. Anyone can do a word study, but Gupta acts as a wise guide through the verbal and historical data as well as the theological import of that data. *The Affections of Christ Jesus* manages to both brim with information and be an enjoyable read. I will be recommending this to students and parishioners for years to come."

—**Amy Peeler,** Wheaton College

"In this valuable volume, Nijay K. Gupta centers that which was central to Paul's life and features in his letters—the love of God revealed in Christ Jesus. This love, to be embraced by believers and extended to one another and outsiders through the empowering presence of the Holy Spirit, far from being a fleeting feeling or a second-hand emotion, is, this book contends, part and parcel to the Apostle's gospel and experience. Indeed, Gupta's timely work helps scholars and students of Paul alike to consider with care how the Apostle thought and taught that 'the greatest of these is love.'"

—**Todd D. Still,** Truett Theological Seminary, Baylor University

"Nijay Gupta is one of the premier Pauline scholars of our generation. In this book, he maps the theme of love, demonstrating how it lies at the heart of Paul's theology; it is the center of the gospel and the truest mark of the church. With verve and clarity, Gupta shows us how Paul's thinking is inspired by God's love for us in Christ, and urges Christians to remember that of all virtues, the greatest of these is love."

—**Michael F. Bird,** Ridley College

"First Corinthians 13 is often referred to as the apostle Paul's love chapter. Yet in this book, Nijay Gupta demonstrates that love is the *sine qua non* of Paul's gospel and permeates all of the apostle's correspondence. The book is both an invitation and a journey to see love as the core of Paul's theology, the center from which all of his theology flows."

—**Lisa Bowens,** Princeton Theological Seminary

"A very welcome summons to pay attention to the overwhelming presence of love language in Paul. Gupta makes a convincing case that love 'is at the bull's-eye center' of Paul's gospel and gives a sophisticated and impassioned description of Christocentric love. An important book."

—**Ann Jervis,** Wycliffe College, University of Toronto

THE AFFECTIONS OF
Christ Jesus

LOVE AT THE HEART OF PAUL'S THEOLOGY

NIJAY K. GUPTA

WILLIAM B. EERDMANS PUBLISHING COMPANY
GRAND RAPIDS, MICHIGAN

Wm. B. Eerdmans Publishing Co.
2006 44th Street SE, Grand Rapids, MI 49508
www.eerdmans.com

© 2025 Nijay K. Gupta
All rights reserved
Published 2025

Book design by Lydia Hall

Printed in the United States of America

31 30 29 28 27 26 25   1 2 3 4 5 6 7

ISBN 978-0-8028-7716-1

Library of Congress Cataloging-in-Publication Data

A catalog record for this book is available from the Library of Congress.

Contents

Foreword by Michael J. Gorman		vii
Preface		ix
List of Abbreviations		xvi
	Introduction	1
1.	Perspectives on Love	13
2.	Love in the Old Testament and Jewish Tradition	37
3.	The Greek Language of Love	56
4.	Love in the Jesus Tradition	74
5.	Paul's Conception of Love	96
6.	Love at the Heart of Paul's Gospel of God	112
7.	Love at the Heart of Paul's Religion	129
8.	Love at the Heart of the Christian Community	149
9.	Paul on Love of the Outsider	165
10.	Ephesians and Paul's Theology of Love	183
11.	Summary, Synthesis, and Implications	206
	Appendix: Early Christian References to Love of God, Love of Neighbor, or Both	217

CONTENTS

Bibliography	219
Index of Authors	233
Index of Subjects	235
Index of Scripture and Other Ancient Sources	236

Foreword

"Love" is a word that gets bandied about and filled with all kinds of content (though sometimes not very much content), not only in secular circles, but in Christian environs as well. I recently heard a baptized Christian quote Jesus as saying, "After all, love is love." And given the way 1 Corinthians 13 is read at some weddings that manifest little or no spiritual and theological depth, it is no wonder that non-Christians and Christians alike speak of love with little substance. Unfortunately, the situation is not always significantly better in discussions among theologically trained clergy and, still more unfortunately, among those who train them. In fact, in the study of Paul and the New Testament more broadly, love is sometimes surprisingly neglected.

In this excellent book, my good friend and colleague Nijay Gupta seeks to help remedy this set of problems with specific reference to the apostle Paul. This makes excellent sense for at least two main reasons. First of all, Paul is certainly one of the eminent theologians of love, someone whose letters—and not merely a single chapter of 1 Corinthians (even though it is theologically profound and aesthetically beautiful)—abound in this greatest of the theological virtues. Second, Nijay has already produced an insightful study of another of those virtues, *Paul and the Language of Faith*. (We can only hope that hope is on the horizon to complete the triad.)

Nijay brings to this book the same sorts of skills he brought to his book on faith and to many other published projects. To begin with, he has done extensive research in the ancient primary sources to place Paul within the several contexts to which the apostle is indebted: Old Testament and other Jewish traditions, Greco-Roman traditions, Jesus traditions, and early Christian tra-

FOREWORD

ditions. The initial chapters prepare us for what Paul inherits from these rich and variegated legacies, and for what he contributes with fresh insight.

Furthermore, in the following chapters, Nijay presents love not merely as a concept but as an embodied reality, beginning with God's love in Christ and continuing to Paul himself and to the Christian community, focusing on both the church's internal life and its external actions. The latter dimension of Christian community—love for outsiders in mission—is an especially neglected topic and thus particularly welcome.

Nijay rightly argues that for Paul love is not simply one topic, or virtue, among many. Rather, it *permeates* his writings and "is at the living heart of all of Paul's theology." In addition, love has associated virtues, such as grace and compassion, that are also found throughout his letters.

A word about the book's title. If "love" is a misunderstood word, then "affections" is even more so, not least because it is seldom used in theological parlance these days. Nijay uses the word because, in Paul's view, both divine and human love are matters of the heart as well as the will. Christian love is emotional—though not sentimental—as well as active.

Throughout the entire book, the discussions of Paul are historically and linguistically responsible, and theologically rich. They are also canonically attuned, with references to so-called disputed Pauline letters (including an entire chapter on Ephesians) and to other parts of Scripture. Moreover, Nijay is in conversation with other writers on love, both Christian (e.g., Augustine and C. S. Lewis) and non-Christian (e.g., bell hooks and Simon May). His style, a bit more conversational and self-revealing than that of many scholars, makes the book more accessible but not at all less scholarly.

Whether speaking of *agapē* in the singular or affections in the plural, Nijay Gupta has unveiled the loving heart of Paul's theology and spirituality, both for academics and for the church. I am confident that this book will do much good—and that it would meet with the apostle's approval.

Michael J. Gorman
St. Mary's Seminary & University

Preface

Typically, in a book like this, there is a long prolegomenon covering methodological matters regarding biblical studies in general and Pauline studies in particular. I felt that that would be tedious and distract from the focus on love language in antiquity, in Scripture, and specifically in Paul in the main chapters of this book. Those who have read my book *Paul and the Language of Faith* will know where I stand on these issues and would not need the same information repeated.[1] At the same time, many scholars and students will want to better understand some of the choices I make in terms of sources and influences on Paul. So I thought it best to include this preface, which briefly covers my approach to studying Paul and a bit about where I land on key debated issues. I don't defend these choices at length in the book, so note the works under "Further Reading" at the end of this preface to read my more thorough arguments. But some readers will want to dive right in, so feel free to skip this preface and begin with the introduction.

THE PAULINE CORPUS

What I received in my graduate education was that scholars divide up the New Testament Pauline corpus into two groups: the undisputed (authentic) epistles and the disputed epistles. That bifurcation can be misleading, because within the disputed-epistles category, scholars often operate with a spectrum of confidence on authenticity. For example, regarding 2 Thessalonians, the views are mixed, with many sympathetic toward authenticity, many more uncertain

---

1. Grand Rapids: Eerdmans, 2020.

PREFACE

about authorship, and a smaller group that is very confident Paul did not write 2 Thessalonians.[2] On the opposite end of the spectrum is 1 Timothy and Titus, texts that many scholars consider pseudonymous or inauthentic. For my dissertation monograph, *Worship That Makes Sense to Paul*, I examined Paul's use of cultic metaphors, but I was warned by my advisers and mentors not to include the disputed epistles, so I didn't.[3] I was content to toe the line as a young scholar and encouraged not to upset or question the consensus. Since then, though, now almost fifteen years past my doctoral defense, I have written extensively on Paul, including commentaries on disputed epistles like 2 Thessalonians and Colossians, so I have had a lot of time to ponder the authorship questions. I agree with scholars like N. T. Wright and Luke Timothy Johnson that it is past time to dispense with the comfortable categories of authentic vs. pseudonymous and disputed vs. undisputed.[4] These artificial lines make it difficult for scholars like me to look at the whole Pauline corpus in a thematic study.

I am convinced that of the factors that should have the most weight in deciding authenticity, we must focus on historical implausibility, that is, those features of a text that indicate the text was written in a later period. Other issues like vocabulary and tone can change from one context to the next and need not indicate a different author. And writing style and even theological variance could be explained by the influence of cowriters or the employment of a particular letter secretary. When we take these factors into consideration, it doesn't make sense to me to leave 2 Thessalonians, Colossians, and Ephesians out of the conversation on Paul's life, thought, and apostolic ministry. And it certainly doesn't make sense to me to fabricate a fictional scenario where a pseudepigrapher was making up people, events, and situations out of nothing.

Scot McKnight has made a strong case that we go too far to presume we have a pure (untainted, unadulterated) Paul in Galatians or 1 Corinthians to treat as a control sample against which we test other letters.[5] How exactly do

---

2. Paul Foster surveyed a large group of mostly British New Testament scholars and discussed his data in this helpful article: "Who Wrote 2 Thessalonians? A Fresh Look at an Old Problem," *Journal for the Study of the New Testament* 35 (2012): 150–75.

3. *Worship That Makes Sense to Paul*, BZNW (New York: de Gruyter, 2010).

4. N. T. Wright, *Paul and the Faithfulness of God* (Minneapolis: Fortress, 2016), 1:56–63; Luke Timothy Johnson, *Constructing Paul* (Grand Rapids: Eerdmans, 2020), 62–92.

5. See Scot McKnight, *Colossians*, NICNT (Grand Rapids: Eerdmans, 2018), 1–18.

Preface

we know these reflect the real Paul? We know Paul used collaborators in his writings, so a pristine Paul the writer does not exist in the texts we have. In this book, I have chosen to include in word studies and other topical compilations the whole of the Pauline corpus. Even if Paul did not write some of these letters (i.e., wasn't involved at all), I don't think that much is jeopardized in my analysis. Paul's love language and themes are consistent and complementary across all thirteen letters.

In terms of where I stand today in the Pauline corpus, I find myself experiencing a strong sense of suspicion about our tools and methods for labeling texts inauthentic or pseudonymous. With a text like Ephesians, for example, scholars may note seemingly new formulations of head-body language, or the presence of a household code, or unique emphasis on *plērōma* (fullness), but none of these things actually indicate pseudonymity, let alone forgery. If we add to that the common practice of using an amanuensis, outside influences on Paul's thinking and writing are reasonable, even expected. And we have to give Paul space, as a human, to have new ideas and to explore new metaphors.

As a practical element of writing this book, I immediately observed that love language (and related terms) occurs very frequently in Ephesians, a text perhaps deserving the label of the most love-saturated New Testament text. But if it is pseudonymous, does that exclude it from discussion and examination in the study of Paul? Or should it be filed away under "reception of Paul"? I sat down and translated Ephesians from Greek over the course of about two weeks during my research for this book. Again, my impression was that there is nothing peculiarly anti-Pauline in this letter, and perhaps oddly enough it can seem at times *too much* like Paul, repeating sound bites from Romans and Galatians in a way that is almost artificial. But rather than concluding that this was the work of a zealous (copycat) student, I was attracted to the notion that perhaps Paul was indeed in prison, that he genuinely wanted to write to the Ephesians (and perhaps other churches as well) to share his apostolic legacy and his deepest hopes for the church in the case of his demise. And for a man with his hands in shackles, it would make sense to enlist support from a friend or pupil in the crafting and writing of this, whether from Tychicus or some other colleague.

I am not fully confident that Paul wrote all of the thirteen letters under his name in the New Testament, but I am also not confident that Paul wrote *any* of those letters *by himself*! I think it is fair to raise questions and operate

PREFACE

at times with caution. But I think it is going too far to discount certain New Testament texts and exclude them from conversation. So I consider various possible scenarios in my chapter on Ephesians, and I hope that circumspection helps to foster an open mind as ongoing conversations about authorship and authenticity continue in Pauline studies.

THE INFLUENCE OF THE OLD TESTAMENT ON PAUL

You will notice in this book (and my related book *Paul and the Language of Faith*) that I begin with the importance and influence of the Jewish Scriptures and Jewish tradition on Jesus, Paul, and the earliest Christian writers in general. I don't think this needs a lot of explanation or justification, as Paul quotes from and alludes to the Old Testament so often. And I have tried to demonstrate in this book that Paul's use of love language, especially his preference for forms of *agapē*, owe a debt to choices made in the Septuagint, especially the Septuagint Pentateuch.

There is no doubt there are many cultural influences on Paul's thought and expression from the Greco-Roman world, but his Jewish heritage and identity played the most formative role in his theology. It would be hard to prove otherwise. Now, there is always the challenge of whether one focuses exclusively on the Septuagint or whether one factors in the Hebrew and Aramaic texts at Paul's disposal. Given we have only Greek texts that Paul wrote, I am inclined to think he commended the Septuagint to gentile churches when he passed on to them the Jewish tradition. As a Pharisee, Paul surely knew Hebrew and interacted with the Hebrew text. But I am persuaded that the Septuagint in particular played a major part in shaping Paul's theological vocabulary and even his theology and thought.

THE JESUS TRADITION

It is a much trickier matter to consider Paul's knowledge of and relationship to the so-called Jesus tradition. Obviously, when Paul was writing letters in the 50s and probably also in the 60s, he did not have copies of texts like Matthew's and Luke's Gospel. Certainly not in the forms we have them today. So it would be inaccurate to look for Paul's dependence on any of the four canonical gospels. But I have a hard time believing he had no access to some

xii

Preface

form of the Jesus tradition—that is, a repository of words and works of Jesus and the traditions about the disciples. Truth be told, Paul almost never quotes from the Jesus tradition, and he rarely appeals to the circumstances of Jesus prior to his crucifixion. But I am still left wondering, when Paul spent time with Cephas and James, what did they talk about? How could they have not discussed Jesus's unique birth; the many healings, exorcisms, and natural miracles he performed; his brilliant, though often perplexing, teachings; and the antics and mishaps of the disciples?

In this book, I wrestled with how much weight to put on the Jesus tradition in terms of influence on Paul. This happens to be one of the very few circumstances where we find strong verbal overlap, especially in the reference to love of neighbor. That doesn't mean that Paul was quoting Jesus (he might have said so explicitly if that was the case). It could simply be that Paul received this emphasis on love of neighbor from the liturgies and teachings of the most primitive traditions of Christianity. Be that as it may, it is more than coincidence that Paul quotes the neighbor-love command more than once.

On the issue of Paul and the Jesus tradition, I try to avoid two extremes. On the one hand, there are those trends in scholarship where it seems like Paul and Jesus are light-years apart and never the twain shall meet. I think that skepticism is missing out on clear thematic and even semantic links across the whole of the New Testament. On the other hand, there is the extreme of overreaching to find connections to and echoes of the Jesus tradition in Paul. But the reality is that Paul clearly wasn't that interested in talking about those thirty-some years of Jesus's earthly ministry. And it is not enough to say he taught about Jesus's ministry in person and just happened not to mention it in his letters. None of Paul's letters contain extensive quotations of Jesus or summaries of Jesus's ministry, so there is very little to hang theories on in that regard. Honestly, it is a mystery to me that most of the New Testament letters (even outside of Paul) make little explicit mention of Jesus's sayings, life, and ministry. But, again, the case can easily be made that certain key terms, themes, and ideas made a broader impact and persisted. I have tried to focus on comparison between the teachings of Jesus and the writings of Paul from that angle.[6]

6. See Nijay K. Gupta, "Jesus and Paul," in *A Beginner's Guide to New Testament Studies* (Grand Rapids: Baker, 2020), 40–56.

xiii

PREFACE

What Do We Call Christ's People?

In a book like this, it is always a challenge to decide what to call Christ's people. It can often seem like using the term "Christian" would be anachronistic, especially because Paul himself didn't use that specific language. At the same time, he didn't have a preferred title for Christians, so scholars often draw from sensible and historically accurate alternatives. A popular option is "believers," since sometimes Paul did use this. The risk here is that one might think all Paul cared about were beliefs, and that is not the case. So is it better to say, "Christ loyalists"? That is clunky and awkward. Then, you have options like "Jesus followers" or "Jesus people," but those aren't Pauline expressions. The most Pauline thing to do would be to say "saints" (as in "holy people"), but that terminology has all kinds of baggage in Western culture. So I struggled with the options. I decided to vary the language, sometimes using "believers" or "believers in Christ" and other times using "Christian." When I use the term "Christian," though, I should clarify that I am trying to reflect the Greek origins of the term *Christianos*, which means devotee or supporter of Christ, similar to the terms "Herodians" and "Nicolaitans."

Acknowledgments

I am grateful to Eerdmans (and in particular my editors Michael Thomson, now at Wipf & Stock, and Trevor Thompson) for supporting this book. And I am indebted to the peer reviewers for their insightful feedback that led to substantial changes, which I hope have strengthened my argumentation and have brought clarity to my writing. Special thanks to my students at Northern Seminary, who have participated in many fruitful conversations about Paul's theology and his emphasis on love. And particular gratitude to Mike Gorman, scholar, mentor, and friend, who has taught me the way of cruciform love.

Further Reading

On Paul's Use of the Old Testament (and in particular the Septuagint)

"The Old Testament in the New." Pages 157–74 in *A Beginner's Guide to New Testament Studies*. Grand Rapids: Baker, 2020.

Preface

Paul and the Language of Faith. Grand Rapids: Eerdmans, 2020.
Galatians. Story of God Bible Commentary. Grand Rapids: Zondervan, 2023.

On Paul and Pseudepigraphy/Authorship

"The Politics of Ephesians and the Empire: Accommodation or Resistance?" *Journal of Greco-Roman Christianity and Judaism* 7 (2010): 112–36.
"What Is in a Name? The Hermeneutics of Authorship-Analysis concerning Colossians." *Currents in Biblical Research* 11 (2012): 196–217.
Colossians. Smyth & Helwys Bible Commentary. Macon, GA: Smyth & Helwys, 2013.
1 and 2 Thessalonians. Critical Introductions to the New Testament. Grand Rapids, Zondervan, 2019.

Abbreviations

1QH	Hodayot
1QH[a]	Hodayot[a]
4Q266	Damascus Document[a]
4Q269	Damascus Document[d]
4Q270	Damascus Document[e]
4Q393	Communal Confession
4Q525	Beatitudes
4QD[a]	Damascus Document[a]
4QD[d]	Damascus Document[d]
4QD[e]	Damascus Document[e]
5Q12	Damascus Document[e]
5QD	Damascus Document[e]
11Q11	Apocryphal Psalms[a]
11Q19	Temple Scroll
11Q22	paleoUnidentified Text
AB	Anchor Bible
ACCS	Ancient Christian Commentary on Scripture
ANTC	Abingdon New Testament Commentaries
AOTC	Abingdon Old Testament Commentaries
b.	Babylonian Talmud
BECNT	Baker Exegetical Commentary on the New Testament
BZNW	Beihefte zur Zeitschrift für die neutestamentliche Wissenschaft
CD	Cairo Genizah copy of the Damascus Document
CIL	*Corpus Inscriptionum Latinarum*. Berlin, 1862–
ConBNT	Coniectanea Biblica: New Testament Series
CSC	Christian Standard Commentary

Abbreviations

IBC	Interpretation: A Bible Commentary for Teaching and Preaching
ICC	International Critical Commentary
JAJSup	Journal of Ancient Judaism Supplements
LNTS	The Library of New Testament Studies
LXX	Septuagint
m.	Mishnah
NA^{28}	*Novum Testamentum Graece*, Nestle-Aland, 28th ed.
NAC	New American Commentary
NASB	New American Standard Bible
NCBC	New Cambridge Bible Commentary
NCCS	New Covenant Commentary Series
NETS	New English Translation of the Septuagint
NIB	*The New Interpreter's Bible.* Edited by Leander E. Keck. 12 vols. Nashville: Abingdon, 1994–2004
NIBCNT	New International Biblical Commentary on the New Testament
NICNT	New International Commentary on the New Testament
NICOT	New International Commentary on the Old Testament
NIGTC	New International Greek Testament Commentary
NIVAC	NIV Application Commentary
NPNF	*A Select Library of Nicene and Post-Nicene Fathers of the Christian Church.* Edited by Philip Schaff and Henry Wace. 28 vols. in 2 series. 1886–1889. Repr., Peabody, MA: Hendrickson, 1994
NRSV	New Revised Standard Version
NTL	New Testament Library
NTTh	New Testament Theology
OTP	*Old Testament Pseudepigrapha.* Edited by James H. Charlesworth. 2 vols. New York: Doubleday, 1983, 1985
PCNT	Paideia Commentaries on the New Testament
SGBC	Story of God Bible Commentary
SNTSMS	Society for New Testament Studies Monograph Series
SP	Sacra Pagina
TLNT	*Theological Lexicon of the New Testament.* Ceslas Spicq. Translated and edited by James D. Ernest. 3 vols. Peabody, MA: Hendrickson, 1994
TNTC	Tyndale New Testament Commentaries
WBC	Word Biblical Commentary
WUNT	Wissenschaftliche Untersuchungen zum Neuen Testament

Introduction

When we ask whether someone is a good man, we are not asking
what he believes, or hopes, but what he loves.

—Augustine[1]

Augustine of Hippo is sometimes dubbed the "theologian of love." A thematic and hermeneutical emphasis on love (especially the Latin *caritas*) permeates his work. Augustine was not simply interested in the Christian ethic of love; rather, love explains the whole nature and the proper direction of human existence in the world.[2] Augustine defined virtue itself as "rightly ordered love."[3] He drew from Matthew 22:37–39 to reason that true Christian faith prioritizes love of God and love of neighbor, as Jesus himself taught. And sin, then, involves *disordered* love, fixating on creatures and things, rather than the Creator.

One gains insight into Augustine's understanding of ontology and anthropology by paying attention to his conception of what is often translated

---

1. *Enchiridion* 31.117.

2. Thomas Williams, "Hermeneutics and Reading Scripture," in *The Cambridge Companion to Augustine* (Cambridge: Cambridge University Press, 2014), 311–30, esp. 321–22; Matthew Levering, *Theology of Augustine* (Grand Rapids: Baker, 2013), 12–28. See Lewis Ayres, "Augustine on God as Love and Love as God," *Doctores Ecclesiae* 5 (1996): 470–87; Tarcisius J. van Bavel, "The Double Face of Love in Augustine," *Augustinian Studies* 17 (1986): 169–81.

3. *City of God* 15.22.

INTRODUCTION

"weight" (*gravitas*) in his writings, and especially in his *Confessions*. In reference to the *gravitas* of objects and substances, he was not talking about a scientific theory of physical heaviness or gravity but an existential resting place specific to each type of thing. He offers several examples: a rock that is dropped from the hand will fall downward to the place where it belongs, but fire naturally flicks upward, and it moves in the opposite direction as the stone: "They are urged by their own *gravitas*, they seek their own places" (9). He likewise comments that if water is poured over oil, the oil and water will strive to trade places to move to where they belong. Again, a substance or object out of place will gravitate toward its natural spot, its home, its place of rest. This is where Augustine makes his famous statement about human nature:

> My weight, is my love; thereby I am borne, whithersoever I am borne. We are inflamed, by Thy Gift we are kindled; and are carried upwards; we glow inwardly, and go forwards. We ascend Thy ways that be in our heart, and sing a song of decrees; we glow inwardly with Thy fire, with Thy good fire, and we go; because we go upwards to the peace of Jerusalem: for gladdened was I in those who said unto me, We go up to the house of the Lord. There hath Thy good pleasure placed us, that we may desire nothing else, but to abide there for ever. (9)

The natural resting place of human existence, Augustine argues, is love, both abiding in the love of God, and expressing and experiencing love with other people. To find peace is to live in love; that is the essential character of humanness. This is reinforced in his reflections on unification in his work *On Order*. Augustine reasons that objects find their meaning and purposes when they combine together within their proper setting. A branch has no individual purpose unless it is united with the other parts of a tree. A solitary soldier has no direction except when positioned within an army unit. And as for humans, they are designed for love, and love is "the will to become one with the object it loves" (*On Order* 2.18.48).[4]

Augustine's most extensive and most memorable teachings on love appear in his commentary-like sermons on 1 John.[5] He was deeply inspired by

4. Quoted in Trasicius J. van Bavel, "Love," in *Augustine through the Ages*, ed. A. D. Fitzgerald (Grand Rapids: Eerdmans, 1999), 509.

5. On Augustine's lectures on 1 John and love, see Levering, *Theology of Augustine*, 46–61.

Introduction

John's reference to God as love (1 John 4:8, 16), and the general Johannine teachings on love and mutuality (John 14–16; 1 John passim). Additionally, Augustine frequently points to the double love command, particularly the teaching of Jesus (again, Matt 22:37–39). Often in discussions of the influences on Augustine's love hermeneutic, Paul is left out. After all, Paul neither has a double love commandment nor explicitly says, "God is love." But it would be a mistake to assume Augustine lacked interest in Paul. In fact, Augustine found ample inspiration in Galatians and Romans, two texts where love is exalted as the goal of religion and the most complete expression of communal life. In view of texts like Galatians 5:14 and Romans 13:10, Augustine was fond of saying, "Charity [*caritas*] is the fullness of the Law" (see *Ep.* 55.21.38).[6] You will also find frequent reference and allusion in Augustine's writings to Romans 5:5b, "God's love has been poured [in the old KJV "shed abroad"] into our hearts through the Holy Spirit that has been given to us."[7]

When Augustine pondered his own story, he found resonance with Paul's own testimony from Phil 3:12–24 of leaving the past in the past and stretching forward toward God's calling.

> Look at how my life is a stretching-apart. Your right hand picked me up and brought me to my Lord, the human mediator. He mediates between you, who are One, and us, who are many. We are in many things and we pass through many things. And You brought me to Him, so that I might take hold of Him by whom I was already held, so that I might be gathered up from my aged days and chase after one thing, having forgotten all that has passed away—so that I might chase not after those things that are going to be and pass away, but after those things that are "before"; so that I might be stretched out, not stretched apart; so that I might chase after that victory palm of the calling from above, not distractedly but intently. If I could win this palm, I would hear a voice of praise and contemplate your delight, which neither arrives nor passes away. Now, of course, my years

---

6. On Galatians 5:14, see Augustine's *On Christian Doctrine* 1.35.39; *Confessions* 12.30.41; see John Riches, *Galatians through the Centuries* (New York: Wiley-Blackwell, 2012), 247–48.

7. In his work *On the Spirit and the Letter*, Augustine quotes Romans 5:5 no less than twelve times!

INTRODUCTION

are full of groans. You are my relief, Lord. You are eternal, my Father. But I am ripped apart in times. I have no idea what their order is. My thoughts and the innermost guts of my soul will be torn to shreds by unstable differences until I flow into you, purified and melted down by the fire of your love. (*Confessions* 11.29.39)

I don't think it is an exaggeration to say that everywhere Augustine looked in Scripture, he saw God's transformative love, including in Paul's letters. In my own early study of Paul, I paid little attention to the place of love in his letters. But in the last few years, I have begun to take this idea more seriously, for several reasons. First, I came to recognize the role that love language plays in Jewish tradition, especially as the core disposition related to covenant fidelity, classically expressed in the Shema (Deut 6:4–9; see pp. 41–52 for a deeper discussion). Second, love discourses in Paul stand out against the backdrop of Greco-Roman religion, where love is virtually absent. (More on that in a moment.)

If one stops to consider the matter in Paul, the evidence is rather striking: The language of love in one form or another occurs over one hundred times in the Pauline corpus. Furthermore, every single letter contains love language—that cannot be said for other contenders for the so-called center of Paul's thought. Paul's favorite love word, *agapē*, appears seven times in 1 Thessalonians, a text widely considered to be Paul's earliest extant letter. It occurs three times in Philemon, Paul's shortest letter. And it appears an astounding fourteen times in Romans, Paul's most theologically weighty letter. Beyond simple statistics, though, Paul's love language is found in core statements of his thought. Consider these, for instance:

But God proves his love for us in that while we still were sinners Christ died for us. (Rom 5:8)

For I am convinced that neither death, nor life, nor angels, nor rulers, nor things present, nor things to come, nor powers, nor height, nor depth, nor anything else in all creation, will be able to separate us from the love of God in Christ Jesus our Lord. (Rom 8:38–39)

Owe no one anything, except to love one another, for the one who loves another has fulfilled the law. (Rom 13:8)

Introduction

I have been crucified with Christ, and I no longer live, but Christ lives in me. And the life I live in the body I live by faith in the one who loved me and gave himself for me. (Gal 2:19–20)

The only thing that counts is faith working through love. (Gal 5:6)

For the whole law is summed up in a single commandment, "You shall love your neighbor as yourself." (Gal 5:14)

Love never fails. (1 Cor 13:8)

It can also be easily demonstrated that Paul's dominant prescription for the problems facing his various churches is *love*. To the Thessalonians he prays, in light of the turmoil they face with persecution and recent deaths in their community, "may the Lord make you increase and abound in *love* for one another and for all, just as we abound in love for you" (1 Thess 3:12). To the Corinthians, he tries to counteract their inflated factionalism with the famous call to selfless love we find in 1 Corinthians 13 ("love is patient, love is kind"). The Philippians struggled with internal cohesion in the midst of their own suffering and persecution, and Paul again makes this his prayer: "that your love may overflow more and more with knowledge and full insight" (Phil 1:9).

If love is so important to Paul, even central, why is it so often neglected in scholarly discussion of his theology? I propose here at least two reasons. First, love can seem like a rather soft and emotional idea, and it might be hard to attribute to it any significant impact on the people of God. Surely terms like "propitiation" or "justification" are fit to do the heavy theological lifting, right? I would like to point to an interesting academic case study here. In 1997, Richard Hays published his now classic *Moral Vision of the New Testament*. Hays established as his "focal images" for this moral vision three core themes in the New Testament: new creation, the redeemed community, and the cross of Christ. Hays purposely chose *not* to concentrate on the topic or virtue of love, not because it is not important in the New Testament but because it is a much-abused word in modern language, "easily debased in popular discourse . . . a cover for all manner of vapid self-indulgence."[8] Some scholars, such as

---

8. Richard B. Hays, *The Moral Vision of the New Testament: Community, Cross, New Creation* (San Francisco: HarperSanFrancisco, 1996), 202.

INTRODUCTION

Richard Burridge, have urged that, even if Hays is correct about the possibility of importing modern connotations into the Pauline use of love language, we ought not to neglect this subject. Rather, the message of the New Testament is that "the love of God ... is breaking into our world here and now to bring about the eschatological restoration of his people under God's gracious reign."[9] David Horrell, likewise, has disagreed with Hays's exclusion of love; in Horrell's own work, he seeks to reinvest in Pauline love language, talking about it in relation to other-regard, focused not on selfish desire but self-giving concern and care for the other.[10]

Second, two thousand years of Christian theology has, perhaps, clouded our assumptions about religiosity and inoculated us to the shocking presence of love language in ancient Christian texts. But as Larry Hurtado has pointed out, such language was entirely foreign to the Greco-Roman religious environment. He writes, "many sophisticated pagans of the day would have regarded any such ideas [of selfless love from God] as ridiculous. . . . In recorded prayer texts from the Roman period, various deities are praised for their power, their ordering of the world, their answers to prayers, and other attributes."[11] But *love* was never assumed. In fact, Aristotle counted it ridiculous and absurd to profess love to Zeus.[12] Gods and mortals are of such different types and orders that any sense of mutuality in love and friendship are impossible; even the thought would be deeply offensive to the high station of the gods.

A few centuries after Aristotle, Plutarch argued that the three most common feelings that a human has toward a god is envy, fear, and respect. Envy— because the gods are immortal and eternal. Fear—because they are sovereign and powerful. Respect, which one *might* call love—because they are righteous and to be admired. But the love about which Plutarch writes is not a personal,

---

9. Richard A. Burridge, *Imitating Jesus: An Inclusive Approach to New Testament Ethics* (Grand Rapids: Eerdmans, 2007), 55.

10. David G. Horrell, *Solidarity and Difference: A Contemporary Reading of Paul's Ethics* (London: T&T Clark, 2016).

11. See Larry W. Hurtado, *God in the New Testament* (Nashville: Abingdon, 2010), 37.

12. *Magna moralia* 1208b. Aristotle argued that friendship could occur only where there was the possibility of reciprocity of affection, something mortals could not exchange with the gods. The divine-human relationship is crucial but absurd to call love.

Introduction

relational love. It is more a sense of admiration or appreciation, bordering on infatuation, because we mortals desire things we don't possess.[13] Plutarch makes these confessions with a sense of lament, because humans want the power and position of the gods, things they cannot possess, but they don't really want to emulate the values and virtues of the justice of the gods, commitments that are, in fact, within reach.

How very unexpected, then, when these Christians referred to *love* as the primary disposition of the divine nature! In Hurtado's *Destroyer of the Gods*, he explains that one simply does not find *anything* in Greek and Roman religious texts akin to what the Christians regularly describe, that God lavishly loves his creatures with a pure and noble affection and compassion.[14]

Cato the Elder records in his *On Agriculture* a farmer's prayer to Mars that is indicative of Roman prayer in general: reverent and utilitarian, with the hopes of reciprocity and return.

> Father Mars, I pray and beseech you to be gracious and merciful to me, my house, and my household; to which intent I have bidden this *suovetarilia* [multianimal offering] to be led around my land, my ground, my farm; that you keep away, ward off and remove sickness, seen and unseen, barrenness and destruction, ruin and unseasonable influence; and that you permit my harvests, my grain, my vineyards and my plantations to flourish and to come to good issue, preserve in health my shepherds and my flocks, and give good health and strength to me, my house and my household. To this intent, to the intent of purifying my farm, my land and my ground, and of making an expiation, as I have said, deign to accept the offering of these suckling victims; Father Mars.[15]

This sample reflects many recorded prayers from Greek and Roman religion. They viewed the gods as celestial rulers, and the overall goal was to safeguard the *pax deorum* (peaceful coexistence with the gods) and beseech them

---

13. Plutarch, *Aristides* 6.3–4.

14. Larry W. Hurtado, *Destroyer of the Gods: Early Christian Distinctiveness in the Roman World* (Waco, TX: Baylor University Press, 2017), 63–65.

15. As translated in Rebecca I. Denova, *Greek and Roman Religions* (Hoboken, NJ: Wiley-Blackwell, 2019), 164; see generally on Greco-Roman prayer, 161–84.

INTRODUCTION

for any goodwill and favors. Again, love—in the deeply personal sense—was not part of the equation. When we look at Paul's writings, then, it becomes rather noticeable that love was clearly at the heart of his teachings in contrast to state and popular religions of the Roman Empire.

The strange reality is that many classic Pauline theologies either leave love out as a core topic, or file it under "Christian ethics" (which tends to be a small section toward the end of the book). For example, in James D. G. Dunn's *Theology of Paul the Apostle*, a section on love appears in the final chapter on the practice of Christian faith, "How Should Believers Live?"—about three pages on "liberty and love."[16] In his two-volume tome, *Paul and the Faithfulness of God*, N. T. Wright's comments about love appear as expected here and there with an excursus on "the electing love of God in the messiah" (Rom 8:31–39) and some reflections on Paul and the Shema.[17] Wright does ground Paul's understanding of God within the loving nature of the one God, but the space given to this subject is noticeably limited.

More promising reflections on Paul's theology of love can be found in the recent works of Douglas Campbell and Paul Sampley. Campbell's *Pauline Dogmatics* defines the apostle's theology in the book's subtitle: *The Triumph of God's Love*. Campbell grounds the identity of Paul's God in the divine relationality, which has a familial character. "At the heart of the universe is a play of love between the Father, the Son, and the Spirit," Campbell claims.[18] Drawing from Romans 5:8, Campbell goes on to offer this programmatic reflection:

> The nature of God is revealed definitively by the death of the Son on the cross for us at the behest of the Father and the Spirit. There the Father has offered up his beloved only Son to die for us, doing so, moreover, while we, the objects of this costly mission, were rebellious and hostile. Before

16. James D. G. Dunn, *The Theology of Paul the Apostle* (Grand Rapids: Eerdmans, 1998), 658–61. See similarly Douglas J. Moo, *A Theology of Paul and His Letters* (Grand Rapids: Zondervan Academic, 2021), 625–27, where Moo talks about love and charity as part of the new life in Christ.

17. N. T. Wright, *Paul and the Faithfulness of God* (Minneapolis: Fortress, 2016), 2:619–20, 902–8.

18. Douglas A. Campbell, *Pauline Dogmatics: The Triumph of God's Love* (Grand Rapids: Eerdmans, 2020), 55.

Introduction

any response had been offered, then, the Father undertook this ultimately costly act for us, which the Son obediently carried out. And this proves that the Father's love for us is utterly fundamental to his character, and limitless, as is the Son's and their Spirit's. This God will stop at nothing in order to reach us and to heal us. God undertook this supremely painful action—the father's sacrifice of his Son—to save a snarling and ungrateful humanity. Astonishing![19]

Campbell's approach sees divine love at the core, the *heart* of Paul's gospel. That's very different from relegating it to a section on Christian ethics or community values. In too many studies of Paul, either the concept of love is left out, or it is given a kind of second-order or third-order significance.[20] What would it mean to recognize that love is more central to Paul's identity, thought, and religion?

As a unique and even provocative way to think about the difference this would make, I want to point to a fascinating set of articles in *Christian Century* from 2012. David Helm recounts a question that P. D. East asked Will Campbell (according to Campbell's autobiography, *Brother to a Dragonfly*):[21] how would he define the gospel or Christianity in ten words? Campbell answered, "We're all bastards but God loves us anyway." East replied, "If you want to try again, you have two words left."[22]

This little experiment inspired Helm to ask various modern theologians to explain the gospel "in seven words." One can get an immediate sense for how these pithy phrases reflect the person's own theology, and specifically the core of their thought. Here are some samples Helm collected:

19. Campbell, *Pauline Dogmatics*, 55–56.

20. Frank Matera's Pauline theology does better than most, but love features only occasionally and incidentally in the first half of his book (which focuses on soteriology) and then is more prominent and intentionally discussed in the latter half (which treats the nature of the Christian life); see *God's Saving Grace: A Pauline Theology* (Grand Rapids: Eerdmans, 2012); see especially 176–80 ("A Love Ethic") and 236–37 ("The Love of God").

21. Will D. Campbell, *Brother to a Dragonfly* (New York: Seabury, 1977).

22. David Heim, "The Gospel in Seven Words," *Christian Century*, September 5, 2012, https://www.christiancentury.org/article/2012-08/gospel-seven-words.

INTRODUCTION

Beverly R. Gaventa: "In Christ, God's yes defeats our no."
Carol Zaleski: "He led captivity captive."
Ellen Charry: "The wall of hostility has come down."

In most of these statements, the word "love" is not explicitly used, but one can get a sense that God's care and concern for his world is in the background.

Bill McKibben chose to quote the Golden Rule, "Love your neighbor as yourself," pointing at the same time to the ethos of the Christian life, and the embodiment of this teaching in the Teacher himself, Jesus. Some tipped their hat to divine love without explicitly using the word: "we live by grace" (M. Craig Barnes), "God through Jesus Christ, welcomes you anyhow" (Martin E. Marty). And a few talked about divine love explicitly: "Divinely persistent, God really loves us" (Donald W. Shriver), "Israel's God's bodied love continues world-making" (Walter Brueggemann).

My point in mentioning these short gospel summaries is not for you (or me) to choose the right one, but to note that our theological distillations will inevitably reveal where we find the center, core, or heart of what the gospel is. And in regard to Paul, our concern in this book is to consider the possibility that *love* is at the bull's-eye center, divine love most crucially revealed in the incarnation and cross and injected into the bloodstream of the church for the life of the world.

In my research on Paul's theology, I was repeatedly surprised by how few books have been written on Paul's language and theology of love. Love and affection language are found in every Pauline letter (not something we can say for "justification" or even "cross," by the way). There are major explicit teachings on love in Galatians, Romans, and 1 Corinthians. And love finds its way into key statements or summaries of the gospel in Paul, such as Galatians 2:20 and Romans 5:1–11. Perhaps another reason that this subject is neglected is simply that it is pervasive and runs the risk of blending into Paul's common discourse, hiding in plain sight, as it were. That is, it's *everywhere* in Paul's letters; forms of *agapē* and *phileō* are found hundreds of times, easy to skip over as yet another mention of love. But, again, it becomes more noticeable when we realize that pagan religious texts simply don't talk about love that much, so its frequency in Paul's writings is certainly distinctive. Take, for example, in Cicero's long treatise *On the Nature of the Gods*, love language is used only a handful of times in a meaningful way, and Cicero was certainly *not* interested

10

Introduction

in divine love as the heart of religion. What about religious expression of the common people in the Greco-Roman world? Did they talk about divine love? Unfortunately, we don't have much preserved from regular folk, but from the repository of inscriptions and other epigraphical sources we do have, love is not a significant factor. Most are records of sacrifices, dedications, and oaths meant to honor gods, and pleas for mercy and protection.[23] They are typically written in a formal tone, bereft of affectionate terms and images.

In Greco-Roman religious history, the influence of Romanness brought more formality to religion, especially state religion. The gods were not friends, lovers, or family; they were like rulers and overlords. Devotees were meant to treat them with honor and respect; emotion and personal affection were completely irrelevant. In fact, Romans were inclined to treat any sort of deep or reactive feelings in worship as dangerously close to superstition.[24]

So, as we open the pages of Paul's letters, it should present a stark contrast, where the apostle is repeatedly talking about the love of God, the affection of Christ, and mutuality and warm communion with the divine. So perhaps Augustine was on to something—if love is the center of the biblical message as a whole, it is worth investigating whether love is at the heart of Paul's theology.

GOALS OF THIS BOOK

To whet your appetite for this topic, we will preview the book in brief. The main argument of this book is that love belongs in the conversation about the center of Paul's theology. Love is at the heart of Paul's understanding of the gospel itself, the nature of the loving God who made a plan to redeem sinful humanity. Love is also at the heart of the expectations of how God's people should relate to God, what we call religion. For a devout Jew like Paul, we can take for granted that the Shema ("love the LORD your God..." [Deut 6:4–9])

---

23. See Mika Kajava, "Religion in Rome and Italy," and James B. Rives, "Religion in the Roman Provinces," in *The Oxford Handbook of Roman Epigraphy*, ed. Christopher Brunn and Jonathan Edmondson (Oxford: Oxford University Press, 2015), 397–419, 420–44.

24. For a more detailed comparison between Roman religion and early Christianity, see my book *Strange Religion: How the First Christians Were Weird, Dangerous, and Compelling* (Grand Rapids: Brazos, 2024).

INTRODUCTION

was deeply ingrained in his knowledge and practice of piety and reinforced all the more by the Jesus tradition and apostolic teachings he inherited when he launched his ministry. Love is also at the heart of how Christians ought to live life together, as they model among themselves the love of the triune God. Finally, we will argue that love is the primary orientation that Christians ought to have toward both insiders *and* outsiders, believers and unbelievers. If love is eternal, if love is the highest form of Christian life, it cannot be restricted to only one's family or friends; if Christ loved those who rejected him, and believers are called to imitate the Son of God, then love is the supreme virtue extended to all.

A Book for Different Kinds of Readers

The heart of this book is essentially a theological analysis or study of Paul's theology and how love permeates his understanding of the triune God, the gospel, the community, and the mission and lifestyle of God's people (as noted above). In order to dissect and examine these items carefully and precisely, I have to spend a lot of time discussing (1) Paul's heritage, (2) Paul's context, (3) Paul's vocabulary, and (4) the ways love language has been variously understood and misunderstood throughout time and space. Scholars who are reading this will be curious about these things and will hopefully appreciate the details, especially the terminology discussions and contextualizing material. But I expect some readers are students, pastors, or laypeople who are interested in Pauline theology but might not want to wade through some of the language details and would prefer to dive right into the theological material. For those readers, I suggest you skim chapters 3 ("The Greek Language of Love") and 5 ("Paul's Conception of Love"), which dwell a lot on Greek semantics. If you find yourself getting lost in the trees of the book, you can use chapter 11 ("Summary, Synthesis, and Implications") as a guide to the forest.

1

Perspectives on Love

The practice of love offers no place of safety. We risk loss, hurt, pain. We risk being acted upon by forces outside our control.

—bell hooks[1]

Love is just one of those things: it's almost impossible to define, but you know it when you see it. The challenge of putting words together to explain love is that in both ancient times and modern times, love language is used in a variety of ways for all manner of people and things. We can say we love our spouse or children. But we can also love french fries or a good parking spot. We hold love as the highest of virtues, which captures the very best of what humanity can do in the world through self-sacrifice and compassion. But we also use terms like "pedophile," which literally refers to someone who loves children with inappropriate sexual infatuation. Love is a remarkably elastic concept, regardless of culture or age. Poet John Ciardi once wrote, "Love is the word used to label the sexual excitement of the young, the habituation of the middle-aged, and the mutual dependence of the old."[2] That makes dictionary definitions practically useless. Dictionaries tend to offer something very generic, defining "love" as a form of affection. But the levels of intensity and importance of that feeling or sense of affection vary drastically.

1. bell hooks, *All about Love: New Visions* (New York: HarperCollins, 2018), 153.
2. As cited in Aaron Ben-Ze'ev, *The Arc of Love: How Our Romantic Lives Change over Time* (Chicago: University of Chicago Press, 2019), 192.

CHAPTER 1

As an interesting exercise, let's look at the various ways Josephus uses forms of *phileō* (like/love) in compound words. For example, he uses *philanthrōpia* for "love of people," and *philoxenia*, "care for strangers/foreigners." *Philonikeō* means "love for victory," which often practically refers to a propensity to argue (*Jewish Antiquities* 1.259). Here are other terms in Josephus's vocabulary:

Philomathēs: "enjoyment of learning"
Philotimeomai: "to be ambitious" (lit., "love of glory")
Philopsycheō: "to be a coward" (lit., "love one's own life [too much]")

We could go on and on.[3] But here we will just note that you can link just about anything to love. That is because we human creatures are drawn to things. Some of them are good, some of them are bad, and some of them don't quite fit either category. Some of them become harmful *because* they move from healthy experiences to obsessions (like food or sex). To be human is to love. Even hate is a form of love, albeit twisted, because it is a deep attachment, a desire for the other to be punished or see harm. Love all by itself is simply a part of our DNA: what we do with it, how we cultivate and nurture it, how we respond to it, and how we strengthen and fortify it will mean the difference between a blessed life and an existence of misery. Voltaire said it better: "Love is a canvas furnished by nature and embroidered by imagination."[4] We are bound to love, but it is another thing to love well.

Trying to understand love psychologically, sociologically, existentially, and theologically is daunting. This can be an unwieldy topic, with lots of voices and angles of approach, so we will take a multifaceted tactic. First, we will consider multiple approaches to the modern conversation of love from different disciples (i.e., philosophy, social science, and cultural studies). Then we will look at the Greek terminology of love used in the New Testament. From there, in subsequent chapters, we will examine how love language appears in the Jewish tradition and the Jesus tradition. Finally, we will turn to Paul and carefully consider his interest in love, both human and divine.

3. See further discussion of Josephus in pp. 64–66.
4. As cited in Aaron Ben-Ze'ev, *The Subtlety of Emotions* (Boston: MIT Press, 2000), 405.

Perspectives on Love

SIMON MAY ON THE MYTH OF DIVINE LOVE

We begin with the important work of Simon May, a philosopher with interest in emotions, culture, and social identity. In 2011, May published an important book called *Love: A History*, where he examines how humans have thought, talked about, and pursued love over 2,500 years of history. For better or for worse, to be human is to be infatuated with the idea of love. "For much of its history love has been captive to an obsession with opposites. It is either self-seeking or self-giving; either possessive or submissive; either illusion-creating or truth-seeking; either conditional or unconditional; either inconstant or enduring; either mired in fantasy or a privileged window into reality. And in every case it is taken to be the apogee, the paradigm, of the quality in question."[5] May is not neutral in his analysis of love's history. He argues that much of history recounts people chasing a phantasm, an idea of love that is unnatural. Too many theologians and philosophers treat the ideal of love as (1) unconditional ("*I will love you no matter what*"), (2) eternal ("*our love will last forever*"), and (3) selfless ("*I expect nothing in return*"). Love, then, becomes so otherworldly that it might as well be a transcendent god itself. This sets up an unachievable ideal; it "booby-traps relationships with an impossible expectation, which is fundamentally untrue to the nature of human love."[6] When humans bind themselves to one another under these kinds of assumptions about love, two tendencies become likely. Either the parties will feel a deep and continuous sense of self-disappointment and other-disappointment, or they will settle into meaningless commitment and pretend to call it love. Either way, any chance at real love is betrayed. Humans, May explains, cannot achieve or maintain an unconditional, eternal, and selfless form of love, because "everything humans do is thoroughly conditioned, interested, time-bound, and dependent on our building a robust self amid the vagaries of fate and vulnerability."[7]

While May surveys numerous philosophies and theologies throughout time and history, he especially draws out the impact of Christianity, which emphasized that "God is love" (1 John 4:8). Not only do Christians identify God with love, but eventually (credit to Augustine) love becomes the highest virtue and ultimate

5. Simon May, *Love: A History* (New Haven: Yale University Press, 2012), 356.
6. May, *Love: A History*, 359.
7. May, *Love: A History*, 363.

CHAPTER 1

reflection of the divine. According to Christianity, because God is love and reflects perfect love in himself (again something Greco-Roman religions did not claim), Christians who aspire to become godly must conform to the same nature of divine love. The early Christians latched on to the Greek word *agapē* as their favored term representing "unconditional, altruistic, obedient, humble selflessness."[8] May sees in the patristic and medieval periods an increasing obsession with the Christian perfection of human love. The modern secular era, though, took god out of the equation and left a vacuum of fulfillment. Whereas once humans craved and pursued (perfect) divine love to find meaning and happiness to dispel darkness and nihilism, now, without god, that burden falls to (imperfect) human love (May here tipping his hat to insight from Nietzsche). May argues that "God is love" has now been replaced by "love is god," the West's most popular replacement for religion. He offers a seven-part doctrine statement of a secular worship of love.

1. Love is unconditional: "a spontaneous gift that seeks nothing for the giver."
2. Love does not judge: it only affirms.
3. Love is selfless: a disinterested concern for the other only.
4. Love is benevolent and harmonious: "a haven of peace." It is by nature a feel-good phenomenon.
5. Love is eternal: it is timeless.
6. Love is transcendent: it carries us into bliss above and beyond our daily problems.
7. Love is salvific: it gives life meaning, redeems us from problems, and brings about the highest good in life.[9]

May argues that adherence to this doctrine does not lead to fulfillment, because we have set a godlike standard that simply won't match up to our human capacities, needs, and actual experiences, so we will be doomed to live with disappointment, even emptiness. Instead, he proposes that human love should not be preoccupied with achieving godlike status but should foster "ontological rootedness" (leaning into love in the here and now), and "love's overriding concern is to find a home for our life and being."[10]

More recently, May has written a follow-up book called *Love: A New Under-*

8. May, *Love: A History*, 45.
9. May, *Love: A History*, 15–16.
10. May, *Love: A History*, 22.

standing of an Ancient Emotion, where he leans more into his own prescriptive teaching on love.[11] Fulfilling human love is about (1) shared identity with another person, (2) common values and virtues, (3) mutual intensification of vitality through shared experiences, and (4) seeking a shared future and destiny in the pursuit of meaning. While many in the past have fixated love on religion or marriage, May argues that it need not be so. A parent-child relationship, for example, showcases some of the richest models and examples of love in human cultural history.

C. S. Lewis on the Four Forms of Love

C. S. Lewis wrote a widely influential classic called *The Four Loves*.[12] In some ways, Lewis's treatment on love is the mirror opposite of May (though Lewis introduced his material several decades earlier, publishing in 1960). Lewis, too, was interested in the powerful and pithy biblical statement "God is love." And, like May, Lewis wanted to push past overly simplistic and sickeningly sentimental conceptions and aspirations of love. At the beginning of the book, Lewis admits that his original intent was to contrast the lower form of need-love (affection that derives from a need, like a child needing a parent) and gift-love (which is more selfless and altruistic). But as he researched, observed, and reflected more, he came to realize that love is complex, it cannot and should not fall under one category or type only, and that *needing* someone is not really something bad, in many cases. Should humans ever grow into a position where they don't *need* God anymore? Surely not, Lewis concluded. God appears to be quite content with a love from his creatures that is "incomplete, preparatory, empty, yet cluttered, crying out for Him who can untie things that are now knotted together and tie up things that are still dangling loose" (13–14). Humans, by God's grace, can mature in loving God, but, of course, they cannot ever match God's love. But *being God* is not really the goal. It is, in fact, being more human that is the object. In fact, "man approaches God most nearly when he is in one sense least like God" (14). (This, I think, is where Lewis would disagree with May on the nature and impact of a Christian theology of love.)

---

11. Simon May, *Love: A New Understanding of an Ancient Emotion* (Oxford: Oxford University Press, 2019).

12. C. S. Lewis, *The Four Loves* (London: Bles, 1960). Page references are given in parentheses in the text.

CHAPTER 1

Before getting into his formal categories of love, Lewis prefaces his work with the fact of human emotion and pleasure-seeking. Attraction is not, all by itself, a moral reaction. Humans are wired to enjoy things, and often the affective and emotional dynamics are reactive, even temporary. "The smell of frying food," he adds, "is very different before and after breakfast" (28–29). Love and desire are wrapped up in ways that humans place value on people and things. Much of Lewis's explanations in his work are observations and guesses—they are not scientific in terms of testing and sampling. But time and time again, I find his observations ring true. "The human mind is generally far more eager to praise and dispraise than to describe and define. It wants to make every distinction a distinction of value; hence those fatal critics who can never point out the differing quality of two poets without putting them in an order of preference as if they were candidates for a prize" (27).

Let's look now at Lewis's four types: affection (*storgē*), friendship (*philia*), romance (*eros*), and charity (*agapē*). One of my concerns with Lewis's work is the association of love types with specific Greek terms. The reality is that some of these Greek words overlap in usage and are somewhat elastic, so they can mean different things in different contexts, or when used by different kinds of authors. That doesn't mean Lewis's observations are irrelevant. I actually appreciated the basic taxonomy he uses in English. My advice, though, would be to ignore the Greek words and just focus on the English terms and categories Lewis uses.

Affection

In Lewis's perspective, affection involves a feeling of closeness based on natural proximity and relationships. We have affection and connection to people in our family, neighborhood, school, or workplace, and we love them simply because they are a regular part of our lives. We experience with them a "warm comfortableness ... satisfaction in being together" (54). It is a form of intimacy bred by familiarity: "soft slippers, old clothes, old jokes, the thump of a sleepy dog's tail on the kitchen floor, the sound of a sewing-machine, a golliwog left on the lawn" (56–57). (I had to google "golliwog," by the way; it's a toy doll.) Affection is the feel-good warmth developed by natural associations, the love of the familiar. Imagine the love you have for bigger family gatherings, even though they include some uncles or cousins that irritate you. And imagine going to a gathering and one of them has passed away. You might miss them more than you expected to. For Lewis, affection is important and necessary, because it gives life stability, routine, comfort, and or-

18

Perspectives on Love

der. Affection creates a kind of base layer in life, but it is not completely fulfilling. Humans naturally pursue deeper or more intense forms of love.

Friendship

Next, Lewis talks about friendship, what the ancients considered the most satisfying form of love. In modern times, friendship is underrated because few truly experience deep friendship. Unlike affection, friendship doesn't just happen. It needs to be formed and cultivated: "Without Eros none of us would have been begotten and without Affection none of us would have been reared; but we can live and breed without Friendship" (88). That is to say, it is *chosen* and *special*. And friendship also has its limitations. You can't be friends with everyone. (I sense Lewis would *not* be on Facebook today.) Friendship by nature requires selecting a small group as intimate companions in life. It might begin with some shared interest (which Lewis dubs "Clubbable-ness"), but it develops into a more specific focus. Friendship must have a "thing," a combined preoccupation. Two friends set out together on a journey of interest, passion, and pursuit. "Those who have nothing can share nothing; those who are going nowhere can have no fellow-travellers" (98).

Lewis attributes to friendship the genuine capacity for transformation. Our friends can change us (for the better or the worse), because we seek their favor and dread their disappointment. A friendship group creates its own microculture that can become very resilient. So much so that it can mute, modify, or defy wider cultural norms. Lewis argues that friendship love gave the church a protective bubble in which to thrive: "The little pockets of early Christians survived because they cared exclusively for the love of 'the brethren' and stopped their ears to the opinion of the Pagan society all around them" (114). In classic Lewis style (which always includes a bit of exaggeration and oversimplification), he asserts that every real friendship holds the power of rebellion. From there it can become a weapon or tool to do great good, or great harm. And friendship can become a snare, because it has the capacity to create an echo chamber or vacuum into which "no voice will carry" (117).

Romance

According to Lewis, romance is infatuation with another person. While it can seem like friendship, the purest form of romance is about desire. Desire in itself

CHAPTER 1

is not evil; God made humans as sensory creatures. But desire must have its limits and control. When romance is combined with commitment and mutuality, it has the capacity to enhance a relationship.

Charity

Last, Lewis talks about charity, the type of unconditional love that God shows for his creation. Lewis sets up the very thing that Simon May found problematic: an ideal and divine form of love that is unconditional, perfect, and eternal. But Lewis firmly believed that love is not just an emotion or feeling but a virtue and Christian pursuit; it can grow and come closer to the way of God, even if it can't be perfect. To have a model in God is not to experience perpetual disappointment in self but to find inspiration to smash idols of selfishness and the propensity to use and manipulate others.

The point of Lewis's book is not to pit one love (charity) against the others, as if life should have just one kind of love. Lewis valued all forms, all four having their rightful places in the balanced and well-rounded life. Friendship, family, school, and work are places that can become training grounds for learning how to love the best things and how to love better.

BELL HOOKS ON HOPE FOR LOVE

Author bell hooks was a cultural critic, feminist hermeneut, and social activist. Her book *All about Love* is a wide-ranging formative reflection on the power of love to overcome cultural evils today. Hooks notes that there is a modern skepticism toward love that she detected in voices all around, young and old. Lovelessness is a wound of the American nation, and courage is needed to learn to love and find hope again. We will pull out six key ideas that are developed in her book.

Love Is Worth It

Hooks traces the modern antipathy and cynicism toward love with a constant feeling of disappointment or betrayal in human experiences. But hooks find redemption in love by defining it correctly. She draws from M. Scott Peck's *The Road Less Traveled* by defining love as "the will to extend one's self for the

Perspectives on Love

purpose of nurturing one's own or another's spiritual growth."[13] Love isn't primarily about feeling good, though often it should leave that effect. It is about giving and growth. That naturally leads to hooks's second point.

Love Is Action

When love is only words, there is a disconnect between thought and experience. If love is genuine, it must be embodied. Love is not just something that happens *to us*, struck by Cupid's arrow. It is a choice, a decision to care and be there for the other, to show up in tangible ways.

Self-Love and Unmasking Are Essential

Loving others, according to hooks, does not preclude loving self. In fact, self-love is crucial. Self-love is not in itself selfish. At its best, it is about positive self-talk. "We need to rid ourselves of misguided notions about self-love. We need to stop fearfully equating it with self-centeredness."[14] A related interest for hooks is the problem of wearing masks and not presenting our true self to others. Just as we may be too embarrassed to love ourselves, so we may be too ashamed to present our true selves to the world. But masks create false intimacy, and false intimacy is bound to fail.

Part of the solution to the problems of lack of self-love and masking involve recognizing the dominating evils in society, like sexism and racism, that harm women and people of color. Self-love empowers the person to sever themselves from false relationships and false impressions of self-value. Love, even self-love, is a choice. And exercising choice and action are important steps in fighting back against dominating cultural forces that seek to diminish and disempower women and people of color.

We May Not Have Been Loved Well

Hooks insists that an important part of finding new hope in the power of love is confronting the demons of our own upbringing, especially contexts where

13. hooks, *All about Love*, 23.
14. hooks, *All about Love*, 70.

CHAPTER 1

we were not loved well. We may have distorted notions of love because of abuse or neglect by family members. We must not hold up our parents as the perfect models of love. Sometimes we need to look back to other people in our lives, like grandparents, aunties, neighbors, coaches, and teachers. Finding new resources and inspirations for love can be rejuvenating. We can discover love's healing power—to grow in the "soulful places" that have been scorched by loss, heartache, or betrayal.

Love Is Finite, and That's Okay

Some preach that love is eternal, but the reality is that our mortal lives are not eternal, hooks argues. The finiteness of mortal existence is precisely what makes love and friendship so special. People lock arms with us and carry us through, and we reciprocate. Also, relationships are not all of one kind. Some relationships last decades; some are very temporary. Each relationship must be seen for what it is, what purpose it serves, and hooks believes that the imposition of "forever" is an unnecessary burden in some cases.

Love Is Necessary for Thriving Communities

Healthy communities need love; that is a fundamental argument by hooks. The kind of love they require is not one of personal emotional attachment (only) but of commitment and generosity. Hooks talks about the will to cooperate in serving the community and safeguarding its future. She affirms the importance of making space for respect and integrity; each party must bring these to the table for the common good. If love is cut out of the equation, a flourishing community will be difficult to establish.

JOHN GOTTMAN ON TRUST AND ATTUNEMENT IN RELATIONSHIPS

John Gottman is a psychologist who specializes in marriage. In his book *Principia Amoris: The New Science of Love*, Gottman outlines what he calls three phases of marital love.[15] Even though our study on Pauline theology is

---

15. John Mordechai Gottman, *Principia Amoris: The New Science of Love* (New York: Routledge, 2015).

Perspectives on Love

not focused on marriage, what Gottman brings to the table of discussion is (1) a social psychologist's perspective based on scientific data collection and (2) a broader interest in trust in love-type relationships.

Phase 1: Falling in Love (Limerence)

Using language from Dorothy Tennov, Gottman talks about "limerence," the strong feelings we have in the initial stage of romance: excitement, obsession, and infatuation. Much of our attraction to another person is physical, and especially chemical (phenylethylamine, pheromones, oxytocin). At this stage, two people are just really into each other, and there is a kind of natural and instant attachment. The reality, though, is that this phase doesn't last forever. Those chemical boosts subside, and a new phase emerges, where the strength of the relationship is tested.

Phase 2: Building Trust

Will you be there for me? Can I count on you? Gottman created a "Love Lab," a homelike environment where he could observe couples (with their consent) in relationship, especially in conflict. When the falling-in-love phase is on the decline, couples start to feel frustration and disappointment, sometimes anger. This is a crucial phase for seeing the relationship through. The key factor becomes building trust. But how? Gottman developed a sixfold process or set of practices that create bonds of trust. He uses the acronym ATTUNE.

1. Awareness of the partner's pain
2. Tolerance and openness to the other's viewpoint
3. Turning toward the partner's need
4. Understanding the partner
5. Nondefensive listening
6. Empathy

One of the hallmarks of Gottman's system is the recognition that grandiose gestures like going on an expensive lovers' vacation or buying jewelry are not as formative as consistency and constancy in the many little things that make up life, such as eye contact, daily positive words, and positive and warm hugs and small physical touches like holding hands.

CHAPTER 1

Phase 3: Building Commitment and Loyalty

This phase moves from the building of the structure of trust to fostering a deeper love that lasts a lifetime. A key part of this phase is what Gottman calls the fairness metric. For positive reciprocal love to thrive, each partner has to accept influence at an equal and fair level as the other. It just doesn't work out where one person does all the giving, and the other all the receiving. That is not marriage love, and it doesn't have the proper resources and balance to make love last.

Gottman doesn't boil successful and long-lasting love down to a certain trick. He uses observation, brain science, and tried-and-true testing of marriage advice to help couples develop bonds of trust that are resilient.

The above multidisciplinary perspectives on love help us to "triangulate" what love *is*. Again, "love" is impossible to define in a brief and neat dictionary entry. These perspectives put some pieces in place to bring rich complexity and texture to our conceptual imagination. We will not be drawing specifically on these scholars and theorists when we get to exegetical and theological discussions, but I hope it will become clear that Paul used love language in the kinds of varied and multifaceted ways demonstrated in the theorists we have already discussed.

An Emotion Theory Approach

Before we turn to some of the specific Greek terms that will become the focus of this study, it is crucial to add to our study insights from the developing scholarship on emotion theory, which draws from psychology, sociology, anthropology, neuroscience, and more. Throughout time, the relationship between thinking, feeling, and behavior has been misunderstood or too often neglected. And especially when it comes to Christian theology, there can be a narrow emphasis on emotionless love as a virtue (self-sacrificial love; see above critiques from Simon May), and when taken to an extreme, this can amount to a neglect of human emotion, or worse, a vilification of emotion, which prefers some sort of stoic posture. But both Jewish and early Christian tradition underscored the condition of the heart and its right orientation.[16]

16. It is remarkable how often the Bible talks about the condition of the heart

Perspectives on Love

One way to ensure we are paying responsible attention to love and the life of human feelings is to learn from modern conversations and research in emotion theory to better understand an anthropology of love.

In the last century or so, there has been an explosion of academic interest in the science of human emotions, which draws from several disciplines but especially psychology and anthropology.[17] Two schools of thought have virtually dominated the academic discussions. The more traditional view, sometimes called "basic emotion," argues that human emotion is instinctual and universal, responses to stimuli that lead to bodily reaction and expression. The second school of thought is called the appraisal theory, which we will discuss at length below. This view posits that emotions are guided by our interpretation or appraisal of our environment and situation. Because individual appraisals will be different, so emotions will differ from one person to the next, even if they encounter the same stimulus. Another category has sometimes been named as a third view, referred to as a psychological-construction approach, which tries to allow for and account for variability in emotion.[18] Many responses can be identified as fear or anger, but there is remarkable diversity and variation within those categories. This construction approach takes seriously both the instinctual-biology perspective of the basic emotion approach and the making-meaning aspect of the appraisal theory. However, this third view allows for more individualization of emotional responses based on things like perception, memory, and cultural influence. The construction approach tries to account more carefully for the complexity of the brain's processes.

Only in the last couple of decades has the field of biblical studies taken broader interest in these conversations about emotions in experience and

---

and the inward self. For a representative sampling, see Deuteronomy 6:5; 10:12; 13:3; 30:6; Joshua 22:5; Judges 16:15; 1 Kings 8:23; 2 Chronicles 6:14; Psalms 13:5; Song of Songs 8:6; Zechariah 8:17; Matthew 22:37; Mark 12:30, 33; Luke 10:27; Romans 5:5; Ephesians 3:17; Colossians 2:2; 2 Thessalonians 3:5.

17. In the brief discussion in this section, I rely heavily on Maria Gendron and Lisa Feldman Barrett, "Reconstructing the Past: A Century of Ideas about Emotion in Psychology," *Emotion Review* 1 (2009): 316–39.

18. See Lisa Feldman Barrett, "Variety Is the Spice of Life: A Psychological Construction Approach to Understanding Variability in Emotion," *Cognitive Emotion* 23 (2009): 1284–1306.

CHAPTER 1

discourse and how insights drawn from modern emotion theories can shed light on reading the Bible. An important contribution in this regard is the edited volume *Mixed Feelings and Vexed Passions: Exploring Emotions in Biblical Literature,* which begins with F. Scott Spencer's erudite, sweeping survey of the history of the study of emotions, and how biblical scholars should benefit (and are benefiting) from research from the fields of philosophy, psychology, classics, anthropology, literature, linguistics, affect theory, neuroscience, and cognitive studies. Spencer ends with a plea for not only taking seriously emotional language in the Bible but also attending to the complex aspects of emotion: somatic, narrative, cognitive, motivational, relational, and value laden/ axiological.[19] In the discussion below, we will attempt to honor Spencer's call for a methodologically reflective approach to examining biblical language and discourse about love.

Love and the Appraisal Theory of Emotion

Again, most books on love in Scripture gloss over or ignore completely the emotional dimensions of love, as if feelings are not important to theology, spirituality, the gospel, and human life.[20] And it is precisely in marginalizing the emotional nature of the Christian life that key values and commands in Scripture are mischaracterized. Emotions are made a point of focus by biblical writers on a regular basis, not least by Paul. The problem with recognizing this is perhaps the popular misconception that human emotions are instinctive cognitive or bodily reactions that don't really affect or represent anything deeper within one's being. Perhaps emotions can seem mercurial or autonomic

19. See F. Scott Spencer, "Getting a Feel for the 'Mixed' and 'Vexed' Study of Emotions in Biblical Literature," in *Mixed Feelings and Vexed Passions,* ed. F. Scott Spencer (Atlanta: SBL Press, 2017), 34. The journal *Biblical Interpretation* devoted two consecutive issues in 2016 to the topic of emotions: "Emotions in Ancient Jewish Literature: Definitions and Approaches" (24, nos. 4–5). Key methodological articles include François Mirguet, "What Is an 'Emotion' in the Hebrew Bible? An Experience That Exceeds Most Contemporary Concepts" (442–65); and Anke Inselmann, "Emotions and Passions in the New Testament: Methodological Issues" (536–54).

20. Doug Campbell's work is an exception to this unfortunate neglect; see his *Pauline Dogmatics: The Triumph of God's Love* (Grand Rapids: Eerdmans, 2020), especially places where he talks about relational joy and delight (e.g., 373, 358).

Perspectives on Love

and therefore irrelevant to spiritual growth and the pursuit of flourishing minds and communities. But deeper study of emotion by psychologists and anthropologists in more recent years has opened up new ways of looking at the complexities and sophistication of human emotion and how emotion is tied to networks of being and life such as thought, bodily functions, relationships, and culture. The better we understand how emotion involves human thinking, being, and being in community, the better we will understand why writers throughout the centuries have talked about love, joy, hope, grief, anger, and fear as intricately woven into the depths of the human experience.

We could fill a whole book with a discussion of many emotion theories that have been presented, especially in the last century. But what I have found most beneficial for studying the emotional language in the Bible is known as the appraisal theory of emotion, first introduced in the modern era by psychologist Magda Arnold in the 1940s.[21] In short, Arnold argued that, while it is true that some emotional responses are purely reactive (like recoiling during a scary part of a movie), it can be recognized that in some cases, different people might have different emotional responses to the exact same event or phenomenon.

For example, my children and I have very different emotional reactions to witnessing a thunderstorm. My children have grown up in Oregon, where thunderstorms are rare, so the flashes of lightning and sudden booms of thunder terrify them. But I grew up in Ohio where they are far more common. So when we visit my parents (their grandparents), and there is a thunderstorm, I watch it with wonder and delight, and my kids are cautious and worried. Arnold would say that our emotional responses to this are going to track with our cognitive appraisal of the situation. Based on past experience and cultural impressions, we filter our situation through a certain grid, and our emotions reflect how we are perceiving our environment.[22] In that sense, emotions are

---

21. For an overview with interest in history of research, see Klaus R. Scherer, Angela Schorr, and Tom Johnstone, eds., *Appraisal Processes in Emotion: Theory, Methods, Research* (Oxford: Oxford University Press, 2001).

22. Batja Mesquita convincingly argues, for example, that emotions are not universal in expression, as human emotion is proven to be influenced not only by individual personality and experience but also culture and language. See *Between Us: How Cultures Create Emotions* (New York: Norton, 2022).

CHAPTER 1

not just automatic responses to stimuli that engage our senses; our brains are making decisions about what we are encountering and what those events or circumstances mean for us. Perception and misperception play a role in our emotional responses. For example, let's say a friend walks up to you and slaps you hard on the arm. Your immediate reaction might be shock or anger (*what the heck!*). But then you look down and see that there is a mosquito squashed against your skin. You realize that friend was not trying to hurt you but was killing a mosquito before it bites you. Your reaction turns from anger to relief, even appreciation. Note: one objective event (your friend smacking you) and two different appraisals—an initial appraisal of a harmful situation (leading you to anger) and then a reappraisal of a helpful situation (leading you to appreciation). As Lisa Feldman Barrett explains, we humans are constantly constructing a world around us, and our emotions are tracking with our situational awareness.[23] Our emotions are in continuous communication with our senses to react appropriately to what we consider dangerous circumstances, peaceful (nonthreatening) ones, or positive events. Emotions are, therefore, not just outbursts that we need to overcome with intelligence (like when we apologize for crying or for getting upset). Many of us were taught from a young age that our feelings were inappropriate or out of place. Through some of these modern theorists, we are gaining a better understanding of how our feelings are working in tandem with our intelligence, not against it: "an emotion is your brain's creation of what your bodily sensations mean, in relation to what is going on around you in the world," Barrett explains.[24]

Psychologist Richard Lazarus has done the most influential work in the last fifty years on this kind of cognitive appraisal theory of emotion.[25] He posits that each of us has goals that our lives are directed toward, some conscious, others unconscious. As we live our lives, our minds are constantly analyzing our environment in relationship to these goals. We naturally detect what appear to be threats or opportunities, and our emotions respond to how we perceive

23. Lisa Feldman Barrett, *How Emotions Are Made: The Secret Life of the Brain* (Boston: Mariner Books, 2018). Credit to my friend Becky Castle Miller for pointing me to insightful resources on emotion theory like this.

24. Barrett, *How Emotions Are Made*, 30.

25. Richard S. Lazarus, *Emotion and Adaptation* (Oxford: Oxford University Press, 1994).

Perspectives on Love

our environment at any given time. Lazarus uses binary terminology for how we appraise our situation: "congruency" or "incongruency." The former means the environment is hospitable toward one's ultimate goals—these lead to emotions like joy and love.[26] Alternatively, if there is perceived incongruency, then the environment is treated as an obstacle or threat to one's goals.[27]

Now, not everything plays a direct role in affecting these master goals. Therefore, Lazarus talks about the relevance factor. To what degree does the environment have a serious effect on personal goals? Take, for example, the situation of witnessing a car broken down on the side of the road. On first glance, you might think you recognize the car as that of a close friend or relative, and you suddenly feel a sense of concern or dread. Then, as you get closer, you realize you don't know the person and your emotional response probably becomes less intense. Why? Your brain recognizes a lower personal relevance once you see it is not someone you know personally. That doesn't mean you don't *care*, but that everyone has a natural gradation of concern and shows more responsiveness to things that have more importance to and direct impact on their personal life.

Related to relevance is also perception of the level of impact: *will the situation I am in have a major impact on my goals, or a minor one?* If you accidentally sleep past your alarm, and you get to work late, it's sometimes an anxiety-producing situation, but the level of emotional response will depend in large part on how you perceive the effect of this on your job security or risk to promotion, that is, factors related to ultimate life goals.

So far we have made the case that the emotions we have often reflect our appraisal of our environment or situation. And the stronger and more long-lasting feelings are tied to perception of progress toward or obstacles in front of our goals. Multiple experiences of incongruence (or congruence) of a similar kind aggregate and affect the whole state of the person; Lazarus refers to this

---

26. According to Lazarus, congruency involves the perception of the environment being conducive to achieving one's goals, and therefore related emotions include joy and happiness. See also Agnes Moore, *Demystifying Emotions: A Typology of Theories in Psychology and Philosophy* (Cambridge: Cambridge University Press, 2022).

27. Incongruency involves the perception of the environment being a threat to achieving one's goals; therefore related emotions are things like fear, jealousy, disgust, or anger.

CHAPTER 1

state as subjective well-being (SWB). Emotions are not simply transient cognitive and somatic reactions to stimuli; they can pile up and shape our overall SWB for our good or for our detriment. And this SWB is directly tied to our sense of personal satisfaction and joy in life. So emotions play a direct part in our human spirit of life satisfaction and overall well-being.

While we cannot force a feeling to happen by sheer willpower, the appraisal theory of emotion tells us that we can affect our emotional responses through *re*assessment of our ultimate goals and *re*appraisal of our environment. Let's say I have a fear of flying because I am concerned that the plane is going to crash. I might overcome that fear by learning more about the safety features of the plane, or by reading the statistics on how infrequent crashes are, or by accumulating multiple positive experiences of flying. And I might even come to enjoy flying. My emotions changed based on a new perception of my environment—*flying is not a threat to my life in the way I had thought before.*

Appraisal Theory and Love

Having laid out in brief the appraisal theory of emotion (with special attention to the work of Lazarus), what can we say about love, in particular love commands in moral discourse? First, if we are talking about feelings of love, these can't really be commanded any more than fright or surprise. Commanding love is often a way of addressing how we perceive the people or things around us in relation to our ultimate goals. Real love, that deep care or concern for something or someone, involves tethering our being to that thing or person. Our soul becomes wrapped up in it. It could be a family member or spouse (things we consider natural and noble), or it could be infatuation with attaining a certain job or income level. Put simply, love is the universal language humans use (across cultures) to talk about the things we most deeply want, the things that give us satisfaction or fulfillment—or at least that is what we *think*. As we shift our priorities and reconsider some of those ultimate goals, our loves will change as well. Jesus put his finger on this reality when he said, "No one can serve two masters. Either you will hate the one and love the other, or you will be devoted to the one and despise the other. You cannot serve both God and money" (Matt 6:24 RSV alt.). Jesus's point here is that if God is one's ultimate focus and pleasing him is the goal, then the servant will love God. If it is money, then the heart will drive the person to be devoted to

Perspectives on Love

acquiring money. You simply can't love everyone and everything, because love is what we express toward our deepest wants and desires. Lazarus quotes the classic words of Saint Augustine: "For what are desire and joy but a volition of consent to the things we wish?"[28]

To seek to shape or reshape love, then, is to touch those things we most ultimately value and desire. And the reality is, our loves and desires can too easily be misguided and misshapen. So teachers, moralists, preachers, therapists, and parents all urge us to love something better if we have pointed our lives at the wrong things. The objective isn't to suppress love, as if loving or wanting or longing or desiring are limitations. Loving is innate to human experience; feeling love works in conjunction with our minds and wills. The objective is to love the right things, to love well, and to better understand and utilize (or bridle) our love—because love is such a powerful emotion that when it is not understood or controlled, it can do damage to others and to ourselves.

Loving God with the Whole Self

This appraisal theory of emotion can be very beneficial for understanding emotion language overall in the Bible, and Paul in particular. It is telling that the focal point of the Deuteronomic covenant is not righteousness, holiness, truth, or even obedience. All of those things are important, of course, but the emphasis is on *love*. For God to command Israel's love (Deut 6:5) is not meant to be forced subservience or merely external compliance. The kings of old often demanded such obeisance from their subjects, but love is not the same thing. To call for love is to invite someone to direct or redirect their whole being toward someone or something and intertwine their whole being with another. It is instructive that Deuteronomy makes this clear with reference to loving God with *heart, soul,* and *might*.[29] They might represent somewhat different *aspects* of our being, but in any case, the sum total of the three implies a sense of wholeness, authenticity, and total commitment. But the mention of "heart" (Hebrew: *levav*; Greek: *kardia*) makes it clear that "love" really does mean love. Not the Cupid kind of fleeting infatuation but something connected to one's deepest sense of self. This is how authentic, relational piety is

28. Lazarus, *Emotion and Adaptation*, 94.
29. We will discuss this at length in chapter 2.

CHAPTER 1

expressed throughout the Old Testament, love of God that manifests without and comes from within. Deuteronomy tells us that in days long past, YHWH "set his heart in love" on the patriarchs (Deut 10:15).[30] Before YHWH called Israel to covenantal love, he had already turned his heart toward affection and care for this people.

The nature of Israel's reciprocal dedication for YHWH is explained in terms of "circumcision of the heart" (Deut 10:16; 30:6). Circumcision of the male foreskin was, of course, a physical ritual that signaled commitment. But the ritual itself was never going to be enough, and external obedience all by itself was also not enough. If love is true, if it is genuine, it must be lived and expressed, but this must come from within; it must come from the *heart*. Circumcision of the heart was a symbol of inner dedication. The image of cutting itself is not about *removal* (that would mean death!), but some element of sacrifice may be implied. This tracks with what we have described about cognitive theories of love. Our deepest loves (and goals) are somewhat exclusive, because we can truly love only a precious few things, those things we intertwine our lives with, like those bonds of affection shown by YHWH toward the patriarchs. To focus on that exclusive sort of love *here* (with YHWH) and not *elsewhere* takes us back again to the singular confession: "The LORD is our God, the LORD is one" (or, "the LORD alone"). To love the Lord with *all* of one's heart, soul, and might is to point and focus love and passion and energy and commitment on this one person and no other.

The final goal in this chapter is to take a deeper dive into the Greek terminology regarding love. Not only will this help to understand the words of Paul and other New Testament writers, but there is also work to be done to correct certain popular myths and misunderstandings.

LOVE, IN OTHER WORDS

The tendency of discussions of love in biblical studies is to fixate on the single term *agapē* (which is especially apparent in May's work)—and this is understandable. After all, it became *the* distinctive term representing the perfect and unique love that God exemplifies and serves as the highest virtue (as Lewis sug-

---

30. The NRSV's "set his heart" reflects the Hebrew *hashaq*, which means "bind." Love, from this angle, is conceived of as bonds of affection. The word for "love" in the same phrase is *ahav*.

32

Perspectives on Love

gests). This is also reinforced in Oda Wischemeyer's excellent monograph *Love as* Agape: *The Early Christian Concept and Modern Discourse.*[31] But languages don't work with single terms only, certainly not concepts as capacious and complex as love. So it is best to think in terms of a word *cluster*, rather than fixate on one word. And, it will become clear, early Christian writers like Paul did not limit themselves to only one word for love. *Agapē* appears in key places and captures something unique and distinctive in early Christian literature, but it is unwise to take a myopic approach when trying to understand Paul's language of love.

There is some subjectivity involved in choosing the terms that fit within the category of love. We will use J. P. Louw and Eugene A. Nida's semantic-domain index as our general guide.[32] Louw and Nida place love under the general umbrella of "Attitudes and Emotions" (#25). From there, they isolate a set of related words that fit the heading "Love, Affection, Compassion" (#25C). Below are the keywords they list.

Phileō, philia. This is the general language of affection and affinity. *Philia* is the classic word for "friendship" and "relationship."

Agapaō, agapē. We will give extensive attention to this term throughout our study, but here we can briefly say that in ancient Greek (before the emergence of Christian literature), this was not a unique term representing the highest and most noble form of love. In fact, the noun was not common at all, and the verb was often used with the meaning "to be content/to be satisfied." Louw and Nida make this important statement in their lexicon: "It would . . . be quite wrong to assume that *phileō* and *philia* refer only to human love, while *agapaō* and *agapē* refer to divine love. Both sets of terms are used for the total range of loving relations between people, between people and God, and between God and Jesus Christ."[33]

Zēlos, zēloō. These terms involve deep passion or concern, hence the English word "zeal." It involves an intensity of feeling; it can be used for "good zeal" or "bad zeal," depending on context.

Ancient Greek had a range of terms representing passion or desire as an instinctual human phenomenon: *epipotheō* (yearn), *splanchnizomai* (feel compassion, concern), *sympatheō* (have sympathy).

---

31. Oda Wischmeyer, *Love as* Agape: *The Early Christian Concept and Modern Discourse* (Waco, TX: Baylor University Press, 2021).

32. J. P. Louw and Eugene A. Nida, *Greek-English Lexicon of the New Testament: Based on Semantic Domains* (New York: United Bible Societies, 1989).

33. Louw and Nida, *Greek-English Lexicon,* 294.

CHAPTER 1

In a different section of Louw and Nida's dictionary, they list terms under "Help, Care for" (#35). Some of these Greek terms overlap with concern for those who are loved (*epimeleomai, epimeleia; thalpō*).

What about *storgē* (verb, *stergō*), the Greek term that Lewis defines as "affection"? Louw and Nida don't address this word group because the specific noun or verb forms don't appear in the New Testament. In the Septuagint, they pop up only a few times (Sir 27:17; 3 Macc 5:32; 4 Macc 14:13). *Storgē* refers to love in a general way, but not in a way that presents a hard distinction from *phileō*.

Again, Paul used a variety of terms and metaphors to talk about love, but it will become clear that the *agapē* and *phileō* word groups became dominant in his letters (*phil-*, 25 times; *agap-*, 115 times). Why Paul latched on to *agapē* is not exactly clear. He is our earliest (extant) Christian writer, so we cannot be sure what sources influenced his Christian language, but we will argue that the word choices made in the Septuagint as well as in the Jesus tradition must have made an impact on primitive Christianity, which then influenced Paul.

The Danger of Overloading *Agapē*

It is important at this point to address a key book from the early twentieth century that made a big impact on biblical scholarship and Christian theology but has now been shown to have overloaded individual Greek words with too much theological meaning.[34] The book is *Agape and Eros* by Anders Nygren (first published 1930; English 1953).[35] Nygren argued for a binary dualism between *eros*, what he considered "selfish love," and *agapē*, "Christian love." Nygren associated *eros* with the flesh-centered teachings of Plato and Aristotle. Christian love (*agapē*), Nygren argued, is spontaneous and unmotivated, indifferent to worth, creative (adding value), and initiating care; *eros*, on the other hand, is "acquisitive" (taking for oneself, selfish), fleshly, and egocentric. *Eros* wants what is valuable, *agapē* makes something more valuable. Nygren was

---

34. Nicholas Woltersdorff's summary about Nygren's work is incisive: "his theology is unacceptable, his exegesis untenable, his intellectual history questionable." See Nicholas Wolterstorff, *Justice: Rights and Wrongs* (Princeton: Princeton University Press, 2008), 98.

35. Anders Nygren, *Agape and Eros: A Study of the Christian Idea of Love*, trans. A. G. Hebert and Philip S. Watson (London: SPCK, 1953).

Perspectives on Love

the master of pithy expressions, but his lexical-semantic work and historical research were deeply flawed. He painted with such broad brushstrokes that it is hard to recognize any true and accurate depictions in his work. Ancient moral philosophers like Aristotle, Plato, Plutarch, Epictetus, and Seneca could talk about love in sophisticated ways, using various terms (including *eros* but more commonly forms of *phileō*). It is misleading to force them into a mold labeled *eros*.

Nygren also contrasted *agapē* with Jewish *nomos* (law). For Nygren, Jewish religion was focused on cold and obligatory performance of law commands, not love. Nygren recognized that love language is present in the Old Testament, but it is a matter of structure. For Nygren, *nomos*, "law," was the Old Testament scheme, and love could happen within that. But then Jesus came along and broke down the law system itself, and all that was left was love. Simon May engages with Nygren and counts his work as the epitome of an antisemitic purist interpretation of Christian love over and against love in any other culture or religion. And May points out that one has to willfully ignore vast portions of both Old and New Testaments to go along with Nygren's theological construct and analysis. May cites several New Testament texts that hold love (*agapē*) and law (*nomos*) together, rather than forcing them into opposition (e.g., John 13:34–35; 15:14; 1 John 3:23).

Unfortunately, Nygren's book was broadly accepted and praised in his era, though not by everyone. Frederick C. Grant (Union Theological Seminary) wrote a perceptive review in 1955 for *Anglican Theological Review*. Grant straightaway identified that Nygren imported his ideas into the ancient texts and failed to read them on their own terms, in their individuality of expression: "The majority of theologians handle ideas only in neat, well-labeled bundles; and the labeling is done, as a rule, with reference to some preconceived dogmatic system. Their inquiry is not, *What did this book, poem, work of art mean to those for whom—or by whom—it was created?* But rather, *What can it be made to mean as a foil to our already established set of ideas or principles?* In other words, their main interest is in argument, not in understanding or appreciation: they are, as Emerson said, 'retained attorneys.'"[36] Grant noted that Nygren downplayed the grandeur of Socrates's teachings on love in Plato's *Symposium*. He

---

36. Frederick C. Grant, review of *Agape and Eros*, by Anders Nygren, *Anglican Theological Review* 37 (1955): 67–68.

explained, "To make Plato's dramatic exposition of the meaning of *eros*, for different men and in different circumstances, the formal statement of the Hellenistic conception of *love*, and to describe it as wholly self-regarding, acquisitive, egocentric emotion, is simply to ignore the real conception of that motive as it is displayed in the heroic figures which dominated Greek drama, art, sculpture, and poetry for thousands of years." Grant exposed Nygren's problematic goal of demonstrating Christian superiority to paganism and Judaism. As for the latter, Jesus himself prayed and taught the Shema and drew inspiration from the Jewish Psalter, which repeats the steadfast covenantal love of God. Grant appropriately asked, "Was the word *agapē* never in use until the Christians invented it? Or did it never mean God's love until Paul so used it?"[37] What do we do, Grant wondered, with the positive uses of *agapē* for divine love in the Septuagint, Philo, and the Jewish pseudepigrapha?

In the end, Grant admitted that Paul and other early Christian writers *did* infuse *agapē* with a certain distinctiveness in relation to the way of Jesus ("a *nova res* in human thought").[38] But Nygren greatly overstated his case at the cost of distorting both Hellenism and Judaism.

Nygren's book is a cautionary tale on how *not* to undertake a study of Paul's theology and language of love. In this chapter, we have attempted to lay the foundation for understanding Paul's conception and expressions of love, but before we can open the pages of Paul's letters, we need to examine the culture, texts, and traditions that would have shaped the apostle's thought world and vocabulary, beginning with the Old Testament and Jewish tradition.

37. Grant, review of *Agape and Eros* (by Nygren), 69, 70.
38. Grant, review of *Agape and Eros* (by Nygren), 73.

2

Love in the Old Testament and Jewish Tradition

[In the Shema, love involves] intense devotion; absolute trust; fear
of his power and presence; and rapturous, if often questioning,
absorption of his will: its demands, meanings, vagaries, and
contradictions. Its moods are a combination of the piety of a vassal,
the intimacy of friends, the fidelity of spouses, the dependence
of a child, the passion of lovers, the intoxicated obedience of a
hostage—and the terror aroused by all these forms of vulnerability.

—Simon May[1]

In the previous chapter, we noted that Anders Nygren's study of *eros* and *agapē*
had a significant impact in his time, and this reinforced the unfortunate juxta-
position of Old and New Testaments, the former focused on *nomos* (law) and
the latter on *agapē* (love), in Nygren's formulation. Now, it is true that torah is
central to the life of Israel, but the goal of the New Testament was never to use
love to abolish the Jewish law, as if torah itself was preventing Israel from truly
knowing God. Both Simon May and Frederick Grant underscored that the
Jesus of the Gospels draws his love language precisely *from* the Old Testament,
and it can be easily demonstrated that love is at the heart of Israel's covenantal
relationship with God.

---

1. Simon May, *Love: A History* (New Haven: Yale University Press, 2012), 33–34.

CHAPTER 2

The *Hesed* Love of God

Too often modern caricatures of the Old Testament portray God as hot tempered, cold, cruel, vengeful, and impersonal. But Jews throughout history (and today as well) have turned to Exodus to explain the gracious identity of their God. In Exodus 33:18, Moses asks to see the divine glory. The Lord obliges, though he cannot be seen directly by mortals. He deposits Moses in the cleft of a rock where the Lord would pass by. As the Lord passed by Moses, he revealed himself with these words:

> The LORD, the LORD,
> a God merciful and gracious,
> slow to anger,
> and abounding in steadfast love and faithfulness,
> keeping steadfast love for the thousandth generation,
> forgiving iniquity and transgression and sin,
> yet by no means clearing the guilty,
> but visiting the iniquity of the parents
> upon the children
> and the children's children,
> to the third and the fourth generation. (Exod 34:6–7)

Moses hears this word and repeats it back to the Lord in Numbers 14 when he is pleading on behalf of Israel (14:18–19). And again in Deuteronomy, the Lord reminds them of his grace-filled disposition, showing steadfast love to the thousandth generation of his covenantal people who heed his word (Deut 5:8–10; cf. 7:9).

The Hebrew word for "love" here is *hesed*, often translated as "kindness," "lovingkindness," "faithfulness," or "loyal love." Katherine Sakenfeld has written extensively on the meaning of *hesed* in the Hebrew Bible and makes the case that three things tend to be true when this word group is used.[2] First, it is more action oriented than focused on the feelings of the lover or loved. That is to say, in Hebrew tradition, *hesed* is something one person *does* for someone they care about. Second, this action-oriented love is a part of an

---

2. Katherine Doob Sakenfeld, *The Meaning of* Hesed *in the Hebrew Bible* (Boston: Brill, 1978).

Love in the Old Testament and Jewish Tradition

existing relationship. It does not take place between strangers or mere acquaintances. And it does not initiate a new relationship. *Hesed* belongs to those who are already committed to each other. Third, *hesed* is love that gives *essential* care to the well-being of another. It is not simply gestures of affection, like the ancient equivalent of a box of chocolates. *Hesed* love invests in the well-being and thriving of the loved. *Hesed* love guards and nurtures the other's *life*.

Hesed appears throughout the Old Testament, but it is especially prominent in the Psalter, where we find repeated affirmations of the steadfast or loyal love of God, so much so that the Psalms could be classified as love songs! The love of YHWH protects Israel, forgives Israel, and offers comfort and care. Psalm 136 repeats praise for the Lord's *hesed* twenty-six times with the same refrain: "for his steadfast love endures forever" (in every verse of the psalm). Each verse points to some activity or attribute of YHWH that reveals his love: his goodness, his supremacy, and especially his tenacious support for Israel: "It is he who remembered us in our low estate . . . and rescued us from our foes" (136:23–24). The exodus event continued to be a core memory of the Lord's enduring love and covenant faithfulness.

What is clear when we look at the uses of *hesed* in relationship to God in the Old Testament is that love and covenant go hand in hand. Covenant is the *context* of God's love relationship with Israel. And torah, the Jewish law, becomes a central part of the covenant, defining clearly *how* God and Israel love one another. Torah is not the enemy of love; they do not repel one another like opposing magnets. On the contrary, Israel professes *love* for the law, precisely *because* it is how God wants to be loved by his treasured people (Ps 119:97, 113, 163, 165). Over and over again we find that loving God is associated with keeping the covenantal commandments. Here is a sampling:

> Know therefore that the LORD your God is God, the faithful God who maintains covenantal loyalty with those who love him and keep his commandments, to a thousand generations. (Deut 7:9)

> You shall love the LORD your God, therefore, and keep his charge, his decrees, his ordinances, and his commandments always. (Deut 11:1)

> Take good care to observe the commandment and instruction that Moses the servant of the LORD commanded you, to love the LORD your God, to

CHAPTER 2

walk in all his ways, to keep his commandments, and to hold fast to him, and to serve him with all your heart and with all your soul. (Josh 22:5)

Now, it might seem like the New Testament preserves the emphasis on love but does away with the law and its commandments. But as both May and Grant point out (as discussed in the previous chapter), we see very similar language in the Johannine literature.

They who have my commandments and keep them are those who love me; and those who love me will be loved by my Father, and I will love them and reveal myself to them. (John 14:21)

If you keep my commandments, you will abide in my love, just as I have kept my Father's commandments and abide in his love. (John 15:10)

By this we know that we love the children of God, when we love God and obey his commandment. For the love of God is this: that we obey his commandments. And his commandments are not burdensome. (1 John 5:2–3)

We will get to the New Testament later on in this book, but suffice it to say for now that the Old Testament can be about the *hesed* love of God *and* about torah as the way Israel expresses and reciprocates love.

THE *AHAVAH* LOVE OF ISRAEL FOR GOD

Hesed is the most common expression of divine love toward Israel, YHWH's generous and faithful covenantal love. But when we look at the love that Israel is expected to have toward YHWH, we do not typically find *hesed* used in that way. Rather, we more commonly find *ahavah*, the more generic Hebrew word for love. It covers a wide range of human intensity of feelings of love, from hobbies and food preferences (Gen 25:28; 27:14), to romantic love (Gen 29:18; Judg 16:4; 1 Kgs 11:1), to friendship (Judg 5:31; 1 Sam 18:1), to evil desires, infatuations, and addictions (Isa 1:23; 56:10; Jer 14:10).

There is an especially high concentration of this word group in Hosea, which makes sense, because Hosea uses the dominant metaphor of Israel as a wayward lover who has chosen idols and forsaken their exclusive relationship

40

Love in the Old Testament and Jewish Tradition

with the Lord (Hos 3:1). Occasionally, YHWH's love for Israel is called *ahavah*: "I have *loved* you with an everlasting *love*" (Jer 31:3). But by and large it is used for the expectations of Israel's love for YHWH. This is a good example: YHWH is "the great and awesome God who keeps covenant and steadfast love [*hesed*] with those who love [*ahav*] him and keep his commandments" (Neh 1:5). The most important and most discussed love text of the Old Testament is the Shema, Deuteronomy 6:4–9:

> Hear, O Israel: The LORD is our God, the LORD alone. You shall love the LORD your God with all your heart, and with all your soul, and with all your might. Keep these words that I am commanding you today in your heart. Recite them to your children and talk about them when you are at home and when you are away, when you lie down and when you rise. Bind them as a sign on your hand, fix them as an emblem on your forehead, and write them on the doorposts of your house and on your gates.

We will spend most of the remainder of this chapter on this core passage of Jewish thought, worship, and religion.

LOVE YHWH, YOUR ONE AND ONLY

Deuteronomy is a foundational text in the Old Testament. As Walter Moberly observes, it is "the most systematic account of the relationship between YHWH and Israel, whose perspectives inform substantial parts of the histories and the prophetic literature."[3] It expresses most clearly and extensively the nature of the covenant relationship, where each party pledges commitment to the other, and Israel can have full assurance of YHWH's protective care.[4] Certainly Deuteronomy, as the book name suggests, reiterates the *nomistic* dynamic of the covenant, but it would be a mistake to see this book merely as a collection of rules for Israel to follow. YHWH's interest in Israel is not focused on making them into his slave labor or extracting from them tangible benefits. Rather, what is reiterated in Deuteronomy is YHWH's *love* (7:8). Put another

---

3. R. W. L. Moberly, *Old Testament Theology: Reading the Hebrew Bible as Christian Scripture* (Grand Rapids: Baker, 2015), 8.

4. See Walter Brueggemann, *Deuteronomy*, AOTC (Nashville: Abingdon, 2001), 17.

41

CHAPTER 2

way, Deuteronomy talks about law, not in contrast to love but in the context of love.[5] This is demonstrated throughout the whole pentateuchal book but is epitomized in the Shema, where it becomes clear that, as Jürgen Moltmann poignantly observes, "all the commandments are explications of the one commandment, to love God and to cleave to him."[6]

The Shema begins with a theological affirmation as Israel is called to attention: "The LORD is our God, the LORD alone" or "the LORD is one." Throughout the centuries, the Shema has been associated with monotheism, the belief in one God. Now is not the place to debate whether ancient Israel had a clear and consistent notion of monotheism at this time, but suffice it to say here that the focus of Deuteronomy is on Israel's life in covenant and their *exclusive* relationship with YHWH. They were positioned at the borders of Canaan, and as they journeyed into and took control over the land, they would face temptation to forget the law of Moses and worship false gods. "When the LORD your God has brought you into the land ... take care that you do not forget the LORD, who brought you out of Egypt, out of the house of slavery. The LORD your God you shall fear; him you shall serve, and by his name alone you shall swear. Do not follow other gods, any of the gods of the peoples who are all around you, because the LORD your God, who is present with you, is a jealous God" (Deut 6:10–15a). Moberly argues that the "one" (*ehad*) of YHWH's identity is not specifically about divine singularity but primarily directed at singular *devotion*. Moberly makes a connection to the appearance of *ehad* (one) in Song of Songs: "My dove, my perfect one, is the only one [*ehad*]" (Song 6:9). Obviously, the lover's point is not that his beloved is the only other person in the world but rather the most treasured, and thus worthy of exclusive devotion. This offers an insightful parallel to Deuteronomy 6:4. "If YHWH our God is 'the one and only,' then Israel's unreserved love is indeed the appropriate response."[7] Dean McBride affirms much the same. He describes YHWH as a jealous God who calls for exclusive allegiance.[8]

---

5. See William Sanford LaSor, David Allan Hubbard, and Frederic William Bush, *Old Testament Survey* (Grand Rapids: Eerdmans, 1996), 122; see also Jon D. Levenson, *The Love of God* (Princeton: Princeton University Press, 2020).

6. Jürgen Moltmann, *Theology of Hope* (Minneapolis: Fortress, 1993), 121.

7. Moberly, *Old Testament Theology*, 18, 20.

8. S. Dean McBride, "The Yoke of the Kingdom: An Exposition of Deuteronomy 6:4–5," *Interpretation* 27 (1973): 294; Gordon McConville, *Deuteronomy*, Apollos (Downers Grove, IL: IVP Academic, 2002), 141.

Love in the Old Testament and Jewish Tradition

From this perspective, there is a clearer connection between Deuteronomy 6:4 ("YHWH is one") and Deuteronomy 6:5 ("love YHWH your God"). Love, as Brueggemann notes, is the "superlative degree of total commitment."[9] Israel is a covenantal vassal expected to honor and regard YHWH as suzerain. Their religion, piety, and devotion is not, as McBride poignantly expresses, "mystical self-denial or spiritual privatism" but communion between God and a people in a relationship of grace and obedience. McBride summarizes the essence and goal of the love command in this way: "Serve him with your whole being in order to prosper his kingdom on earth."[10]

But what *exactly* does Deuteronomy mean when it speaks of love here and throughout the book? There is a fascinating and insightful debate in scholarship that is moving toward a consensus. It is helpful to begin with an influential article written by William L. Moran from 1963.[11] Looking at forms of *ahav(ah)* in Deuteronomy, Moran argued that this pentateuchal book aligns with love language in ancient Near Eastern political and legal texts, where vassals are called to loyalty toward their superiors. In these contexts, then, love is not fixated on feeling, intimacy, or personal fulfillment. "Compliance" and "obedience" are the keywords that would be the main concerns of this love.[12] When we look at Deuteronomy, then, Moran argues that the Shema love command "epitomizes the book's central preoccupation, namely, observance of the Law."[13] Covenantal obedience is what love looks like in Deuteronomy (Deut 10:12; 19:9). Moran argues that readers of Deuteronomy ought not to sentimentalize the text's love language, as if love is expressed as an internal emotion. The legal-religious setting of Israel makes it clear that if love can be commanded, it more closely relates to action than feeling. When a regent dictates love from his subjects, he is expecting loyalty, service, and obedience to his laws.[14]

---

9. Brueggemann, *Deuteronomy*, 84.

10. McBride, "Yoke of the Kingdom," 304.

11. William L. Moran, "The Ancient Near Eastern Background of the Love of God in Deuteronomy," *CBQ* 25 (1963): 77–87.

12. Moran walks through evidence from Egyptian texts. He also gives an example from the historical books of the Old Testament; in 1 Kings 5:1, King Hiram of Tyre is called David's "friend" (*ohev*), this term reflecting a diplomatic relationship, not a personal one. See Moran, "Ancient Near Eastern Background," 81.

13. Moran, "Ancient Near Eastern Background," 77.

14. Moran "Ancient Near Eastern Background," 77, 78.

CHAPTER 2

Several scholars have affirmed Moran's approach to Deuteronomy's love language.[15] They recognize that what YHWH especially calls for in this context is practical allegiance; YHWH is not a friend who wants (simply) warm feelings of affection. He is their God and expects obedience. Susan Ackerman observes that while Deuteronomy's setting is more political, there are other texts where the imagery of marriage and family are more dominant and, thus, the meaning of "love" would come across differently (e.g., in Hosea, Ezekiel, and Jeremiah).[16]

While virtually all Old Testament or Hebrew Bible scholars agree that the love language of Deuteronomy should be interpreted in relation to a political covenantal context, there has been some pushback against the notion that Deuteronomy is fixated on allegiance and not feelings of love. Jacqueline Lapsley, for instance, argues that, even though *ahav* can emphasize duty and service, that does not thereby eliminate an affective element.[17] Lapsley argues that definitions of "love" cannot be so easily siloed into categories of internal (emotional) versus external (obedience) that are unrealistic and unnatural to human life. Also, she detects in Moran's discussion a sense that he assumes emotions do not influence (or should not influence) ethics.[18] But this is not really how obedience and action operate. In everyday life, we don't bracket out our feelings or personal thoughts. In fact, on the contrary, our inner life comes to expression precisely *in* our behavior. It is possible that one might carry out an act out of sheer duty without liking the idea or wanting to personally, but the evidence in Deuteronomy itself doesn't seem to bear that out; YHWH wants more than cold obedience.

15. Moshe Weinfeld, *Deuteronomy 1–11*, AB (New Haven: Yale University Press, 1991). See Susan Ackerman, "The Personal Is Political: Covenantal and Affectionate Love in the Hebrew Bible," *Vetus Testamentum* 52 (2002): 437–58; Brueggemann is largely positive about Moran's insights but still finds it too one-sided; see also McBride, "Yoke of the Kingdom."

16. Ackerman, "Personal Is Political," 457.

17. Jaqueline Lapsley, "Feeling Our Way: Love for God in Deuteronomy," *CBQ* 65 (2003): 350–69.

18. Lapsley, "Feeling Our Way," 366; see also R. W. L. Moberly, "Toward an Interpretation of the Shema," in *Theological Exegesis in Honor of Brevard S. Childs*, ed. C. Seitz and K. Greene-McCreight (Grand Rapids: Eerdmans, 1999), 134n19; Walter Brueggemann, *Theology of the Old Testament* (Minneapolis: Fortress, 1997), 416–17, 420.

Love in the Old Testament and Jewish Tradition

Time after time, in fact, the commands and expectations emphasize the inner life of Israel, specifically devotion to YHWH with heart (*levav*) and soul (*nephesh*).[19] Here is a sampling:

So now, O Israel, what does the LORD your God require of you? Only to fear the LORD your God, to walk in all his ways, to love him, to serve the LORD your God *with all your heart and with all your soul*. (Deut 10:12)

You shall love the Lord your God, therefore, and keep his charge, his decrees, his ordinances, and his commandments always. (Deut 11:1)

Heed his every commandment that I am commanding you today—loving the LORD your God, and serving him *with all your heart and with all your soul*. (Deut 11:13)

If you will diligently observe this entire commandment that I am commanding you, *loving the Lord your God*, walking in all his ways, and holding fast to him . . . (Deut 11:22)

Moreover, the LORD your God will *circumcise your heart and the heart of your descendants*, so that you will love the LORD your God *with all your heart and with all your soul*, in order that you may live. (Deut 30:6)

In ways similar to Lapsley's argument, Bill Arnold has also challenged Moran's internal-external approach to love in Deuteronomy. While Deuteronomy may emphasize the importance of obedience to the commandments, that does not eliminate internal aspects like affection.[20] He looks at the language of fear in Deuteronomy, noting that it has cognitive *and* affective dimensions. Fear is related to our emotional responses to intimidation and threats (Deut 1:21, 29; 20:3). And it is also something that can be commanded, representing a virtue and value that one holds. YHWH calls the people to *learn* proper fear

19. See also Old Testament texts highly dependent on Deuteronomy: Joshua 22:5; 23:11; Daniel 9:4; Nehemiah 1:5.

20. Bill T. Arnold, "The Love-Fear Antimony in Deuteronomy 5–11," *Vetus Testamentum* 61 (2011): 552.

CHAPTER 2

of their God (4:10; cf. 6:24; 31:12). There is some sense in which fear can be controlled, or at least channeled toward obedience of God's commandments (5:29; cf. 6:13). This is summed up well in Deuteronomy 10:12–13:

> So now, O Israel, what does the LORD your God require of you? Only to fear the LORD your God, to walk in all his ways, to love him, to serve the LORD your God with all your heart and with all your soul, and to keep the commandments of the LORD your God and his decrees that I am commanding you today, for your well-being.

So Arnold sees in Deuteronomy two different, but not unrelated, meanings or connotations of fear language. One type involves a "pathological anxiety" responding to a threat, which leads to "crippling inactivity." And also we find a more formative or positive use of fear language, which respects and obeys an authority or powerful figure. A key point that Arnold makes is that understanding fear as an *emotion* doesn't change or go away when it is used in the sense of obedience or commitment. Rather, relational nuance is *highlighted* without setting aside affect. Arnold argues that fear and love language works in similar ways in Deuteronomy, in that it calls Israel to exclusive commitment to YHWH that includes genuine emotion and relational connection. In fact, Arnold believes that Deuteronomy uniquely brings together fear and love as intertwined responses to covenantal fidelity, perhaps for the very first time. Deuteronomy took what previously was not related and forged a new "contiguous relationship" where these complement one another: where "love prevents terror and fear prevents irreverent familiarity."[21]

Most scholars, including Lapsley and Arnold, recognize that Moran did add something important to the discussion of love in Deuteronomy. He was able to relate it to love discourse more broadly in legal texts and recognize the expected outcome of obedience. But what these scholars have tried to do is *also* read Deuteronomy's love language in the context of YHWH's unique relationship with Israel. Along those lines, we can make a number of points that give texture to what "love" means.

Familial Love. To begin with, one of the unique elements of the Israelite religion is the emphasis on a kinship or familial relationship with God.[22] The

---

21. Arnold, "Love-Fear Antimony," 564, 567.

22. See Lapsley, "Feeling Our Way," 359; also Frank Moore Cross, "Kinship and

Lord their God is not just a political sovereign who demands obedience. He is a heavenly Father who cares for Israel as his child: "The LORD your God, who goes before you, is the one who will fight for you, just as he did for you in Egypt before your very eyes, and in the wilderness, where you saw how the LORD your God carried you, just as one carries a child, all the way that you traveled until you reached this place" (Deut 1:30–31). YHWH has compassion on Israel like a parent for a child. At times, this is stated forthrightly (Deut 14:1–2). So too, YHWH desires that Israel grows up in faith and maturity, so like a parent YHWH disciplines them (Deut 8:5; cf. 32:5, 9). This is meant to communicate genuine care, not attempts to coerce.

YHWH as Example. Lapsley also notes that the kind of love that YHWH expects *from* Israel would naturally resemble the kind of love YHWH shows *for* Israel. We get a clear glimpse of that in Deuteronomy 7:7–8: "It was not because you were more numerous than any other people that the LORD set his heart on you and chose you—for you were the fewest of all peoples. It was because the LORD loved you and kept the oath that he swore to your ancestors, that the LORD has brought you out with a mighty hand, and redeemed you from the house of slavery, from the hand of Pharaoh king of Egypt." It is obvious that YHWH's love is a deep affection—he *set his heart* on them, and not because of some benefit received from helping them. Quite the opposite—Israel had nothing to give back of worldly value. Yet YHWH graciously devoted his whole self to rescuing and protecting this people. That same kind of internal plus external attachment is what YHWH expects *from* Israel: no more, no less. As Lapley writes, "God's love for Israel is not expressed solely in action but in the divine emotional response to Israel. Somehow, God's love for Israel is born out of a feeling, and that feeling has moral weight and relates in a significant way to the actions God takes on Israel's behalf."[23]

Responsive Love. From this perspective, the love that is expected and commanded by YHWH is not mere obedience to a king's decrees but a heartfelt response to loving God.[24] YHWH acted first, showering Israel with compassion,

---

Covenant in Ancient Israel," in *From Epic to Canon* (Baltimore: Johns Hopkins University Press, 1998), 3–21; Ronald E. Clements, "The Book of Deuteronomy," *NIB* 2:343.

23. Lapsley, "Feeling Our Way," 368.

24. Peter C. Craigie, *The Book of Deuteronomy*, NICOT (Grand Rapids: Eerdmans, 1976), 170.

CHAPTER 2

grace, and empowerment. What is expected is reciprocity, a kind of responsive love. While ancient covenants can and often did have unequal partners, they were still meant to be mutual and reciprocating relationships. McBride explains this as *gratitude*.

> Israel's fidelity is motivated out of gratitude for what Yahweh has done and promises to do and out of fear of the dire consequences of covenant breaking. To love God is to obey his decrees. But we would be remiss without underscoring the positive and trusting relationship which the command to love Yahweh so vividly expresses. The God who entered into treaty with Israel is not an obscure, otiose divine principle to be contemplated and revered from afar; neither is his rule whimsical or burdensome for those who acknowledge him. Love is an appropriate demand because it measures the personal, the intimate, and hence the particular dimension of covenant faith, the nearness of the cosmic divine king who is passionately concerned with day-to-day well-being of those who serve him.[25]

McBride describes the faith-filled love of Israel as more than mere submission to a ruler. It is a symbiosis between YHWH and Israel, ensuring life and wisdom and flourishing when the relationship is healthy. In 1902, S. R. Driver described Deuteronomy's covenantal expectations as true devotion "with undivided allegiance, and with the pure and intense affection denoted by the term 'love', to the service of the one Jehovah."[26]

Hear, O Israel

Now that we have a better orientation toward love language in Deuteronomy, let's return to the Shema to see how Israel is exhorted to know, trust, and obey YHWH.

25. McBride, "Yoke of the Kingdom," 301; similarly, see McConville, *Deuteronomy*, 141.

26. S. R. Driver, *A Critical and Exegetical Commentary on Deuteronomy*, 3rd ed., ICC (Edinburgh: T&T Clark, 1902), 91.

Love in the Old Testament and Jewish Tradition

"Hear, O Israel: The LORD Is Our God, the LORD Alone" (Deut 6:4)

The Shema is at the same time a prayer (insofar as the Hebrew people chose to use it in prayer throughout history), a confession of faith, and a call to action. The first command is to "hear" (*shema*). On one level, hearing is about paying attention: alertness, attentiveness, attunement (Exod 18:19; Deut 4:1; 5:1). Several times throughout Deuteronomy, the same statement appears: "Hear, O Israel!" (9:1; 20:3; 27:9). These interjections appear at key moments throughout the book, calling Israel to remember the commands that follow.

Shema, in these contexts, is not only about attention and hearing but also *heeding* and *obeying*. Note how this verb is used in Genesis 26:5: "Abraham *obeyed* [lit., *heard*] my voice and kept my charge, my commandments, my statutes, and my laws." Hearing is seen here as an obedient attentiveness, a reaction-ready form of listening.[27] A number of times in Deuteronomy, Israel's *hearing* is essential to covenantal faithfulness.

> If you will only heed [*hear*] his every commandment that I am commanding you today—loving the LORD your God, and serving him with all your heart and with all your soul, then he will give the rain for your land in its season, the early rain and the later rain, and you will gather in your grain, your wine, and your oil; and he will give grass in your fields for your livestock, and you will eat your fill. (Deut 11:13–15)

> Today you have obtained the LORD's agreement: to be your God; and for you to walk in his ways, to keep his statutes, his commandments, and his ordinances, and to obey [*hear*] him. (Deut 26:17)

> I call heaven and earth to witness against you today that I have set before you life and death, blessings and curses. Choose life so that you and your descendants may live, loving the LORD your God, obeying him, and holding fast to [*hearing*] him; for that means life to you and length of days, so that you may live in the land that the LORD swore to give to your ancestors, to Abraham, to Isaac, and to Jacob. (Deut 30:19–20)

27. Moberly, *Old Testament Theology*, 22.

CHAPTER 2

So, in these contexts, hearing is not just something you do with the ears, though of course you have to listen to get the instructions in the first place. Ultimately, covenantal *hearing* is a readiness and willingness to do as instructed, to hold fast to the teaching, and to pour one's whole self into obedience.

The first thing that is stated is not a direct command but rather an affirmation: "The LORD is our God, the Lord alone" (or "the LORD is one"). We have already talked about this oneness affirmation. Suffice it to say here, Israel is invited to recognize singular devotion to their faithful God. He shall be their one and only. This is especially important as they enter Canaan, and they will face temptation to worship other gods (Deut 5:7; 6:14; 11:16, 28; 13:6; 28:14). These gods could so easily tempt and corrupt Israel (7:25; 29:17); these false gods could steal away their hearts (30:17). This is grounds for divine wrath (8:19). In fact, Deuteronomy prophesies that Israel will indeed commit idolatry of heart, worship, and act (31:16–20), which will initiate covenant curses and severe repercussions. Yet the Shema became an essential summary of God's covenantal yearning for Israel's devotion.

"You Shall Love the LORD Your God with All Your Heart, and with All Your Soul, and with All Your Might" (Deut 6:5)

The prime command in the Shema is that of love for God. As we have argued above, love (*ahav*) is not *only* external compliance, nor is it *only* inner feelings. Moberly wisely explains it as "a thoroughgoing internalization and appropriation of obedient action towards YHWH, so that action and intention fully cohere, and so do practice and thought."[28] Ultimately, this love is cultivated internally, becoming commitment and manifesting in active obedience. God's love imperative may seem strange. How can you force love? How can you command it? But it is about opening oneself up to another and nurturing certain values that help to grow in fondness for that one.[29]

The Shema explicates the depths and extent of this covenantal love. The first thing mentioned is whole-hearted love. This refers to genuine affection and personal commitment, active in the seat of the will.[30] The second aspect

28. Moberly, *Old Testament Theology*, 23.

29. See Lundbom, *Deuteronomy*, 311, 389.

30. Jeffrey Tigay, *Deuteronomy*, JPS Torah Commentary (Philadelphia: Jewish Publication Society of America, 1989), 77.

50

Love in the Old Testament and Jewish Tradition

is soul-grounded love. The "soul," *nephesh*, is not a spiritual existence separate from a bodily one—that is not how Hebrews understood the person. And yet, in cases like this, "soul" does carry a sense of something intangible, "the totality of one's thoughts, feelings, intentions, and desires."[31]

The last category that Deuteronomy references is "might" (*meod*). It is unclear exactly what this refers to. It could mean human *power*, as in "self-discipline."[32] Or perhaps the abundance of one's resources and abilities.[33] Daniel Block includes in this "muchness" everything at one's disposal, including physical strength, money, tools, livestock, and property.[34] McBride and Block both argue that "heart," "soul," and "might" are not three separate areas of life, but rather the terminology moves from inward to outward, the last item being all encompassing.[35] "This is the 'yoke of the kingdom,'" Block explains, "covenantal commitment rooted in the heart, but extending to every level of one's being."[36]

> Keep these words that I am commanding you today in your heart. Recite them to your children and talk about them when you are at home and when you are away, when you lie down and when you rise. Bind them as a sign on your hand, fix them as an emblem on your forehead, and write them on the doorposts of your house and on your gates. (Deut 6:7–9)

Israel is meant to carry these commandments, especially the Decalogue (Deut 5:1b–21), in their hearts, again an affirmation of the assimilation of the covenantal teachings and commandments into their whole life, not as a thoughtless obligation, but as a life philosophy.[37] Four actions are promoted

31. Tigay, *Deuteronomy*, 78.

32. Duane Christensen, *Deuteronomy 1–11*, WBC (Dallas: Word, 1991), 143.

33. McConville, *Deuteronomy*, 142.

34. Daniel Block, *Deuteronomy*, NIVAC (Grand Rapids: Zondervan, 2012), 184; see also Weinfeld, *Deuteronomy 1–11*, 332. As support for this, Weinfeld notes that Aramaic (targum) versions of Deuteronomy 6:5 make mention of "with all your property" (Targum Onkelos, Targum Neofiti, Targum Pseudo-Jonathan) and "with all your money" (Targum Pseudo-Jonathan and Targum Neofiti); cf. also rabbinic texts Sipre Deuteronomy 32; m. Berakhot 9:5.

35. McBride, "Yoke of Heaven," 304.

36. Block, *Deuteronomy*, 184.

37. See Patrick Miller, *Deuteronomy*, IBC (Louisville: Westminster John Knox, 2011), 104. The connection between the Shema (Deut 6:4–9) and the Decalogue is

CHAPTER 2

here. *Recite*—memorize and voice these commandments to your family to embed them into their memories and lives. *Discuss*—talk about the nature, importance, and expression of them. *Wear* and *display*—surround yourself with them, because they will mean the difference between prosperity and life, and decay and death. This is not normally how political texts talk about subjects interacting with laws and decrees. Deuteronomy expects from Israel a deeper level of commitment and engagement.

While Deuteronomy does not use the word "meditate" for God's law, it is expected and affirmed throughout the rest of the Old Testament, perhaps inspired by the Shema's insistence on hearing, reciting, discussing, and displaying.

> This book of the law shall not depart out of your mouth; you shall meditate on it day and night, so that you may be careful to act in accordance with all that is written in it. (Josh 1:8a)

> Happy are those who do not follow the advice of the wicked . . . their delight is in the law of the LORD, and on his law they meditate day and night. (Ps 1:1–2)

> I will meditate on your precepts, and fix my eyes on your ways. (Ps 119:15)

> I revere your commandments, which I love [*ahav*], and I will meditate on your statutes. (Ps 119:48)

Ben Sira promoted the same thing centuries later: "Reflect on the statutes of the Lord, and meditate at all times on his commandments. It is he who will give insight to your mind, and your desire for wisdom will be granted" (Sir 6:37). Loving the divine commandments and meditating on them reflect a personal commitment to the covenant, not unlike marriage vows. This is the path to blessing and prosperity for Israel. The alternative is being wooed away to follow false gods, a road to ruin.

---

affirmed in the Nash Papyrus (150–100 BCE), which contains both texts together in one place.

Love in the Old Testament and Jewish Tradition

IS LOVE A CONDITION OF THE COVENANT?

It is worth asking how love works as a covenantal command and obligation. Jon Levenson has written an important monograph on love in Judaism. He explains that the Hebrew Bible uses love language to express Israel's loyalty to the Lord, "accepting the yoke of the kingship of Heaven," as it is said in Jewish tradition (m. Berakhot 2:2). God will not tolerate divided allegiance. He is a jealous God. The love command is not a matter of earning the acceptance of Israel's God. Rather, the beloved is meant to show true commitment to the will of the sovereign. Their well-being is not safeguarded by their ability to perform perfectly before God. If that were the case, they would be hopeless. Rather, Israel constantly depends on God's grace. Precisely how this works in terms of conditionality is not neat and precise. Jon Levenson explains, "It is unconditional in that the love comes into, and remains, in force even when nothing has been done to deserve it. . . . But the relationship is also conditional in that it involves expectations and stipulations, and suffers and turns sour if they are not met."[38] Levenson points to ambiguous but real expectations of reciprocity that exist in personal relationships. There is a "morality of gratitude" at work that is not as simple as a commercial exchange of goods and benefits. Relationships do not thrive when they are based on reward or punishment alone. The guardrails of the covenantal blessings and curses keep Israel focused on the consequences of their actions and behavior. But genuine affection and loving commitment is ultimately what tethers YHWH and Israel together. It is no wonder, then, that Hosea concentrates on the imagery of marriage. YHWH conceives of Israel's propensity toward idolatry as adultery, covenantal infidelity. God is angry like a jealous spouse. Though he is also committed to compassion with the expectation that Israel will change its ways: "It bears mention that we are not dealing here with cheap grace—forgiveness without reform, restoration without repentance."[39]

38. Jon D. Levenson, *The Love of God* (Princeton: Princeton University Press, 2020), 62.

39. Levenson, *Love of God*, 97.

CHAPTER 2

A Testimony to the Caring God

In most ancient religious texts, the emphasis is on human reverence for the divine, the reinforcement of cosmic stratification of power where mortals act as subjects, and the expectation that rituals and sacrifices are done with regularity, specificity, and respect. Of course, the Old Testament contains some of these dynamics, but John Goldingay observes how comprehensively we find YHWH's covenantal love expressed and affirmed throughout. He offers over a dozen categories (I will combine some below) where the First Testament (Hebrew Bible/Old Testament), as he calls it, bears witness to the compassionate and caring nature of YHWH, Israel's God.[40]

> *Parental carrier*—YHWH carries his people like a parent or older family member carrying weaker or more vulnerable kin. Hosea depicts YHWH as a father loving a child, rescuing them from danger and harm (11:1–9). He carried them in his protective grasp, even when they kicked in rebellion (11:3). He enveloped them in love and kindness, providing for and nourishing them (11:4).
>
> *Motherly compassion*—YHWH is portrayed as a mother who bore this beloved child (Deut 32:18).
>
> *Attentiveness*—YHWH not only commands and dictates but listens with concern and compassion (Pss 5:3; 17:6; 55:17).
>
> *Mercy*—"For thus says the high and lofty one who inhabits eternity, whose name is Holy: I dwell in the high and holy place, and also with those who are contrite and humble in spirit, to revive the spirit of the humble, and to revive the heart of the contrite" (Isa 57:15).
>
> *Healing and cleansing*—YHWH seeks Israel's wholeness, healing, and blessing (Jer 33:6; Hos 6:1).
>
> *Lovingkindness and faithfulness*—YHWH promises steadfast love for the people whom he has chosen (Exod 20:6; Ps 146:6–7).
>
> *Passion*—"I am jealous for Zion with great jealousy, and I am jealous for her with great wrath" (Zech 8:2).
>
> *Atonement and forgiveness*—YHWH does not harbor bitterness toward Israel

40. John D. Goldingay, *Israel's Faith*, vol. 2 of *Old Testament Theology* (Downers Grove, IL: IVP Academic, 2006), 110–34.

Love in the Old Testament and Jewish Tradition

in their sin but lovingly forgives and seeks to reconcile. "Yhwh gets angry, but does not hold on to anger so that it becomes a permanent running resentment that makes it impossible to restore their relationship. . . . God declines to be offended, and the offenses therefore cease to exist."[41]

Sadness and grief—YHWH experiences grief because of Israel's sins (Isa 63:10). He does not stand at a cool distance, like a neutral judge. The covenantal relationship is personal and intimate, even as it is legal and professional. Goldingay is clear about the *emotions* of God transparently reflected in the Old Testament: "Scripture . . . corrects the idea of the impassibility of God, the idea that pain does not belong properly to God, which comes from outside Scripture."[42] In his personhood and covenantal relationality, YHWH opens up to love and being loved, which carries risk. Love has the capacity to bring exponential flourishing and joy, but it also comes with the risk of being hurt and rejected.

What we find in the Old Testament looks nothing like Nygren's analysis of YHWH's *nomos* (law) needing to be replaced by Jesus's *agapē* (love). On the contrary, it is easy to see why Jesus (and the New Testament writers) focus so much on love and draw from the deep well of Hebrew tradition (especially the Shema), whereby it is repeatedly affirmed that YHWH loves Israel and Israel is called to love YHWH in response; this is the master dynamic of the covenant. This love should be practiced and culminates in obedience, but there is an assumed inward dimension as well, a matter of the heart and soul. This God is no mere cosmic magistrate who makes demands of his mortal subjects. It is more like a parental relationship, where it is clearly not an equal partnership (YHWH is sovereign), but there is mutuality, trust, and a genuine desire for flourishing.

In the next chapter, we will shift from the Jewish religious world to the Hellenistic world, specifically the Greek language of love that offered the semantic and cultural vocabulary for Paul's expressions of love in his letters.

41. Goldingay, *Israel's Faith*, 127–28.
42. Goldingay, *Israel's Faith*, 134.

3

The Greek Language of Love

Love [*agapē*] is as powerful and stubborn as death,
passion [*zēlos*] is fierce, as terrifying as Hades.
Its sparks are sparks of fire,
its flames.
It burns so hot that oceans of water won't extinguish love [*agapē*],
and rivers will not wash it out.
If any man offered to pay all he owned to buy out love [*agapē*],
they would hate and mock him bitterly.

—Song of Songs 8:6–7
(my translation from the Septuagint)

What is love? It sounds like an existential question, and it is, but answering the question also involves semantics, so in this chapter, we will focus our attention on the Greek language of love as we find it in classical antiquity up to the time of the New Testament. We already mentioned some Greek terms for love in chapter 1 in brief; here we will explore this in more detail.[1]

1. See also James W. Thompson, *Moral Formation according to Paul* (Grand Rapids: Baker, 2011), 158–61. Thompson is especially skilled at discussing how love language was used by Greco-Roman moral philosophers. See also Oda Wischmeyer, *Love as Agape: The Early Christian Concept and Modern Discourse* (Waco, TX: Baylor University Press, 2021), 61–75.

The Greek Language of Love

Though *agapē* has become the most famous Greek term for love, Greek has a cluster of terms that relate to love, affection, and desire/passion.[2]

Our goal in this chapter is to consider the bigger picture of the nature of love and how it is expressed in Greek words. We often associate "love" today with a strong feeling that is especially experienced in marriage, other close family relationships, or friendship. But when we look at how love language is actually *used* then and now, it is remarkably elastic and covers a vast breadth of relationships, contexts, and levels of interest and intensity. Love language in the Septuagint, for example, clearly reflects this semantic breadth and diversity. We will make some brief comments here of a general nature about the Septuagint love vocabulary and usage, with more details below.

Love as Desire and Enjoyment

Perhaps the most familiar and comfortable definition of "love" is about enjoying and desiring someone or something. The psalmist proclaims, "Oh, how I loved [*ēgapēsa*] your law, O Lord! All day long it is my meditation" (Ps 118:97 LXX). Clearly Israel takes pleasure in and treasures the law, cherishing it. But love of this kind is not always attached to something good and pure. In Hosea, we find the prophetic word against Israel that they have reveled in shameful acts of sexual indulgences and improper allegiances and idolatry: "They loved [*ēgapēsan*] dishonor" (Hos 4:18). You can feel an attraction to something and enjoy it, but sometimes it is harmful and even self-destructive.

Love as Value Affirmation

In biblical discourse, sometimes "love" is used not so much in association with personal and spontaneous feelings but more with certain values that one holds. When we read in Isaiah that the Lord *loves* justice and *hates* crime, it

---

2. We have already mentioned the following terms (see pp. 32–34): *phileō/philos* (love); *agapaō/agapē* (love); *storgē* (affection); *zēloō/zēlos* (desire/zeal, devotion); *epipotheō* (yearn); *splanchnizomai/splanchna* (feel compassion/compassion); *sympatheō* (feel sympathy toward, share in feeling or pain).

CHAPTER 3

is less about what God enjoys and more about a moral commitment that is expressed in the form of love language. Similarly, Israel is exhorted in Amos to pursue goodness and shun evil in order to fully experience covenantal flourishing. Insofar as Israel has heeded that call, they can say, "We have *hated evil things* and *loved the good things*" (Amos 5:14, emphasis added). These kinds of statements identify core values that involve a person's feelings, will, character, and action. In these contexts, "love" is how one expresses value, investment, and commitment. Similarly, the famous covenantal expectation in Micah 6:8 reminds Israel of their obligation to seek what is good, to perform righteousness and justice, to walk with God in humility, and to "love mercy."

> Has it been told to you, O man, what is good
>   or what the Lord seeks from you,
> but to do judgment and to love mercy
>   and to be ready to walk with the Lord, your God?

To "love mercy" is to be fully invested in showing and acting upon compassion; it is not about producing a certain feeling, though feelings are involved. Love language sometimes expresses deep personal and communal values.[3]

The inverse is true as well. Sometimes we love things that we would never admit to, things that reveal deeper urges. So in Micah the Lord calls out the wickedness of the prophets and rulers. They are twisted in character, *hating* what is good and *pursuing* (*zēteō*) evil (Mic 3:2).[4]

We see similar usage of love language in non-Jewish Greek literature. The Greek philosopher Epictetus talked about love and moral philosophy at length in his discourses. He gives much attention to *utilitarian* love, the idea that we might place value and investment in someone or something because of what we get out of it. For example, Epictetus warns slaves (himself a former slave) that they ought not to be fooled into thinking that their master loves (*phileō*) them. Epictetus wonders, Does the master actually care about you, or are you a resource that he invested in protecting, like an effective sponge he uses to wipe his shoes, or an animal that can carry heavy loads? (paraphrase,

---

3. "Love mercy" in Hebrew: *ahav* + *hesed*; Greek Septuagint: *agapaō* + *eleos*.
4. Where the Septuagint has *zēteō* the MT has *ahav*.

Discourses 2.22.31a). Epictetus warns naive slaves that that love will magically evaporate when a slave gets sick or too old to be useful.

Epictetus argues that often love is a self-interested phenomenon. We love those things that secure and enhance our survival and happiness. Whenever we might feel threatened by something, we will hate it. And you can't love everything, just as you can't value everything. Humans often function like animals, engaging a survival instinct that protects what is theirs. We must be careful, Epictetus warns, because our primitive loves (of security, for example) can coerce and manipulate us into twisting the truth and giving into vice (*Discourses* 2.22.15–21).

And just as masters might not actually love slaves with pure intentions, so too slaves love masters (perhaps as sycophants) only because it might be to their advantage. He gives the example of the Roman emperor as a kind of high master of society. Do people actually *fear* or *revere* Caesar? No, Epictetus argues, they couldn't care less about the person. What they fear is Caesar's power—to execute, banish, penalize, imprison, and shame. And, alternatively, no man really *loves* Caesar either—at least, not the person. What they love is his power, wealth, status, and influence: "When we love, and hate, and fear these things, it must be that those who have the power over them must be our masters" (*Discourses* 4.1.60).

Epictetus also underscores what we saw in the Jewish tradition: if we are not careful, we can come to love evil, because we benefit from it. So Epictetus warns his readers to devote themselves to goodness, and their love will be attached to goodness (*Discourses* 2.22.1).

Love as Devotion

Love is not so easily partitioned out into separate meanings; rather, different shades of meaning are often blended together. We have to evaluate the connotations of its contextualized usage, which sometimes articulate pleasure, other times affinity and affection, and other times values and commitments. Clearly, from one context to another, there can be a certain emphasis on action or emotion, but in many cases "love" refers to a kind of comprehensive package of devotion that has wrapped up within it enjoyment, value, commitment, and action. A good example of this is found in the famous love passage from Song

CHAPTER 3

of Songs 8:6–7; here I will quote from the English translation of the Septuagint (my translation):

> Imprint me as a seal on your heart,
> as a seal on your arm,
> because love [*agapē*] is as powerful and stubborn as death,
> passion [*zēlos*] is fierce, as terrifying as Hades.
> Its sparks are sparks of fire,
> its flames.
> It burns so hot that oceans of water won't extinguish love [*agapē*],
> and rivers will not wash it out.
> If any man offered to pay all he owned to buy out love [*agapē*],
> they would hate and mock him bitterly.

We can see, then, that love can be many things. There are tiers of love, some more playful and minor (loving sweets or pleasant music), and there are more serious kinds of love. Song of Songs sings of love as a resilient, fierce, and even dangerous force—intangible, unstoppable, inexplicable, and yet something many of us can identify with deeply. According to Jewish tradition, love is a *superpower*. And just as we discussed in the previous chapter, there is a reason that core Old Testament texts like Deuteronomy 6:5 center love for God as *the* core covenantal response. Hosea, a kind of prophetic counterpart to Deuteronomy, expresses the divine hopes for covenantal restoration and consummation as unity through love.

Much of Hosea, truth be told, is warning of judgment and condemnation. But in those moments of hope and encouragement, we see the tender mercies of God on display. YHWH will rescue his people from death (Hos 13:13–14). But they must willingly repent and return (14:1–2). They must break their alliances with wicked nations and smash the idols they have made with their hands (14:3–4). When YHWH makes peace with Israel, their communal home and land will be healed, and he will love (*agapaō*) them without barrier or hesitation (14:4).

This is a point we will return to again and again in this book: love is important and revealing as we look at human behavior precisely because it indicates one's value system, what we choose to pursue, where we direct our lives, and

The Greek Language of Love

how we relate to others. Today, Western culture often associates love with pleasure and enjoyment, and ancients could certainly refer to that; but that is not always the case. Sometimes, love can indicate a deep commitment that doesn't always feel good. Think about love that we have for an aging parent in our care—the commitment is there even when it doesn't immediately come with tingly, warm feelings; we call that love, even when it doesn't include any element of infatuation or romance. Or what about an ex-husband or ex-wife who needs help from their former partner? There is sometimes that sense of concern but not exactly a relationship of affection. At its most basic, love is about connection, association, and attachment. That is what C. S. Lewis was getting at when he discussed *affection* as comfortability with the people in one's life. But love can range widely in intensity and commitment. At its strongest (as we read in Song of Songs 8:6–7), it is deeply passionate and an unstoppable force. In order to properly understand what the apostle Paul really means when he talks about love, we need to dig deeper into two keywords in Greek: *phileō* and *agapē*.

Phileō, Philos, Philia

We will now take a deeper dive into the two most important and most common love terms in ancient Greek: the *phileō* word group and the *agapē* word group. *Philos* is a noun or adjective that means "love" (affection, affinity) and is also associated with the concept of friend/friendship. For example, in the book of James, Abraham is called *philos theou*, "friend of God" (Jas 2:23). *Phileō* is a common verb meaning "to love." *Philia* is a noun that can refer to friendships in a number of contexts and involves varying levels of attachment and affection. Before we get into the details about this word group, it is helpful to engage with a New Testament debate that is now all but settled but serves as an insightful case study on how we think about love language in the Greek New Testament. In John 21:15–19, we find the post-resurrection story of Peter conversing with Jesus on the beach over breakfast. Jesus asks, "Simon son of John, do you love me more than these?" (21:15). Peter replies, "Yes, Lord; you know that I love you." Again, Jesus asks the same question, and again Peter answers. Jesus asks a third time, and again Peter says yes. Many a sermon has tried to explain the threefold questioning dynamic here by pointing to the change of wording:

61

CHAPTER 3

"Do you love [*agapas*] me more than these?" (21:15a).
"You know that I love [*philō*] you" (21:15b).
"Do you love [*agapas*] me?" (21:16a).
"You know that I love [*philō*] you" (21:16b).
"Do you love [*phileis*] me?" (21:17a).
"You know that I love [*philō*] you" (21:17b).

In the first two questions, Jesus uses the verb *agapaō*, and Peter responds affirmatively with *phileō*. In the third question, Jesus uses *phileō*, and Peter responds with the same. This has sometimes been explained as Jesus presenting some kind of supreme or ideal form of love to Peter (*agapaō*) at first, and Peter's able to admit only to a lower, more flawed or human form of love (*phileō*). Finally, Jesus lowers his standard, and asks whether Peter has even *phileō* love.[5] This explanation can offer some sparkle and pizzazz for a sermon, but unfortunately there is nothing to support it in terms of how these verbs were used in the ancient world in general and in the Gospel of John in particular. In fact, as many scholars point out today, these verbs function more or less as synonyms in the New Testament and could often be used interchangeably. We ought not to overinterpret the change of verbs here when it is probably a matter of verbal variety. For example, we see a similar phenomenon in Proverbs 8:17 LXX: "I love [*agapaō*] those who love [*phileō*] me." The reader is not meant to distinguish between the love of the "I" and the love of the "those" here in any significant way. In the Hebrew counterpart text, it is one Hebrew verb repeated: *ahav*.[6]

---

5. Nineteenth-century German theologian Johann Peter Lange wrote this in his commentary on John's Gospel: "This does not look like an accident. The distinction seems to be that [*agapaō*] is more used of that reverential love, grounded on high graces of character, which is borne towards God and man by the child of God;— whereas [*phileō*] expresses more the personal love of human affection. Peter therefore uses a less exalted word, and one implying a consciousness of his own weakness, but with it a persuasion and deep feeling of personal love." See J. P. Lange, *The Gospel according to John*, trans. P. Schaff (Bellingham, WA: Logos Bible Software, 2008), 639.

6. See *New International Dictionary of New Testament Theology and Exegesis*, ed. M. Silva (Grand Rapids: Zondervan, 2014), 1:104–5.

62

The Greek Language of Love

This idea that *phileō* and *agapaō* were synonyms and close in meaning is supported by many instances in non-Jewish literature as well. Plato, for example, sets these verbs in parallel (*Lysis* 215d), as does Plutarch (*Moralia*; *Lives*). Also, there is plenty of evidence that *phileō* was used in reference to noble, sincere, and self-giving love. For example, Epictetus uses *phileō* to talk about a parent's pure and selfless love for their child: "Do you think that Admetus did not love [*phileō*] his own child when he was little? That he was not in agony when the child had a fever? That he did not often say, 'I wish I had the fever instead of the child'?" (*Discourses* 2.22.12).

When it comes to *agapaō*, which we will discuss in more detail in the next section below, it is not the case that this verb was always used for selfless love. In fact, in the Gospel of John, *agapaō* could be used for carnal, selfish, or worldly kinds of love. In John 3:19, Jesus teaches that some people love (*agapaō*) darkness more than light. And in John 12:43, John explains that some love (*agapaō*) human glory more than glory from God. Alternatively, *phileō* is used not uncommonly in John for divine love: the Father loves (*phileō*) the Son (5:20), and the Father loves (*phileō*) the disciples (16:27). Jesus loved (*phileō*) Lazarus (11:3, 36).[7] Marianne Meye Thompson argues that context plays the most important role in determining the meaning of these verbs as John uses them; "if Peter loves Jesus and still wants to follow him to death (13:37), then he may demonstrate it by carrying out the particular command to care for Jesus' flock, even to the point of giving his life for the sheep (10:11)."[8]

So by way of summary, we can say that *phileō* was the most common word for love and affection in the ancient world. It could be used for people who are close, or not; deep love, or utilitarian interest; things, people, or places. It was as elastic and capacious as our English word "love." Let's return now briefly to *philos*. This term involved a relationship that was forged or cultivated by choice. David Konstan explains that it was not used for biological family members.

---

7. Philo can use *phileō* in reference to pure love for God (*Allegorical Interpretation* 2.55). See James Barr, "Words for Love in Biblical Greek," in *The Glory of Christ in the New Testament*, ed. N. T. Wright and L. D. Hurst (Oxford: Oxford University Press, 1990), 3–18, esp. 13–14.

8. Marianne Meye Thompson, *John*, NLT (Louisville: Westminster John Knox, 2015), 442.

CHAPTER 3

Philoi . . . occupy an intermediate zone between kin and country. The relationship between *philoi* is voluntary or achieved as opposed to an ascribed connection grounded in status such as common membership in a family or community.[9]

Friends (*philoi*) liked one another and maintained some commitment to each other. It is demonstrated in action: "what counts is what one does for a friend, for that is the surest evidence of devotion."[10] The opposite of a friend (*philos*) is an enemy (*echthros*), someone who does not have your best interests in mind; enemies do not want to protect and promote your well-being. And relationships can change, where a friend becomes an enemy and vice versa. So Konstan points to a statement made by Demosthenes that "friend" or "enemy" is not a static category, and only action truly tells one apart from the other. A friend helps; an enemy hurts (*Against Aristocrates* 23.56).[11]

There were many kinds of friendships in the Greek world, so sometimes it doesn't always make sense to translate *philos* as "friend" in English. In Greek, sometimes *philos* refers to someone we might call an ally, comrade, or associate/colleague. In these kinds of cases, personal affection or likability is not a prime factor, but what brings two people or entities together is a pact, treaty, or alliance based on some shared interest and a commitment to benefit the other.

When we look at the noun *philia*, it is commonly glossed in lexicons as "friendship," but again it can refer to many kinds of relationships, including political or personal alliances. In Josephus's *Jewish Antiquities*, he tends to use *philia* in reference to pacts and treaties. David and Jonathan, for example, were bound by *philia* (*Jewish Antiquities* 7.111). This is obviously a more emotionally involved relationship of friendship and mutuality. Josephus also used *philia* to describe the alliance that the Israelites made with the Canaanites (*Jewish Antiquities* 6.30) and with the Tyrians (*Jewish*

9. David Konstan, *Friendship in the Classical World* (Cambridge: Cambridge University Press, 1997), 55; see also Simon May, *Love: A History* (New Haven: Yale University Press, 2012), 95.

10. Konstan, *Friendship*, 56.

11. Konstan, *Friendship*, 56–57.

64

The Greek Language of Love

Antiquities 7.66). Josephus regularly paired *philia* with the language of *pistis*, which implies faithfulness and allegiance (*Jewish Antiquities* 2.66; 7.107; 8.304; 13.45).[12] Sometimes we see *philia* paired with *eirēnē* (peace), where the emphasis is on a peace treaty (*Jewish Antiquities* 12.393; cf. 8.400). We also see *philia* paired with *symmachia*, literally "mutual assistance in battle [against a common enemy]."[13] And we occasionally see *philia* combined with *eunoia*, "goodwill," recognizing that allies benefit from the thriving of their partners, so they seek out their benefit.

AGAPAŌ, AGAPĒ

Let's turn now to the Greek language of *agapē*. We have already talked about how we must be careful not to read too much into the appearances of these words, especially outside of the New Testament. Even within the New Testament itself, *agapaō* and *phileō* do not carry easily distinguishable meanings or nuances. The former is not necessarily about perfect, divine love, and the latter flawed, human love. Both can refer across the spectrum from interest, to association, to enjoyment, to deeper forms of love. Both can involve wholesome love for what is good, or attraction to what is evil. In the Greek world at large, the *phileō* word group is far more common; it was the default language of love and friendship. But when *agapaō* (the verb) did occur, which it did with moderate frequency, readers would treat it as a synonym, like we would today with the language of "love" and "care about." The noun *agapē* is another story, and a bit of a mystery. Before the New Testament was written, we don't find much use of this noun (compared to the verb). Note the representative sampling of information in the chart below.

---

12. For more details, see Nijay K. Gupta, *Paul and the Language of Faith* (Grand Rapids: Eerdmans, 2020).

13. *Symmachia* is often translated as "alliance" in traditional English translations of Josephus's works: *Jewish Antiquities* 4.102; 7.66; 7.107; 8.304; 12.419; 13.32, 45, 110, 170; 14.197.

CHAPTER 3

FREQUENCY OF *PHILEŌ* AND *AGAPAŌ/AGAPĒ* IN ANCIENT TEXTS

Writer	Number of occurrences: *phileō* (verb)	Number of occurrences: *agapaō* (verb)	Number of occurrences: *agapē* (noun)
Non-Jewish Texts			
Plato (429–347 BCE)	1479	152	0
Epictetus (50–135 CE)	26	1	0
Plutarch (46–119 CE)	2081	477	0 (*Artaxerxes* 21.1, contested)
Cassius Dio (155–135 CE)	204	63	0
Jewish Texts and Early Christian Texts	**Jewish texts have more occurrences of *agapaō/ agapē* because of the influence of the Septuagint		
Septuagint (3rd c. CE)	32	276	19
Philo (20–50 CE)	63	65	3
Josephus (37–100 CE)	31	75	0
Old Testament Pseudepigrapha (5th c. BCE to 9th c. CE)[14]	12	105	38
New Testament (40–100 CE)	25	143	116
Apostolic Fathers (70–150 CE)	1	82	99
Athanasius (293–373 CE)	5	35	15
Basil (330–379 CE)	0	3	13

The ancient (non-Jewish, pre-Christian) occurrences of *agapaō* tend to use this verb in very mundane ways. In fact, the most common meaning

14. Some of these texts may be written or edited by Christians and bear marks of the influence of New Testament texts and early Christian discourse.

66

The Greek Language of Love

of *agapaō* is something like "to be content" or "to like/prefer."[15] It was not a particularly strong form of love; it was more about personal satisfaction and inclination. On rare occasions, it appeared in relation to friendships (Plutarch, *Alcibiades* 4.4). And it should be no surprise by now to learn that *agapaō* as love language was common in political friendships/alliances. One can love (*agapaō*) an ally insofar as they contribute to one's own political interests (Appian, *Roman History* 3.62). Appian tells the story of King Mithridates IV, ruler of Pontus, who sought to punish the Greek Chians for their lack of loyalty. He sent a letter claiming the following: "You favor the Romans even now, and many of your citizens are still sojourning with them. You are reaping the fruits of Roman property of which you do not make returns to us. Your trireme [warship] ran against and shook my ship in the battle before Rhodes. I willingly imputed that fault to the pilots alone, hoping that you would observe the rules of safety and *remain my submissive subjects* [*agapan*; i.e., "love me"]" (*Mithridates* 47). Here Mithridates explains that he expected *submission* from the Chians, and he called this love. Love in this context implies devotion and obedience—nothing to do with feelings of warmth or affection.

Agapaō is also sometimes found in relation to familial love. Plutarch offers an extended example of this in his *Advice to Bride and Groom*, where he gives instruction on the nature of love. Mothers love (*agapaō*) their sons because their sons help them; fathers love their daughters because their daughters need their help. Husband and wife love (*agapaō*) each other because of the unique characteristics of the other. Plutarch goes on to explain that one can grow in trust by practicing trust, and the same for love (*phileō*); it has a way of expanding (*Advice to Bride and Groom* 36).

Plutarch also uses *agapaō* to talk about worship and devotion toward the gods. He explains that the powers on high provoke many feelings and attitudes among mortals—envy, fear, respect—and humans are jealous of their immortality and terrified of their wrath. But they also love (*agapaō*) and respect them for their maintenance and pursuit of justice (*Aristides* 6.3–4).

---

15. Lucian, *Disowned* 24; Plutarch, *Reply to Colotes in Defence of the Other Philosophers* 25, 26; *Anthony* 40.4; 69.4; *Agesilaus* 40.1; Arrian, *Anabasis of Alexander* 4.29.4; Dionysius of Halicarnassus, *Roman Antiquities* 2.4.2; 7.46.3; 8.47.3, 49.5; Appian, *Roman History* 2.92; Epictetus, *Discourses* 4.4.45.

CHAPTER 3

By way of summary, we can say that non-Jewish texts often treat *agapaō* as a synonym for *phileō*. There is no clear rhyme or reason why an author might choose one over the other. Because *philos* is the default term for "friend" (and *philia* for "friendship"), it makes sense that *phileō* is a common verb referring to friendship-affection but not to the exclusion of *agapaō*. What *is* odd is that the noun *agapē* is extremely rare in non-Jewish texts before the first century CE.[16] Once we look at Jewish texts, we see, starting with the Septuagint, that there is a preference for *agapaō* and a clear interest in *agapē*—Jews apparently latched on to this word group to represent their preferred language of covenantal love.

The Septuagint, contrary to legendary tales of its origins, was probably not written by one specific group of people at once in one place. Rather, it was translated and circulated over many years, beginning sometime in the third century BCE. Almost certainly the Pentateuch was translated first, given its foundational status in Jewish liturgy and worship. *Agapaō* and *agapē* (and other terms built on the same root) appear about forty times in the Septuagint Pentateuch, most of those occurrences in Deuteronomy. This terminology preference presents the best explanation for why Hellenistic Jews (and eventually early Christians) latched on to this particular language. In fact, it may be that the use of *agapaō* in the Shema in particular gave this word group central importance.

But that still leaves the question, Why did the Septuagint Pentateuch translators favor *agapaō* over *phileō*? There are no clear answers, only theories, but the theories are worth mentioning. One option is that perhaps *phileō* communicated some physical or sexual connotation (kissing?) that the Septuagint translators did not want to convey inadvertently.[17] I find that unlikely given how often *phileō* still appears in the Septuagint and other Jewish literature of

16. Ceslas Spicq offers a careful study of where and when the noun *agapē* appears in Greek texts. He argues that there are exceptionally few appearances before the writing of the New Testament and in non-Jewish texts (like the Septuagint). Spicq mentions three possible non-Jewish texts (Berlin Papyrus 9869; Paris Papyrus 49, 3; Philodemus, *On Frank Criticism* 13a.3), but in all these cases, either one could contest whether the word *agapē* actually appears, or it cannot be clearly dated before the first century CE (*TLNT* 1:8).

17. See R. Joly, *Le vocabulaire chrétien de l'amour est-il original?* (Brussels: Brussels University Press, 1968), 1n3. Barr refutes this reasoning, noting that *agapaō* is used in the Septuagint in erotic settings as well as nonerotic ones. See Barr, "Words for Love," 4–6; and Septuagint Song of Songs.

68

the Second Temple period. Another line of reasoning I have come across is that the *agapē* Greek word group has some phonic similarities to the Hebrew word *ahav*, especially the repeated "a" sound (*agapē; ahav*).[18] James Barr takes a third position, that *agapaō* was growing in popularity in general in the last few centuries BCE. He saw the Septuagint translators' preference for *agapaō* as "*continuity* with contemporary usage" and "the effort to portray it as a supreme example of *discontinuity* was completely wrong."[19]

Barr explains, as we have emphasized already above, that non-Jewish usage of *agapaō* before the Septuagint already bears witness that this was a "strong, warm, vivid, and colourful term," a good match for what the Septuagint writers wanted to convey in regard to covenantal love. Barr does not deny that the Septuagint use of *agapaō/agapē* became influential for Judaism and Christianity; he only clarifies that there was no anti-Hellenistic agenda behind the verb choice for love.[20] The New Testament was influenced by the Septuagint's investment in *agapē* and *agapaō*, but the New Testament writers further positioned *agapē* (the noun in particular) as a core theological term.

THE LANGUAGE OF DESIRE

We cannot end a discussion of the Greek language of love without addressing desire. Love and desire are closely related. Love is, essentially, an attraction or attachment to someone or something, and this is often (though not always) expressed in terms of longing, wanting, and desiring. Hopefully, one thing is clear by now, that the Jewish conception of love and the Greek expression of love do not and cannot exist and function without the desires of the heart. Now, when we are talking about love in a more professional atmosphere, the internal desire is still there, but it won't necessarily look like emotional attachment. And yet love is broadly still understood as a desire-oriented phenomenon.

Jewish and non-Jewish literature alike emphasize that desire in itself is not bad. For Jews, it is not sinful; for gentiles, it is not considered a vice per se. It is taken for granted as a natural part of what it means to be human. But what is often

---

18. See G. B. Caird, "Homocophony in the Septuagint," in *Jews, Greeks and Christians* (Leiden: Brill, 1976), 74–88. Barr finds this unlikely ("Words for Love," 4); there are too few clear Hebrew Bible to Septuagint homocophonic parallels.

19. Barr, "Words for Love," 7, 8.

20. Barr, "Words for Love," 6, 8.

CHAPTER 3

condemned is desire for what is evil, and letting passions run away in such a way that these wants cause people to do things that hurt themselves and others.

It might seem natural that we would focus here on *eros*, the classic term for erotic love—especially since this term was a matter of interest for both C. S. Lewis's and Nygren's work that juxtaposes *agapē* and *eros*. But *eros* wasn't the most common or most important word for sexual love in the Greek world, and it certainly wasn't used as an antonym for *agapē*. And perhaps most important for our purposes, the New Testament never even uses the word! It appears only twice in the Greek Bible (Prov 7:18; 24:51 LXX). Nevertheless, it is still worth commenting briefly on the meaning of *eros* as part of the Greek vocabulary of desire.

The basic meaning of *eros* is love with a focus on desire, but perhaps it is better to think of it as "obsession" or "infatuation." It is not a love that is chosen but one of instant and deep attraction. Now, as I said, we often hear it talked about today as erotic or sexual love. It can be used in that way, and many occurrences in ancient Greek literature carry that connotation. But it could be used for other objects of passion. For example, Josephus uses *eros* in reference to someone who has an obsession with wealth (*Jewish War* 5.558) and to another who loves tyrannical power (*Jewish War* 4.208).[21]

The term *eros* was not always used for something bad or inappropriate. Philo, for example, makes reference in a positive way to a person who loves knowledge (*On Drunkenness* 159). It is unclear why the New Testament writers didn't use *eros* (especially given how often they *do* talk about desire). One possibility is that they wanted to avoid reference or allusion to the deity known as *Eros*, god of sexual love. But the more mundane explanation is that there were multiple other terms that covered the same semantic ground (i.e., *zēloō*, *epithymeō*, *epipotheō*).

Let's start with *zēloō*. We get the English word "zeal" from this Greek word group, and that is not too far from its original meaning. It represents a kind of passionate fixation (see Louw and Nida).[22] It appears over one hundred times in the Greek Bible. In many cases, it carries the connotation of jealousy or covetousness. Proverbs and Ecclesiastes repeatedly warn against envy (Prov 23:17;

21. *Kerdainein erōs* (*Jewish War* 5.558); *erōta tyrannidos* (*Jewish War* 4.208).

22. It has the following uses: "set one's heart on" (25.76); "have a deep concern for or devotion to someone or something" (25.46); "covet" (25.21); "be jealous" (88.163).

70

The Greek Language of Love

24:1, 19; 27:4; Eccl 4:4; 9:6 LXX), but when *zēloō* is used of YHWH, it refers to God's passion for his people and his anger at their idolatry and adulterous spirit. Multiple times through the Septuagint, YHWH is described as a "jealous god": "For you shall not do obeisance before another god. For the Lord God, jealous [*zēlōtos*] [is his] name, is a jealous [*zēlōtos*] God" (Exod 34:14; cf. Exod 20:5; Deut 4:24; 5:9; 29:20; Josh 24:19; Nah 1:2). The priest Phinehas was celebrated for preserving the purity of Israel by killing an impious Israelite. His actions were referred to as "zeal" (*zēlos*) that curtailed the wrath of God (Num 25:11; cf. 1 Macc 2:54). If we go back again to that famous passage in Song of Songs 8, it is affirmed that love is strong as death and *zeal* (*zēlos*) as powerful as Hades (8:6). In the New Testament, the Gospel of John connects the temple incident with Psalms 69:9: "Zeal [*zēlos*] for your house will consume me" (John 2:17). Jesus becomes here the manifestation of passion for true worship and unhindered communion with God. Zeal is neither good nor evil all by itself. It depends on the object of that passion and the responsible stewardship of it (Rom 10:2; 1 Cor 13:4).

More frequently occurring in the Greek Bible is the verb *epithymeō* (and root-based related terms). This is another term of desire, typically representing a yearning, a want, a feeling of lack (Louw and Nida). This is the language used in the (Septuagint) Decalogue: "You shall not covet [*epithymeō*] your neighbor's wife, you shall not covet [*epithymeō*] your neighbor's house" (Exod 20:17; cf. Deut 5:2). But the same is true for *epithymeō* as for *zēloō*—desire itself is not the enemy of faith, love, or obedience. Rather, holy and virtuous living is a matter of avoiding any desiring and yearning that harms (others or self) or that is pointed in the wrong direction. Desire, in many ways, reveals the longings of the heart (1 Sam 20:4). When worship is rightly oriented, desires deepen and enhance love.

> Day after day they seek me
> And desire [*epithymeō*] to know my ways.
> Like a people that practiced righteousness
> And did not forsake the judgment of their God.
> They now ask of me righteous judgment,
> And they desire to draw near to God. (Isa 58:2 NETS)[23]

23. See also Ps 118:40; Wis 6:11 LXX.

CHAPTER 3

To desire is a natural part of humans having connections to the things around them, including peoples, values, and hopes. Sometimes we have desires within us that compete with other desires. Jewish tradition regularly reflected on Israel's sinful desires in the wilderness period as misdirected passions.

> They were quick to forget his works;
> they did not wait for his counsel.
> And they craved with craving in the wilderness
> and put God to the test in a waterless region,
> and he gave them their request
> and sent surfeit into their souls.
> And they craved [*epithymeō*] with craving [*epithymos*]
> in the wilderness
> and put God to the test in a waterless region.
> (Ps 105:13–14 LXX)[24]

Cravings themselves are not the problem, but rather allowing a certain kind of desire to interfere with covenantal trust in YHWH is ruinous. The apostle Paul presents the nature of desire as a war being waged in our hearts: "for what the flesh *desires* [*epithymeō*] is opposed to the Spirit, and what the Spirit *desires* [*epithymeō*] is opposed to the flesh; for these are opposed to each other, to prevent you from doing what you want" (Gal 5:17; cf. Rom 6:12; 13:14). Paul sees the goodness of other-affirming desires and passions (like in friendship; Phil 4:1); but believers must put to death the selfish and destructive cravings of the flesh (Gal 5:24). The book of James narrates the movement from interest to temptation to action and consequences: "But one is tempted by one's own desire [*epithymia*], being lured and enticed by it; then when that desire [*epithymia*] has conceived, it gives birth to sin, and that sin, when it is fully grown, gives birth to death" (Jas 1:14).

The last term we will examine is *epipotheō*, a verb expressing longing and yearning. It appears to be a less common synonym of *epithymeō*. As with *epithymeō*, *epipotheō* has that same dynamic of a light version and a dark version.

---

24. Paul draws from this same tradition to warn the Corinthian Christians: "Now these things occurred as examples for us, so that we might not desire evil [*epithymētēs*] as they did" (1 Cor 10:6).

The Greek Language of Love

Positively, we find it in Psalm 41:2 LXX: "Just as the doe *longs* [*epipotheō*] for the springs of water, so my soul *longs* [*epipotheō*] for you, O God" (cf. Ps 83:3; 118:174 LXX). It refers to a deep connection to something, like a gut reaction that represents a longing and need (Sus 35). But it can reflect sinful desires as well (Sir 25:21). *Epipotheō* points to some feeling of emptiness and a visceral desire to fill that void. Whether it is seen as a good or a bad desire depends especially on what the thing is and what role it plays in bringing good things to the person and their effect on others.[25]

As you can see from our survey of Greek love language, there are many terms for love with many connotations and shades of meaning, and several terms have flexibility. This presents two warnings when reading the New Testament: (1) we ought not to label specific terms too rigidly and put them into hermetically sealed boxes; and (2) we ought not to focus on just one or two words in our understanding and expression of Christian love. In order to responsibly examine what an author (like Paul) thinks about love, we have to look at the whole range of terms in the semantic cluster. We are almost ready to turn to Paul's writings but not quite. First we need to talk about the Jesus tradition and its potential influence on Paul's understanding of love.

25. See David E. Fredrickson, *Eros and the Christ: Longing and Envy in Paul's Christology* (Minneapolis: Fortress, 2013).

4

Love in the Jesus Tradition

The religion of Jesus says to the disinherited: "Love your enemy.
Take the initiative in seeking ways by which you can have the
experience of a common sharing of mutual worth and value.
It may be hazardous, but you must do it."

—Howard Thurman[1]

Our ultimate goal in this book is to examine the writings of the apostle Paul closely to see how love permeates his thinking and correspondence and to further investigate how love is related to his theology more broadly. We have already spent time looking at the Jewish roots of Paul's thought in the Old Testament and in early Jewish traditions. We have also provided a brief look at key terms in Greek. Our final preliminary step before opening up the pages of the Pauline canon is to consider the Jesus tradition we find in the Gospels. This seems to me to be a natural consideration, since Paul's own articulation of love is *Christocentric*; he taught believers to love according to the love of God demonstrated in the life, death, and new life of the Lord Jesus Christ. But there are a few obstacles to navigate when considering the relationship of Paul to Jesus (and specifically his knowledge of the Jesus tradition as we know it from the four canonical gospels).

1. Howard Thurman, *Jesus and the Disinherited* (Richmond: Friends United Press, 1981), 100.

Love in the Jesus Tradition

First, Paul doesn't cite the teachings of Jesus, certainly not explicitly, when it comes to instruction on love, or on virtually any matter. There are a couple of times where it appears Paul quotes a dominical *logion*, but these are very few and very far between. That is true, and it is an oddity because (1) we know that Jesus was hailed as a *teacher* (so there's probably a lot of material that would be useful for passing on in the Pauline churches) and (2) we can be pretty sure that Paul was given this teaching at some point. Scholars have come up short on solving this mystery, but if it can be shown that Jesus (according to the Gospels) was passionate about teaching about love, and that love was central to his kingdom proclamation, *and* that Paul was similarly enthusiastic about instructing his communities about love, then it makes sense to connect these two. We will come back to this in a moment.

A second challenge is this: if Paul's writings precede the publication or wide circulation of the Four Gospels, how helpful are these gospels for telling us how Paul was impacted by the Jesus tradition? Scholars fall across a wide range of views on the historical reliability of the Gospels; some treat the Gospels (especially the Synoptics) as more or less a factual account of the life and teachings of Jesus with a bit of literary license from the evangelists. Others view the Gospels as derived from the historical life of Jesus but heavily embellished, so as to not serve as a legitimate historical account. At the risk of oversimplification, I will assume here a moderate approach that takes for granted both that the Synoptics depend on real historical information by and large (probably a combination of oral and written traditions) and that each gospel takes some freedom to "narratize" features to align with the wider story each evangelist tells. Taking this sort of approach means that we can trust these sources to relay the basic substance of the events and teachings related to Jesus, but each writer looks at Jesus with a specific theological lens. The bottom line is that the Synoptics reflect the general material of the Jesus tradition; therefore it is possible to talk about the life and teachings of Jesus with some knowledge and historical confidence. What about John's Gospel? The Fourth Gospel is often left out of the conversation about the historical Jesus, but recent conversations in scholarship have shown reluctance at throwing this material out in toto.[2]

2. See the publications from the SBL program unit John, Jesus, and History, especially Paul N. Anderson, Felix Just, and Tom Thatcher, eds., *Critical Appraisals of*

CHAPTER 4

While John may offer the most overtly theologized story of Jesus, that does not mean it is worthless for studying Jesus of Nazareth. I am sympathetic to those who urge that there is a distinctive Johannine tradition alongside a Markan one.[3] We will cautiously include John in our conversation about Jesus and Paul, less as some kind of unbiased historical report and more as a theo-drama inspired by the early testimonies about Jesus.

Now let's turn back to Jesus and Paul. While it is obvious Paul was not quoting the Jesus tradition at length, and Paul had his own preferred theological vocabulary, I think many scholars have been too quick to see a vast chasm between the Nazarene and the Tarsian. But in more recent years, there has been a bit of a pendulum swing toward an open or more moderate position. While Paul does not quote Jesus extensively or frequently, there are some clear connections between their teachings and passions.[4]

Jimmy Dunn, who wrote extensively on both Jesus and Paul, has argued that there is one obvious connection between these two that often is neglected or minimized in scholarship—namely, moral teachings on *love*. "The most striking evidence of the influence of Jesus' teaching on Paul is Paul's reference to the love command. In both Romans and Galatians he makes the same point—the same point that Jesus made! All the commandments are 'summed up in this word, in the command, "You shall love your neighbour as yourself"' (Rom 13.9)."[5]

Critical Views, vol. 1 of *John, Jesus, and History* (Atlanta: Society of Biblical Literature, 2007); and Anderson, Just, and Thatcher, eds., *Aspects of Historicity in the Fourth Gospel*, vol. 2 of *John, Jesus, and History* (Atlanta: Society of Biblical Literature, 2009).

3. See Paul N. Anderson, *The Fourth Gospel and the Quest for Jesus* (New York: T&T Clark, 2006).

4. See the important recent work, Todd D. Still, ed., *Jesus and Paul Reconnected: Fresh Pathways into an Old Debate* (Grand Rapids: Eerdmans, 2007).

5. James D. G. Dunn, *Jesus, Paul, and the Gospels* (Grand Rapids: Eerdmans, 2011), 114. A similar discussion appears in the work of David Wenham, *Paul, Follower of Jesus or Founder of Christianity?* (Grand Rapids: Eerdmans, 1995), 237–38: "In their emphasis on love Paul and Jesus come very close" (237). See also Michael Gorman, *The Death of the Messiah and the Birth of the New Covenant* (Eugene, OR: Cascade Books, 2014), 126–27; Frank Matera, *New Testament Ethics* (Louisville: Westminster John Knox, 1996), 201. Similarly, Thomas W. Ogletree, "Love Command," in *Dictionary of Scripture and Ethics*, ed. Joel B. Green (Grand Rapids: Baker, 2011), 492.

Love in the Jesus Tradition

Dunn argues that Paul's reference to Leviticus 19:18 in both Romans 13:9 and Galatians 5:14 must have come from the impact of Jesus's own teaching that became a fixture in early Christian tradition. He makes this case (with Mark 12:29–31 in view) on the basis of the notion that combining Deuteronomy 6:5 (love of God) and Leviticus 19:18 (love of neighbor) was a hermeneutical and didactic innovation starting with the historical Jesus. When asked about the most important commandments that give meaning to the rest of torah, it would have been natural to point to the Shema, Dunn reasons; but "the second was a complete surprise."[6] Dunn believes no other Jewish text *prior* to Jesus has been found that combines these two texts and love commands of torah in this explicit way. Dunn is aware that something similar can be found in rabbinic literature, but it is possible these rabbinic traditions were influenced by early Christian teaching, even if inadvertently.[7] We will have a more thorough discussion below of the interpretation of the love commandments in early Jewish context, but suffice it to say for now, Dunn's simple comments do not reflect the complexity of the state of the discussion about whether Jesus was the first Jew to pair love of God and love of neighbor as the summation of the law. Still, the fact that all three Synoptic Gospels include some form of a double love command means that it was firmly imprinted into the earliest Jesus tradition.

Dunn goes on to argue that this is reflected in Paul's references to love of neighbor and is especially notable in the Galatians 5:14 reference. A word-for-word translation of the Greek text would read something like this: "For the whole law is fulfilled in one statement, in the 'You shall love your neighbor as yourself.'" Dunn observes how Paul's mention of Leviticus 19:18 starts with "in the" (*en tō*), which indicates a familiar tradition or saying (otherwise this "in the" is superfluous).[8] The upshot for Dunn is that this is an indicator that this was a well-known teaching, not something Paul was introducing for the first time. So, Dunn concludes, *"nowhere is the line of continuity and influence from Jesus to Paul clearer than in the love command.... Paul followed in his train*

---

6. Dunn, *Jesus, Paul, and the Gospels*, 112.

7. Dunn, *Jesus, Paul, and the Gospels*, 112. In the Sifra on Leviticus 19:18, Rabbi Akiba referred to the command to love neighbor as "the greatest principle in the Law."

8. See Dunn, *Jesus, Paul, and the Gospels*, 114n67. It should be noted that this "in the" is often omitted in English translations. The NASB glosses it as "in the statement" (adding the word "statement").

CHAPTER 4

and summed up the whole law in the same command and, like Jesus, used the criterion it gave him to discern the commandments that really mattered in directing the relationship between God and his people and between the individual members of his people."[9]

That Paul's love-of-neighbor teaching traces back to Jesus is almost without a doubt—how many degrees of separation we can't really say. Still, I hope this has established enough connection between Jesus and Paul to justify examining what the Jesus tradition in the Gospels has to say about love. This will ultimately help to paint a vivid picture of the social, religious, and ethical world that formed Paul's thought and moral imagination.

JESUS ON LOVING GOD AND NEIGHBOR

In the Synoptic Jesus tradition, we have three similar (though not identical) scenarios in each gospel where Jesus engages in conversation about the most important commandment of the law (Mark 12:28–34; Matt 22:34–40; Luke 10:25–28).[10] In all of these, Jesus either verbalizes the double love commandment or affirms it. Even in the case of someone else articulating the double love commandment, it very well could be that they were repeating back to Jesus a teaching they heard from him on an earlier occasion. We know that different rabbis had their own unique interpretation of the law. Jesus's, according to the Gospels, focused on love as the essential covenantal priority and guide to Jewish piety.

Some scholars believe that the differences between the synoptic accounts can be explained in terms of Jesus having similar conversations about the law on various occasions. Others think, assuming Markan priority, that Matthew and Luke reshaped Mark's episode according to their own narrative and theological interests. Choosing between these approaches is not necessary for establishing the key point of this chapter—*love* is a distinctive teaching of Jesus, reflected in the Synoptics. (We will engage with the Johannine tradition later on in this chapter.) We will examine each synoptic story about Jesus and the most important commandment by looking at each gospel account in turn, starting with Mark.

9. Dunn, *Jesus, Paul, and the Gospels*, 114, 115.

10. The command to "love your neighbor" (Lev 19:18b) is found three times in total in Matthew (5:43; 19:19; 22:39).

78

Love in the Jesus Tradition

Mark and the Most Important Commandment

Up to this point in Mark's Gospel, the scribes were largely suspicious and critical of Jesus (Mark 2:6, 16; 7:5; 9:14; 11:18; 14:1). They accused Jesus of being in league with Beelzebul and demons (7:1). And some scribes were intent on putting him to death (11:18; cf. 8:31; 10:33). After Jesus was arrested, these scribes joined with the chief priests to mock and demean him (15:1, 31). But in chapter 12, we find a scribe who is genuinely interested in Jesus's teaching and interpretation of the law.

> One of the scribes came near and heard them disputing with one another, and seeing that he answered them well, he asked him, "Which commandment is the first of all?" Jesus answered, "The first is, 'Hear, O Israel: the Lord our God, the Lord is one; you shall love the Lord your God with all your heart, and with all your soul, and with all your mind, and with all your strength.' The second is this, 'You shall love your neighbor as yourself.' There is no other commandment greater than these." Then the scribe said to him, "You are right, Teacher; you have truly said that 'he is one, and besides him there is no other'; and 'to love him with all the heart, and with all the understanding, and with all the strength,' and 'to love one's neighbor as oneself,'—this is much more important than all whole burnt offerings and sacrifices." When Jesus saw that he answered wisely, he said to him, "You are not far from the kingdom of God." After that no one dared to ask him any question. (Mark 12:28–34)

The scribe appears to interrupt a debate, interjecting his honest question: "Which commandment is the first of all?" Discussing the heart or center of the law was apparently a common rabbinic preoccupation. Jewish tradition records that Rabbi Simlai (third-century CE talmudic teacher) numbered the commandments at 613. He derived this number from the gematria numerical value of the word "torah," plus the key mitzvot, "I am the Lord your God" and "You shall have no other gods" (Exod 20:2, 3). Simlai further explained that these several hundred commandments were guided by eleven key ideas in Psalm 15—such as following God wholeheartedly, practicing righteousness, and speaking truth. This was further reduced to six commandments in Isaiah (33:15–16), three in Micah (6:8), and finally down to one primary

CHAPTER 4

commandment in Habakkuk (2:4): "the righteous will live by faith [*emunah*]."[11] Simeon the Just boiled all of Jewish religion down to three priorities: observance of the law, participation in temple piety, and acts of lovingkindness (m. Avot 1:2).[12] Rabbi Hillel concentrated the torah on what has come to be known as the negative Golden Rule: "What is hateful to you do not to your neighbor; that is the whole Torah, while the rest is commentary on it; go and learn it" (b. Shabbat 31a). These examples reveal a natural curiosity about the coherence of the many laws and how to know whether one is maintaining faithfulness to the covenant. *Is there a simple life philosophy that all these commandments point to?*[13]

Jesus is willing to engage with this curious scribe. While the scribe's question assumes *one* most important command, Jesus immediately answers with two. The first is a quotation of the beginning of the Shema (Deut 6:4–5): "Hear, O Israel: the Lord our God, the Lord is one; you shall love the Lord your God with all your heart, and with all your soul, and with all your mind, and with all your strength." The Greek text of Mark aligns relatively closely with the Septuagint of Deuteronomy. The only differences are in the elements of Deut 6:5.

> Hear, O Israel, the Lord our God, the Lord is one. You shall love the Lord your God with all your heart [*kardia*], and with all your soul [*psychē*], and with all your mind [*dianoia*], and with all your strength [*ischys*]. (Mark 12:28)

> Hear, O Israel, the Lord our God, the Lord is one. And you shall love the Lord your God with the whole of your mind [*dianoia*] and with the whole of your soul [*psychē*] and with the whole of your power [*dynamis*]. (Deut 6:4–5 LXX)

11. B. Makkot 24a; Midrash Tanhuma B on Judges 16b.

12. As cited in Matthias Henze, *Mind the Gap: How the Jewish Writings between the Old and New Testament Help Us Understand Jesus* (Minneapolis: Fortress, 2017), 139.

13. Charles H. Talbert, *Matthew*, PCNT (Grand Rapids: Baker Academic, 2010), 255, observes that this was not just a Jewish phenomenon. As Plutarch examined the many inscriptions from the oracle of Delphi, he observed that the two most important pieces of advice were "Know thyself" and "Avoid extremes."

Love in the Jesus Tradition

John Meier has observed that, despite the popularity of this text in early Jewish prayer, we do not have a verbatim citation of Deut 6:4–5 in the rest of the Old Testament/Hebrew Bible, the Old Testament Apocrypha, Pseudepigrapha, Philo, or Josephus. Even in Qumranic literature, we do not have explicit citation of this text in the sectarian works, only in copies of Deuteronomy itself. That makes the Synoptic Gospels' citation a remarkable rarity.[14]

With this quotation, Jesus first affirms the oneness of God. This is summarized afterward by the scribe ("he is one, and besides him there is no other" [v. 32]). Scholars disagree over the exact nature of Jewish monotheism—how it developed, to what degree it was exclusive, and how this line from the Shema should be understood and translated.[15] Regardless of whether Jesus and the scribe had in mind *belief* in one God only, we can say that they affirmed a Jewish commitment to honoring *only* the God of Israel.[16] This would align with Walter Moberly's argument that the original purpose and use of the Shema in Deuteronomy was not so much a religious belief claim (about the existence of only one God) but more so a confession of exclusive love and devotion (see earlier, pp. 41–46). Thus, Jesus goes on to cite the next part of the Shema regarding genuine and comprehensive love for God. The Septuagint version of the Shema refers to mind, soul, and strength. Mark's version adds a fourth, heart (*kardia*). It could be that a fourfold focus is simply the version of the Shema that Mark was familiar with. Or perhaps Mark added *kardia* because of his interest in the gospel, the

14. See John P. Meier, *A Marginal Jew*, vol. 4, *Law and Love* (New Haven: Yale University Press, 2009), 500; see also Oda Wischmeyer, *Love as* Agape: *The Early Christian Concept and Modern Discourse* (Waco, TX: Baylor University Press, 2021), 21. For a more detailed reception study, see Lori A. Baron, *The Shema in John's Gospel*, WUNT 2/574 (Tübingen: Mohr Siebeck, 2022); see especially 1–114, which covers the Hebrew Bible and the range of texts of early Judaism.

15. See Loren T. Stuckenbruck and Wendy E. S. North, eds., *Early Jewish and Christian Monotheism* (London: T&T Clark, 2004); Larry W. Hurtado, *One God, One Lord: Early Christian Devotion and Ancient Jewish Monotheism*, 2nd. ed. (London: T&T Clark, 1998).

16. Meier wonders whether emphasis on exclusive worship in Mark's Gospel is a criticism of the Roman controlled temple or the many pagan cults established in Caesarea Maritima: "The emphasis on monotheism, far from irrelevant or merely a later Christian catechetical device, is thus well suited geographically and theologically" (*Marginal Jew*, 4:495).

CHAPTER 4

kingdom, and the inward life (see *kardia* in Mark 2:6, 8; 3:5; 6:52; 7:6, 19, 21; 8:17; 11:23).[17] In any case, Joel Marcus is correct that these four parts of the person are not meant to be treated as separate elements but should be taken together to reflect a sense of wholeness, "the human mind and will, viewed from slightly different angles."[18] The scribe might have expected Jesus to stop there—after all, he was looking for *one* most important commandment. But Jesus adds a second, the command from Leviticus 19:18b to love neighbor as self (Mark 12:31). This was not an afterthought, or even a secondary commandment, but was treated by Jesus as a foundational concept *alongside* love of God; the covenant depends both upon sincere and steadfast love of God *and* love of neighbor.[19]

While the Shema was undoubtedly widely known as a common prayer in early Judaism, the same is not true for Leviticus 19:18. Again, Meier and others have claimed that no verbatim and complete citation of this text can be found in early Jewish literature that predates the Gospels' record of Jesus's words.[20] In general, this appears to be correct, but the novelty of Jesus's appeal to love of neighbor has been exaggerated. Pheme Perkins is right to identify the problem of assuming "Christian originality." Jesus was not deviating from Jewish conceptions of religion by summing up the law with love; Perkins argues that Jesus was drawing from Jewish wisdom traditions.[21] In a recent monograph, Kengo Akiyama studied all known quotations of and allusions to Leviticus 19:18 (and the similar commandment in 19:34) in ancient Judaism. He concludes that while there is some distinctiveness to Jesus's appeal to neighbor love, it fits within a stream of interest in neighbor love in early Judaism. Akiyama confirms that complete verbatim quotation of Leviticus 19:18 is lacking in early Jewish literature, but partial quotes and clear allusions exist.[22]

---

17. We learn from Mark 11:23 that faith is not just a matter of the head but also of the heart.

18. Joel Marcus, *Mark: A New Translation with Introduction and Commentary*, AB (New York: Doubleday, 2000), 837.

19. Victor Furnish, *The Love Command in the New Testament* (Nashville: Abingdon, 1972), 27.

20. Meier, *Marginal Jew*, 4:500; see also Heinz Hiestermann, *Paul and the Synoptic Jesus Tradition* (Leipzig: Evangelische Verlagsanstalt, 2017), 184.

21. Pheme Perkins, *Love Commands in the New Testament* (New York: Paulist, 1982), 21.

22. Kengo Akiyama, *The Love of Neighbour in Ancient Judaism: The Reception of Leviticus 19:18 in the Hebrew Bible, the Septuagint, the Book of Jubilees, the Dead Sea Scrolls, and the New Testament* (Boston: Brill, 2018), 3.

Love in the Jesus Tradition

To begin with, Akiyama engages with the list of quotations and allusions identified by Armin Lange and Matthias Weigold.[23] Lange and Weigold present about a dozen texts from the Dead Sea Scrolls, the Old Testament Apocrypha, and Pseudepigrapha, but only four of these could be technically classified as a quotation.[24]

CD VI, 14–21 (DAMASCUS DOCUMENT, DEAD SEA SCROLLS)

They should take care to act in accordance with the exact interpretation of the law for the age of wickedness: to keep apart from the sons of the pit; to abstain from wicked wealth which defiles, either by promise or by vow, and from the wealth of the temple and from stealing from the poor of his people, making widows their spoils and murdering orphans; to separate unclean from clean and differentiate between the holy and the common; to keep the sabbath day according to its exact interpretation, and the festivals and the day of fasting, according to what was discovered by those who entered the new covenant in the land of Damascus; to set apart holy portions according to their exact interpretation; *for each to love his brother like himself*; to strengthen the hand of the poor, the needy and the foreigner; *Blank* for each to seek the peace. (CD VI, 14–21)[25]

Here, the Damascus Document exhorts community members to love each other by caring for the needy, including the foreigner.[26]

23. Armin Lange and Matthias Weigold, *Biblical Quotations and Allusions in Second Temple Jewish Literature*, JAJSup 5 (Göttingen: Vandenhoeck & Ruprecht, 2011), 84.

24. The full list includes the following: Dead Sea Scrolls—CD VI, 20–21; IX, 2; 4QD^a (4Q266) 8 II, 10; 4QD^d (4Q269) 4 II, 2; 4QD^e (4Q270) 6 III, 16–17; 5QD (5Q12) I, 2. Old Testament Apocrypha—Sirach 13:15 (MS-A). Old Testament Pseudepigrapha—Jubilees 7.20; Letter of Aristeas 228; Testament of Issachar 5.2; Testament of Gad 4.2; Testament of Benjamin 3.3–4. See also John J. Collins, "Love of Neighbor in Hellenistic-Era Judaism," *Studia Philonica Annual* 32 (2020): 97–111. Similarly, see Sirach 13:15–16: "every living thing loves what is like it, and every person his neighbor. All living beings associate with their own kind, and people stick close to those like themselves"; but Sirach is describing nature, not issuing a command contrary to nature (Collins, "Love of Neighbor," 100).

25. Florentino García Martínez and Eibert J. C. Tigchelaar, *The Dead Sea Scrolls Study Edition (Translations)* (Leiden: Brill, 1997–1998), 559.

26. Akiyama, *Love of Neighbour*, 111.

CHAPTER 4

4Q269 4 II, 1–7 (DAMASCUS DOCUMENT, DEAD SEA SCROLLS)

> according to their exact interpretation; *to lo[ve, each one, his
>   brother like himself;]*
> to [streng]then [the poor, the needy and the foreigner; to seek,]
> ea[ch] one, the pe[ace of his brother and not to be
>   unfaithful against]
> [his] blood [relation; to refrain from fornication in accordance
>   with the regulation; to
> each one, [his brother in accordance with the precept, and
>   not to bear resentment from one day to the next;] to keep
>   ap[art. . . .]. (4Q269 4 II, 1–7)[27]

Akiyama recognizes love as a repeated interest in the Damascus Document, a virtue that "governs intra-communal relations or a fundamental belief that shapes and regulates the Yahidic frame of mind."[28]

BOOK OF JUBILEES 7.20 (OLD TESTAMENT PSEUDEPIGRAPHA)

> And in the twenty-eighth jubilee Noah began to command his grandsons with ordinances and commandments and all the judgments which he knew. And he bore witness to his sons so that they might do justice and cover the shame of their flesh and bless the one who created them and honor father and mother, and each one *love his neighbor* and preserve themselves from fornication and pollution and from all injustice. (7.20 [*OTP*])

Jubilees offers a summary of Genesis 1 through Exodus 24, and love of fellow Israelite is a theme throughout, alongside righteousness and peaceful life in community.[29]

The text that has received the most discussion among early Jewish texts is the Testaments of the Twelve Patriarchs. Here we have a document that not

---

27. García Martínez and Tigchelaar, *Dead Sea Scrolls*, 607.

28. Akiyama, *Love of Neighbour*, 133.

29. See Akiyama, *Love of Neighbour*, 79–94. For Jubilees texts mentioning communal love, see also 20.1–2; 35.1–27; 36.1–19; Collins, "Love of Neighbor," 102.

84

Love in the Jesus Tradition

only mentions love of neighbor but also in the same breath the love of God; like Jesus's teaching, we have in the Testament of Issachar affirmation of the double love commandment, though in very short form.

TESTAMENT OF ISSACHAR 5.1–2 (OLD TESTAMENT PSEUDEPIGRAPHA)

Therefore, guard the law of God, my children, and acquire generosity, and walk in innocence, do not meddle in the commandments of the Lord and the business of your neighbor; but *love the Lord and your neighbor*, show mercy to the poor and weak. (5.1–2)[30]

This is an important text, because it shows a clear parallel to Jesus's teaching about love. It is important that scholars do not exaggerate the uniqueness of Jesus's focus on love of God and neighbor. However, some scholars wonder whether an ancient Christian editor added the double love command to the Jewish Testaments of the Twelve Patriarchs, or whether somehow this text is dependent on or influenced by the Jesus tradition in some way.[31]

Another text that comes up in this conversation about the double love command in early Judaism comes from Philo's *Special Laws*. At one point, Philo identifies two "heads" (*duo ta anōtatō kephalaia*) of all of the law's teachings and doctrines, "the regulating of one's conduct towards God by the rules of piety and holiness, and of one's conduct towards men by the roles of humanity and justice" (*Special Laws* 2.63). While Philo does not quote Deuteronomy 6:4–5 or Leviticus 19:18, nor does he use the language of love (*agapē*) here, and it is interesting to observe that his rubric for interpreting the law

---

30. Similarly, the Testament of Gad references "loving of one's neighbor" (4.2), and the Testament of Benjamin calls the readers to "fear the Lord and love your neighbor" (3.3; cf. 3.4); see also Testament of Reuben 6.9 ("show love, each to his brother"); Testament of Zebulun 7.2 ("provide for every person with a kind heart"); Hiestermann, *Paul and the Synoptic Jesus Tradition*, 184.

31. Akiyama considers the Testaments of the Twelve Patriarchs dependent on the Gospels (*Love of Neighbour*, 17); see also Collins, "Love of Neighbor," 110; Heinz Hiestermann, *Paul and the Synoptic Jesus Tradition*, 183. Michael Thompson, *Clothed with Christ: The Example and Teaching of Jesus in Romans 12.1–15.13* (Sheffield: Sheffield Academic, 1991), 133–34, thinks Testaments of the Twelve Patriarchs is more original.

CHAPTER 4

and the Jewish religion focuses on the paired concern for God and others. Collins adds the important observation that Philo in particular was interested in a broader understanding of *philanthrōpia*, where concern is expressed for all humanity on a much broader scale, though Philo no doubt treated fellow Jews as special.[32]

Turning back to Mark 12, what can we conclude about Jesus's teaching on the "most important commandment" in light of currents in Jewish moral philosophy and torah interpretation of the time? Furnish is undoubtedly correct that Jesus wasn't the only Jewish teacher to talk about love as central to Jewish piety: "one finds other teachers who in one way or another single out love as the sum of the law's requirements."[33] And yet, we can see that love is distinctive and repeated in the Jesus tradition, such that it is a major theme in Jesus's teaching and lifestyle. Meier is more reserved than Furnish, hesitant to buy into "blithe homiletical generalizations proclaiming love to be the center of Jesus' message."[34] But what cannot be ignored is that all four evangelists draw out the theme of love from Jesus's ministry, and Jesus's teachings on love left a clear impact on early Christian writings.

The Double Love Commandment in Matthew and Luke

We will briefly look at the other two synoptic passages that talk about the most important commandment:

> When the Pharisees heard that he had silenced the Sadducees, they gathered together, and one of them, a lawyer, asked him a question to test him. "Teacher, which commandment in the law is the greatest?" He said to him, "'You shall love the Lord your God with all your heart, and with all your soul, and with all your mind.' This is the greatest and first commandment. And a second is like it: 'You shall love your neighbor as yourself.' On these two commandments hang all the law and the prophets." (Matt 22:34–40)[35]

32. Collins, "Love of Neighbor," 109; see also Hiestermann, *Paul and the Synoptic Jesus Tradition*, 182.

33. Furnish, *Love Command*, 64–65.

34. Meier, *Marginal Jew*, 4:481.

35. If you recall from the introduction of this book, this was one of the passages that Augustine returned to as he taught about the importance of Christian *caritas* (love).

86

Love in the Jesus Tradition

In Matthew's account, we again have dialogue between Jesus and Jewish scholars, but it is a law expert (*nomikos*) who speaks up, not a scribe (*grammateus*), as in Mark. Matthew's story is brief, and it is made clear here that the law expert is not engaging in genuine conversation but rather trying to test Jesus. This response from Jesus does not include Deuteronomy 6:4 ("Hear, O Israel, the Lord our God, the Lord is one"), and also excludes Mark 12's "with all your strength."[36] In Matthew, Jesus makes a clarifying comment that the second commandment is "like it" (*deutera homoia hautē*), putting the neighbor-love command on par with love for God. And the final statement orients the double love commandment toward the whole of torah: the law and the prophets *hang* (i.e., depend) on these.[37]

> Just then a lawyer stood up to test Jesus. "Teacher," he said, "what must I do to inherit eternal life?" He said to him, "What is written in the law? What do you read there?" He answered, "You shall love the Lord your God with all your heart, and with all your soul, and with all your strength, and with all your mind; and your neighbor as yourself." And he said to him, "You have given the right answer; do this, and you will live." (Luke 10:25–28)

Luke's story is brief, like Matthew's, and also features a law expert (*nomikos*) who wants to test Jesus; but unlike Matthew or Mark, here it is not Jesus who utters the most important commandment. Luke's version also includes a number of important details about the *hermeneutical* nature of this conversation. Jesus turns a question back to the law expert—"what do you read there?" literally, "how do you read [it]?" (Luke 10:26; *pōs anaginōskeis*). Second, Jesus's final comment ("do this, and you will live") makes it clear that love, in Jewish piety, is not just something to think or feel but also an *action* (*poieō*), which is made clear in the ongoing discussion with the law expert, which leads to Jesus's parable of the good Samaritan (Luke 10:29–37).[38] This parable is a visualization of Jesus's attitude toward fulfilling the command to love one's neighbor. Neighbor love is not just scratching the backs of one's own family and friends.

---

36. W. D. Davies and Dale C. Allison, *Matthew 19–28*, ICC (Edinburgh: T&T Clark, 1997), 241, observe that Mark's citation of Deuteronomy 6:5 is closer to the Septuagint, and Matthew's resembles the Hebrew version.

37. See Furnish, *Love Command*, 27, 30–34.

38. See John Carroll, *Luke: A Commentary*, NTL (Louisville: Westminster John Knox, 2012), 881.

CHAPTER 4

It is about feeling compassion and acting on that impulse toward *anyone* that you might encounter, whether family, friend, or even enemy. That leads us to consider in more detail love of outsider and enemy in the Jesus tradition.

LOVE OF OUTSIDER AND ENEMY IN THE JESUS TRADITION

Jesus's teaching on love of enemy has left a massive impact in history and culture. This is well illustrated in the teachings and lifestyle of Mahatma Gandhi, who revered the Sermon on the Mount. According to the account of Rev. J. J. Doke, Gandhi was deeply affected by reading about Jesus's teachings on benevolence. "When I read in the Sermon the Mount such passages as 'Resist not him that is evil but whosoever smiteth thee on thy right cheek turn to him the other also,' and 'Love your enemies and pray for them that persecute you, that ye may be sons of your Father which is in heaven,' I was simply overjoyed, and found my own opinion confirmed where I least expected it. The Bhagavad Gita deepened the impression, and Tolstoy's *The Kingdom of God Is Within You* gave it permanent form."[39]

We will argue that generous love was a remembered emphasis in Jesus's teaching, but Jesus wasn't the first person to express this value. Pheme Perkins points to precedents inside and outside of ancient Judaism.[40] For example, Proverbs 20:22 and 24:29 express that revenge is unrighteous and that judgment belongs to the Lord. Similar sentiments are expressed by the Jewish sage Ben Sira (Sir 28:1–2). In the ancient Counsels of Wisdom (a Babylonian collection of 160 moral exhortations; c. 1500 BCE), the sage advises the people,

> Be fair to your enemy,
> Let your mood be cheerful to your opponent.
> Be it your ill-wisher, treat him generously.
> Make up your mind to no evil,
> Such is not acceptable to the gods,
> Evil is abhorrent to Marduk.[41]

---

39. See C. F. Andrews, *Mahatma Gandhi at Work: His Own Story Continued* (New York: Routledge, 1931), appendix 2.

40. See Perkins, *Love Commands*, 28–34.

41. See Richard J. Clifford, *The Wisdom Literature: Interpreting Biblical Texts* (Nashville: Abingdon, 1998), 30; cf. also Meier, *Marginal Jew*, 4:531.

Love in the Jesus Tradition

William Klassen sees a strong parallel to Jesus's teaching in the Testaments of the Twelve Patriarchs. "For a good person does not have a blind eye, but is merciful to all even though they may be sinners. And even if people plot against such a one for evil ends, by doing good this one conquers evil, being watched over by God. He loves those who wrong him as he loves his own life" (Testament of Benjamin 4.3).[42]

The ancient Greek tragedian Sophocles tells the story of the hero Ajax who repents of his anger and hatred toward his foes: "I learnt one need not hate a foe forever / He may become a friend."[43]

In Greco-Roman moral philosophy, the Stoics taught grace toward others. In Seneca the Younger's *On Leisure*, he acknowledges that Stoics like him were known for persistence in working toward the common good and holding strong to duty no matter what. Part of this commitment is not getting distracted by squabbles; good Stoics support even their enemies until their aged hands give out (*On Leisure* 1.4). Seneca also wrote a treatise called *On Clemency* to inspire the newly crowned emperor Nero to rule with grace and mercy. (Apparently the message didn't take.)

These teachings on love and grace from various writers belong in the wider conversation of enemy love in ancient discourse, but they were all fighting against popular cultural trends that reinforced social boundaries and saw justice in revenge and retribution.[44] For example, we read in the Qumranic Community Rule that those will be accepted into the community who "love the Sons of Light each according to his lot in the Council of God, and [who] hate all the Sons of Darkness each according to his guilt at the vengeance of God" (1QS I, 9b–11a).[45] Furnish wonders whether when Jesus quotes popular tradition to the effect "love your neighbor, hate your enemy," it could be referencing sayings just like this.[46] Jesus's kingdom teaching breaks away from

42. William Klassen, "'Love Your Enemies': Some Reflections on the Current Status of Research," in *The Love of Enemy and Nonretaliation in the New Testament*, ed. W. M. Swartley (Louisville: Westminster John Knox, 1992), 14.

43. Sophocles, *Ajax* 678–79.

44. Perkins, *Love Commands*, 21–22.

45. Akiyama, *Love of Neighbour*, 125. Akiyama is right to note that "hate" here doesn't mean animosity or malice but is a literary device that draws a line between friend/insider and enemy/outsider.

46. Furnish, *Love Command*, 47.

CHAPTER 4

this to show grace and generosity to outsiders, even opponents. The following texts are relevant from the Synoptic tradition:

> You have heard that it was said, "You shall love your neighbor and hate your enemy." But I say to you, Love your enemies and pray for those who persecute you, so that you may be children of your Father in heaven; for he makes his sun rise on the evil and on the good, and sends rain on the righteous and on the unrighteous. For if you love those who love you, what reward do you have? Do not even the tax collectors do the same? And if you greet only your brothers and sisters, what more are you doing than others? Do not even the Gentiles do the same? Be perfect, therefore, as your heavenly Father is perfect. (Matt 5:43–48)

> But I say to you that listen, Love your enemies, do good to those who hate you, bless those who curse you, pray for those who abuse you. If anyone strikes you on the cheek, offer the other also; and from anyone who takes away your coat do not withhold even your shirt. Give to everyone who begs from you; and if anyone takes away your goods, do not ask for them again. Do to others as you would have them do to you.
>
> If you love those who love you, what credit is that to you? For even sinners love those who love them. If you do good to those who do good to you, what credit is that to you? For even sinners do the same. If you lend to those from whom you hope to receive, what credit is that to you? Even sinners lend to sinners, to receive as much again. But love your enemies, do good, and lend, expecting nothing in return. Your reward will be great, and you will be children of the Most High; for he is kind to the ungrateful and the wicked. Be merciful, just as your Father is merciful. (Luke 6:27–36)

Jesus presents love of friends as convenient, even self-serving. Pagans and sinners do this by nature. But God calls his people to be perfect in covenantal righteousness and to model the virtuous character of the Father himself.[47] The undercurrent of these teachings involves some sense of self-sacrifice in

---

47. On the meaning of "perfect" in Jewish and Christian tradition, see Kent L. Yinger, *God and Human Wholeness: Perfection in Biblical and Theological Tradition* (Eugene, OR: Cascade Books, 2019). Yinger argues that the biblical use of perfection

Love in the Jesus Tradition

love of enemy. It is, by nature, difficult and costs something. Enemy love is counterintuitive. Human nature pushes back when shoved. Enemy love is a moral virtue, exercise, and commitment that must be learned and practiced. Jesus is, as Meier observes, "commanding his disciples to will good and to do good to their enemies, no matter how the disciples may feel about them, and *no matter whether the enemies remain enemies despite the goodness shown them.*"[48]

Of Jesus's parable teaching, none demonstrates his instruction on love better than the parable of the good Samaritan.[49] It is important to recognize that Luke ties this parable to Jesus's teaching about love of neighbor and Jewish obedience to Leviticus 19:18. The *nomikos* (law expert) asks, "who is my neighbor?" (clearly a trick question), and Jesus answers with a story (Luke 10:30–36). A few things can be briefly highlighted in this well-known parable. First, Jesus emphasizes the sad circumstances of this unnamed victim: attacked, disrobed, beaten, left half dead. Second, two Jewish cult professionals (a priest and Levite) notice the man but do not help. Now, Jesus leaves unstated what exactly their concerns were. Safety? Purity? We don't know. But what is clear is that instead of going *near* to evaluate the situation, they cross over to the other side of the road to put a greater distance between him and them. The story sets up a pattern of *seeing* and *reacting*. After the priest and Levite *see* the victim, their reaction is fear or repulsion. A third traveler enters the story, this time a Samaritan, of a people we know that Jews did not like to associate with. He also *sees* the man, but his reaction is the opposite. Rather than moving away, he moves toward, because he is driven by compassion (*splanchnizomai*). He goes out of his way to care for this poor victim, providing not only immediate first aid but also setting him up in an inn for longer-term care and prepaying for his treatment. The story, as Jesus tells it, is meant to be ludicrous: *Who would do such a thing? Especially—gasp!—a Samaritan?!*

Jesus's postparable question to the law expert ties the story back into the earlier discussion about the heart of torah: "Which of these three, do you think, was a neighbor to the man who fell into the hands of the robbers?"

---

language has less to do with absolute sinlessness and more to do with maturity and integrity; see similarly, Furnish, *Love Command*, 54.

48. Meier, *Marginal Jew*, 4:530.

49. A close second would be the parable of the prodigal son, which highlights the forgiving love of the father.

CHAPTER 4

(Luke 10:36). Jesus means here, Which man was a *good* or *torah-abiding* neighbor? The law expert is wise to not answer, "the Samaritan," because the point is not whether the helper is a Jew or Samaritan, or whether the victim is a Jew or Samaritan; what matters is that the observer "showed him mercy" (10:37a). The NRSV uses conventional English ("showed him mercy"); in Greek the verb for doing (*poieō*) is used here, so a more accurate rendering would be this: "The one having performed [an act of] mercy." That makes better sense of Jesus's final words, "Go and do likewise" (10:37b). For Jesus, love and mercy are not just sentiments and feelings, though they start to take life in the heart. As torah commands love and mercy, they are meant to be performed; they are acts of care and compassion for the other. Furnish puts it well: "Love is not just an attitude but a way of life. Love requires the real expenditure of one's time, effort, and resources. And love is not guided in its course, like an antiballistic missile, by something inherently attractive in its object. It is empowered and guided, rather, by its own inherent rightness as a response to human need."[50] Furnish's point is that love as a *virtue* does not reserve itself for those whom we consider worthy of that love. All persons, even outsiders and enemies, deserve love, just like all humans deserve the sun and rain that God gives over the earth, whether they are righteous or unrighteous (Matt 5:45).

Jesus backs up his teaching on love of outsiders with his own behavior. Jesus was known for spending time with "tax collectors and sinners."[51] He showed immediate compassion for the so-called sinful woman who came to anoint him in the house of a Pharisee (Luke 7:36–50). He conversed with a Syrophoenician woman (Mark 7) and Roman soldiers.[52] Jesus seemed to care genuinely for anyone he encountered, regardless of ethnicity, gender, or status. If that were not enough, he also demonstrated compassion for his enemies. When we look at Luke's Gospel, Jesus taught numerous times on forgiveness (Luke 6:37; 7:47; 11:4; 17:3). At the end of his life, he was willing to put into practice his own instruction as he uttered the words from the cross, "Father, forgive them; for they do not know what they are doing" (Luke 23:34).[53]

50. Furnish, *Love Command*, 60–61.

51. Matthew 9:10; 11:19; Mark 2:15; Luke 5:30; 7:34; 15:1.

52. Matthew 8:5–13; 27:54; Mark 15:39; Luke 7:2–6; 23:47.

53. While some early Greek manuscripts of Luke omit this verse (P75, B, D*, W, Θ, Syriac), I agree with Bock that it is easier to explain a scribal exclusion (concerned

Love in the Jesus Tradition

It is time to process in summary the theme of love in the synoptic Jesus tradition. Scholars like John Meier and Victor Furnish recognize that love stands out in these texts. But they come to different conclusions about what exactly this tells us about Jesus. Furnish is convinced that it is evident that love must have been a main teaching of Jesus, as it left such a strong impact on the evangelists. The love ethic was taught by Jesus, embraced by his disciples, and set firmly into the foundation of early Christianity.[54] Meier, too, recognizes that Jesus taught about love and has some striking statements about love of enemy, but there is not enough material to warrant claiming it as the heart or center of his message. When combined with Jesus's loving actions and deeds, Meier confesses, a stronger case can be made for the importance of love in the synoptic tradition; but even then he is hesitant.[55] I find myself standing somewhere in between Furnish and Meier. I agree with Meier that Jesus's love teachings are not frequent, but the emphasis on related matters of forgiveness, compassion, and mercy should be taken into consideration. And though it is true that Jesus's love teaching is not *frequent*, we can at least say it was *distinctive*. Furnish may have overstated the case, but for our purposes (as we look ahead to Paul), the case I think has been made that we can trace Paul's focus on love back to the Jesus tradition, at least in part.

Now we turn to the Johannine Jesus tradition.

JESUS AND LOVE IN THE GOSPEL OF JOHN

The Fourth Gospel's Jesus tradition is clearly different from the Synoptics, though there are a few overlaps. When it comes to Jesus and love, John does not include the verbatim quotation of either Deuteronomy's command to love God or Leviticus's command to love neighbor. However, the theme of love is a more prominent and pervasive theme throughout, given lengthier blocks

---

about this being too forgiving toward Jews) than for its inclusion. This is simply too big of a theological statement for a scribe to have included ex nihilo, though it is possible that it is a Jesus agraphon. See Darrell Bock, *Luke 9:51–24:53*, BECNT (Grand Rapids: Baker, 1996), 1867.

54. Furnish, *Love Command*, 17–18; cf. R. T. France, *The Gospel of Matthew*, NICNT (Grand Rapids: Eerdmans, 2007), 843.

55. Meier, *Marginal Jew*, 4:478–81.

CHAPTER 4

of teaching and appearing at numerous climactic points. In fact, I don't think Moody Smith exaggerates when he claims that love is the most important command taught by John's Jesus.[56] Love language pervades John, but the key didactic sections are found in the farewell instruction (13:1–17:26; especially, 13:1–38; 15:12–17; 17:1–26).

The focal point of John's interest in love is the love of the Father, especially the mutual love that God the Father and Jesus the Son share (3:35; 5:20). It is difficult to pinpoint exactly what John means when he uses the word "love" (*agapē*/*agapaō*). It is primarily a relational word, but John can also use it in reference to a primary set of values or commitments—for example, people *loved* darkness rather than light (3:19; cf. 5:42). In many cases, love involves the whole spectrum of personal experience and social expression: affection, commitment, obedience, and action—an all-encompassing investment in someone or something that is so firm that it could lead to loss or sacrifice (15:12–15).[57]

Discipleship, in John, is conceived of as abiding in Jesus the Son, sharing in the Father's love, and experiencing and expressing love toward one another in the community.[58] Humility and service are hallmarks of love, as modeled in the footwashing narrative (13:1–20).[59] Pride leads to division, but love focuses on the other and the community. It is true that John's tradition of the ministry of Jesus is concentrated on the community of disciples and showing love to one another, but I don't see this as exclusionary. The disciples are to know and learn love in the believing community, but not in a way that isolates them from the rest of the world. Just as they are expected to learn love from the Son, surely they must assimilate the action of the Son in the incarnation, where Jesus went to a needy world that did not accept him, and gave his life for them (see John 20:21). It is true, though, that John dwells on Jesus's message of intimacy and mutuality of love in the faith community as a central focus.

---

56. D. Moody Smith, *The Theology of the Gospel of John*, NTTh (Cambridge: Cambridge University Press, 1995), 148.

57. See Craig R. Koester, *The Word of Life: A Theology of John's Gospel* (Grand Rapids: Eerdmans, 2008), 190.

58. Francis J. Moloney, *Love in the Gospel of John: An Exegetical, Theological, and Literary Study* (Grand Rapids: Baker, 2013), 132.

59. Moloney, *Love in the Gospel of John*, 102.

Love in the Jesus Tradition

This runs parallel, I think, to Paul's instruction to the Galatians that goodness ought to be shown in the family of faith as a spiritual discipline; but Paul also believed that goodness and respect is for everyone (Gal 6:10).

Our goal in this chapter has been modest: to examine the claim that love is an important part of the Jesus tradition in the Gospels. Moody Smith captures well what we have tried to demonstrate: "in each Gospel Jesus issues a commandment of love."[60] A simple statement but accurate and telling. Matthew, Mark, Luke, and John do not record Jesus saying the *exact* same thing about love, but they all remember and identify that Jesus had something important to say about love as part of his kingdom teaching. It was, in fact, a hallmark of his instruction, and we can be sure this left an impact on the earliest Christians, including Paul.

---

60. Smith, *Theology of the Gospel of John*, 147.

5

Paul's Conception of Love

> There is no Pauline letter in which the term "love" (almost
> always *agapē*) does not appear and in which exhortations to love
> do not figure prominently.
>
> —Victor Furnish[1]

After what might seem like a long prolegomenon in this book, we are finally ready to focus our attention on Paul and his writings. It took several chapters to set the stage, and now we will go into detail about Paul's theological conception and articulation of love in relationship to the gospel. In this chapter, we will take a look at Paul's conception of love from the thirty-thousand-foot view. This chapter is meant to paint a broad picture of Paul's conception and articulation of love. This is also the place to address questions about key sources and influences.

How and Where Does Paul Talk about Love?

Victor Furnish is correct in the quotation above—love language appears in every single Pauline text in the New Testament. And he is also correct that love features prominently in several key passages. This, perhaps, goes unnoticed

---

1. Victor Furnish, *The Love Command in the New Testament* (Nashville: Abingdon, 1972), 91.

Paul's Conception of Love

in Bible reading because it is so common to see "love" in Paul's letters that it is hidden in plain sight. Much like Paul's frequent references to thanksgiving, grace, and joy, "love" constantly bleeds out of Paul's pen with ease. And yet, as we have noted again and again, love rarely features in studies of Pauline theology, and when it *does*, it tends to be filed under ethics or outworkings of the Christian life. No doubt, exhortations to love *are* common in Paul's writings, but love language appears in various sections of his letters and relate not just to Christian communal behavior but to all areas of Christian religion, theology, worship, and communal life.

For example, if we *just* look at Paul's Letter to the Romans, one might guess that love language would be concentrated in the more practical sections of the text, chapters 12–15 in particular. Indeed, Paul gives attention to the virtue of love in 13:8–10, quoting the neighbor-love command of Leviticus 19:18 (Rom 13:9). And, again, in his comments about unity in diverse community, Paul underscores living a lifestyle of love in disagreement on food and table practices (Rom 14:15). But love comes up even more frequently in Romans 5–8, what many consider the doctrinal heart of the letter, his articulation of the gospel of Jesus Christ.[2] We will give a more robust analysis of this section of Romans in the next chapter; here we will just skim across the surface to flag Paul's references to love. As Paul explicates the heart of the rightwising and peacemaking work of the gospel (5:1), he expresses full confidence in God's commitment to his people to the very end, because of his love (5:5). Here, divine love is known and experienced through the gift and presence of the Holy Spirit. But the ultimate demonstration of God's love and affection is the death of Christ on behalf of sinners (5:8).

Jumping ahead to Romans 8, still part of this gospel-explicating section of the letter (chapters 5–8), Paul signals that the key covenantal response to God's love is human love (8:28). It is not a tit for tat or quid pro quo. It is not some kind of love exchange as if humans can repay God for his salvation. Paul viewed faith and love as the *natural* responses to God's much greater grace and favor. Ultimately, what maintains the connection between heaven and earth is not human capacity for love but God's unique and superlative love in Jesus Christ.

2. See N. T. Wright's recent work, which is focused on Romans 8, *Into the Heart of Romans* (Grand Rapids: Zondervan, 2023), 198–222.

CHAPTER 5

And it is ultimately to this love of Christ that Paul points when he reminds the Romans of where their hope and confidence lie. *Nothing* can separate them from Christ's love (8:35, 39).

Here in one letter, we have a well-rounded conception of the many directions of love in the gospel economy. First and foremost, you have the love of God, which seeks and saves sinners because of God's own compassion. Believers are called to respond with their own love for God, and also to love one another as Christ affirmed the law's commandment to love one's neighbor. Romans 14:15 offers a Pauline phrase that is very insightful for understanding his conception of the Christian life: *kata agapēn peripateis*—"walking according to love." "According to" (*kata*) is meant to identify a certain standard or style; the Jewish idiom of "walking" indicates a practical or habitual lifestyle. Christians live all aspects of their being in a spirit of love. Love is not just a concept relevant to ecclesiology or ethics but all of life and spirituality.

Paul's Language of Love

What kind of language and terminology does Paul use when he talks about love? There has been a tendency for scholars to focus on just one term, *agapē*. Of course, *agapē* is the most important term Paul uses. Thanks to the Septuagint's repeated and central use of *agapē*, and also the focus on *agapē* in the early Jesus tradition, Paul preferred *agapē* as a distinctly Jewish and Christian way of understanding love. But to limit the discussion to *agapē* ignores how language works. Human communication naturally includes variance of terminology. So we will talk about a cluster of terms that work together as part of a wider semantic domain of affection.

Agapē *and Its Cognates*

Agapē (love) as a noun appears sixty-three times in the undisputed Pauline letters.[3] It will become clear that this is Paul's favored term for love. The verb form *agapaō* appears about half that number of times (thirty-four), and the term of endearment *agapētos* (beloved) twenty-seven times. The highest concentration of *agapē* is 1 Corinthians (13:1–13), then Romans and 2 Corinthians (nine

3. *Agapē* (63), *agapaō* (34), *agapētos* (27).

98

Paul's Conception of Love

times each; Ephesians also nine times); then a handful of references spread across the rest of his letters. What does *agapē* mean? Obviously it means "love," but can we say more than that? *Agapē* is not some sort of spiritual language. And yet it became a kind of technical term early on in the Jesus movement. We will be looking at specific usage in the following chapters, but suffice it to say for now that it takes its *Christian* meaning from the love that God shows, especially in the sacrificial death of Christ. We might gloss *agapē*, then, as *authentic and deep love as modeled by Jesus Christ who gave himself over to death out of his care for sinners.*

When reading Paul's letters, it is easy to pass by his many references to "beloved" (*agapētos*), but given the importance of *agapē* in his writings, it is worth considering the significance and usage of this term of endearment. *Agapētos* is often translated "beloved" and is used by Paul as an affectionate term for his churches. On several occasions, Paul refers to specific individuals as "beloved" (e.g., Ampliatus, Stachys, Persis [Rom 16:8, 12], Timothy [1 Cor 4:17]). One wonders why Paul calls Ampliatus "beloved" but not Urbanus or Tryphaena and Tryphosa. Given this is a commendation list, I doubt Paul wanted that to reflect negatively when *agapētos* was absent. My hunch is that when it was used person to person ("my beloved Stachys"), it signaled a close personal friendship or bond, the way we might say "my good friend" (see Phlm 1). This implies personal knowledge and shared experience, as well as fondness. That sense of personal affection seems to be the sentiment of Paul's description of the Corinthian church as his "beloved children" (*tekna mou agapēta*; 1 Cor 4:14; cf. 1 Thess 2:8).

But sometimes Paul uses the plural *agapētoi* for the whole church as God's "beloved."[4] Again, given *agapētos* is a form of *agapē*, there is reason to see theological importance in this ecclesial descriptor. Paul *could* have called fellow Christians *philoi* (a common term for "friends"), but using *agapētoi* was probably a way of reminding them of their participation in the gospel love of God in Jesus Christ. The theological significance of this term is reinforced by a few factors. First, Paul wasn't the only one to use it. It appears as a common term for Christians in Hebrews (6:9), James (1:16, 19; 2:5), 1 Peter (2:11; 4:12), 2 Peter (3:1, 8, 14, 17), 1 John (2:7; 3:2, 21; 4:1, 7, 11), and Jude (3, 17, 20). It might be

---

4. Romans 12:19; 1 Corinthians 10:14; 15:58; 2 Corinthians 7:1; 12:19; Philippians 2:12; 4:1; cf. Ephesians 5:1.

CHAPTER 5

the case that all these texts were influenced by the Pauline tradition, but it is equally plausible that *agapētos* was a common Christian expression in earliest Christianity that preceded Paul's writings.

A second consideration in terms of theological importance of *agapētos* is how it is sometimes used by Paul with weighted meaning and clear rhetorical impact. Romans, for example, has a very long prescript (even for Paul!). In Romans 1:7, he acknowledges the addressees this way: "To all God's beloved [*agapētois*] in Rome, who are called to be saints [*hagioi*]." To be holy is to be invited into the presence of God, and to be beloved is to be welcomed into the family of God, like his beloved son, Jesus. We also see a theological weighty use of *agapētos* in Philemon 15–16: "so that you might have him [Onesimus] back forever, no longer as a slave but more than a slave, a beloved [*agapēton*] brother." Paul wanted to see a transformed relationship between the estranged slave Onesimus and the master Philemon. Philemon, in particular, needed to see his relationship with Onesimus primarily as brothers in Christ, not master-slave.[5] The addition of the term "beloved" was a reminder of what it means to be family, a relationship of mutuality, generosity, appreciation, and affection.

One more item to observe: often Paul uses "beloved" as a callout to the letter audience when he is about to give an exhortation or corrective command. In these heated and sensitive situations, it appears that he was trying to remind them of his love for them and the wider context of God's love for them. Paul often deftly combines exhortation with comfort and encouragement, as demonstrated well by Philippians 4:1: "Therefore, my brothers and sisters, whom I love [*agapētoi*] and long for, my joy and crown, stand firm in the Lord in this way, my beloved [*agapētoi*]."

Phileō *and Its Cognates*

As we have already indicated, the most common terminology for love in the ancient Greek world is *phileō*. Although many a sermon has been preached on *phileō* representing a lower form of love than *agapaō*, the actual evidence

5. See John M. G. Barclay, "KOINΩNIA and the Social Dynamics of the Letter to Philemon," in *La lettre à Philémon et l'ecclésiologie paulinienne*, ed. D. Marguerat (Leuven: Peeters, 2016), 151–69.

Paul's Conception of Love

from the Greek Bible shows that there is no formal difference between these two verbs. *Phileō* can be used for petty or self-centered forms of infatuation or affection (e.g., Matt 23:6; Luke 20:46). But the Fourth Gospel repeatedly uses *phileō* for the perfect love of the Father (John 5:20), the love of the Son (11:3), and the ideal love of believers (12:25; 16:27). The one time we find *phileō* in the undisputed Pauline letters, it is treated as genuine love for Christ: "Let anyone be accursed who has no love for the Lord. Our Lord, come!" (1 Cor 16:22). Given the commonness of *phileō* in ancient Greek texts in general, it is noticeable that it appears only once in Paul (note also Titus 3:15), twice in Revelation (Rev 3:19; 22:15), and not at all in the Catholic Epistles. John has the most occurrences in the New Testament (thirteen), then Matthew (five), Luke (two), then Mark (one). It appears that the verb *agapaō* became the preferred expression of love in early Christianity, which reduced the usage of *phileō*, but the meanings of these words continued to be essentially the same and varied only based on context and rhetorical nuancing.

It is also interesting to note that the common Greek terms *philos* (friend) and *philia* (friendship) are not found at all in the Pauline corpus. This is a bit odd, because other texts, like James, do not shy away from them (Jas 2:23; 4:4), and writers like Luke and John use them frequently.[6] One possibility for why Paul avoided *philos* is that it could be used for political or patronage alliances that might not capture the heart of real friendship—note the infamous accusation against Pilate that if he tried to release Jesus he would be no "friend/ally" (*philos*) of Caesar (John 19:12). However, the most general and common meaning of *philos* is what we think of as "friend," so the Letter of James had no concern with referring to the patriarch Abraham as "friend of God" (*philos theou*; Jas 2:23). I think the more sensible explanation for why Paul did not use *philos* (or *philia*) is simply that he preferred forms of *agapē*, like *agapētos* (beloved), and when it comes to language and images of affection, Paul leaned heavily on familial metaphors like "my brothers and sisters" (*adelphoi*).

To say that Paul did not use *philos* at all is somewhat misleading; he did not use the adjective *philos* or the noun *philia*, but he did use common compounds that include a form of *philos*.

---

6. Luke 7:6, 34; 11:5, 8; 12:4; 14:10, 12; 15:6, 9, 29; 16:9; 21:16; 23:12; John 3:29; 11:11; 15:13; 19:12.

CHAPTER 5

PAULINE USAGE OF COMPOUND FORMS OF *PHILOS*

Word	Meaning/Gloss	Occurrences
philadelphia	sibling love	Rom 12:10; 1 Thess 4:9
philostorgos[7]	love	Rom 12:10
philoxenia	hospitality (lit., love of stranger)	Rom 15:20 (*philoxenos*, 1 Tim 3:2; Titus 1:8)
philotimeomai	ambition (lit., love of honor)	Rom 15:20; 2 Cor 5:9; 1 Thess 4:11
philēma	kiss	Rom 16:15; 1 Cor 16:20; 2 Cor 13:12; 1 Thess 5:26
philoneikos	contentious (love of arguing)	1 Cor 11:16
prosphilōs	lovely	Phil 4:8
philosophia	philosophy (lit., love of wisdom)	Col 2:8
aphilargyros	not greedy (lit., no love of gold)	1 Tim 3:2; 6:10; 2 Tim 3:2
philautos	selfish (lit., love of self)	2 Tim 3:2
aphilagathos	not a friend of the good (lit., no love of good)	2 Tim 3:2; Titus 1:8
aphilēdonos	no love of pleasure	2 Tim 3:2
philotheos	lover of God	2 Tim 3:2
philandros	lover of husband	Titus 2:4
philoteknos	lover of one's children	Titus 2:4
philanthrōpia	lover of humanity	Titus 3:4

The takeaway from looking at this data is that while Paul clearly preferred *agapē* language for talking about love, he did not use it exclusively and was more than comfortable with variation, including forms of *phileō*. When it comes to translating this word group, there is no reason to differentiate it from *agapē*. While *phileō* is the more general and generic Greek term for love, what matters is how the author uses it when it comes to meaning and translation,

---

7. Paul doesn't use *storgos*, but *astorgos* appears in 2 Timothy 3:4.

Paul's Conception of Love

and based on 1 Corinthians 16:22 alone, we can confirm that Paul was more than comfortable using *phileō* in reference to ideal forms of Christian love.

Terms of Affection and Desire

Many studies of love language in Paul focus exclusively on *agapē* and *phileō*, but if we want a more complete picture of how Paul talks about love (as a concept), we must include closely related terminology involving affection and desire. Paul uses a number of Greek terms that involve desiring, yearning, cherishing, and fondness. We discussed these earlier (pp. 32–34, 61–73), but here our focus is on Pauline usage.

Epipotheō. This verb refers to desires and longings, often in a positive way. Paul *longs* (*epipotheō*) to see the Romans to have fellowship with them (Rom 1:11; cf. Phil 1:8; 2:26; 4:1; 2 Tim 1:4). He was often encouraged by his churches' *desires* to see him (2 Cor 7:7; 1 Thess 3:6). This verb indicates an attachment to someone or something at the heart level. Just like we can feel physically hungry in the pit of our stomachs, so we can feel a longing to be with someone, and that passion comes from affection and love.

Splanchna. Another term in this semantic category used by Paul involves the exercising of the gut, similar in idiomatic expression to how modern Westerners talk about the heart as the center of the emotional experience. *Splanchna* reflects a deep connection to something or someone, as if one treats them almost as a part of oneself. Thus, *splanchna* often is translated as not only "affections" (2 Cor 6:12) and "heart" (2 Cor 7:15; Phlm 7, 12, 20) but also "compassion" (Phil 1:8; 2:1). Again, we see here that love, for Paul, is not only or primarily a cerebral phenomenon (e.g., of knowledge and sheer duty), though he believed that what you think about someone affects how you feel about them. Still, love is a complex phenomenon that operates deep in the gut or heart. To love is to form a heart bond with someone and experience a real connection to that person's life, to experience joy when they are flourishing and to experience compassion and sorrow when they are suffering.[8]

Zēlos. Finally, in this category of desire, we have a term that refers to passion or zeal. Sometimes it is translated as "jealousy," signaling a focused, intensified, or exclusive form of desire. In Paul's view, zeal is not inherently good or bad.

---

8. Paul was fond of *splanchna,* and it appears in the Gospels and Acts but not in Revelation or other New Testament letters aside from 1 John (3:17).

CHAPTER 5

He took it for granted that humans naturally will be passionate about certain people or things. These desires must be properly cultivated, controlled, and directed. So, for example, he tells the Corinthians to show *zeal* (*zēlos*) for the greater gifts (1 Cor 12:31; cf. 14:1). Sometimes we (moderns) can think of real love as cold, calculated, and emotionless (i.e., doing the right thing); and, in contrast, we sometimes think that emotions deceive us and somehow dilute real love because we are acting on impulse or by feelings. Paul didn't see it that way. Emotions are natural and tell us something about our deepest longings and desires—what we hold most precious. Passion and desire should not be ignored, suppressed, or extinguished. Neither God nor your loved ones want passionless fidelity. There are certainly times when passion is misplaced or overwhelms reason. But the best scenario is when mind, heart, and body are working in unison and reflect genuine love for others in a way that feeds our soul and cherishes, serves, and respects the one whom we love.

Patheō/sympatheō and *epithymia*. In addition, we can address two less common terms in Paul involving passion, particularly as they relate to overwhelmingly powerful sinful desires (often translated "lusts"). *Patheō* and *pathos* simply mean "experience/deep feeling" but often carry the connotation of sinful desires that override the mind and will (Rom 1:26; cf. 1 Thess 4:5). Similarly, *epithymia* is the form of uncontrollable desires and passions that is part of the flesh and must be crucified (Gal 5:24).[9] The verbal form is used by Paul when he quotes from the Decalogue, "Do not covet" (*epithymeō*; Rom 13:9). Looking at the original Old Testament commandment, Patrick Miller describes this prohibition as "a combination of feeling and action in pursuit of what one is greedy for but may not have."[10] It goes beyond simply a strong desire; it is a compulsion and obsession. Miller connects this prohibition to what the torah explains about the problem in Eden—Eve craving what she sees to be a pleasurable delight of the forbidden tree. Eve has plenty to eat; God has provided abundantly for Adam and her, but she longs for that which is held back from her. Her sin involves "violation of the constraints of life in the garden, a violation due wholly to desire and its power to make one forget

9. *Epithymia*: Romans 1:24; 6:12; 7:7; 13:9, 14; 1 Corinthians 10:6; Galatians 5:16; 1 Thessalonians 4:5.

10. Patrick D. Miller, *The Ten Commandments* (Louisville: Westminster John Knox, 2009), 341.

Paul's Conception of Love

and ignore, in this case forget the divine commandment and ignore its consequences. The first act of disobedience is the couple's unrestrained craving. Desire out of control changes the human way in the world."[11]

Desire out of control. That is an appropriate way to look at terms like *patheō* and *epithymia* as Paul uses them. It is important to know that *desire*, even *passion*, in itself is not wicked. In fact, Paul talks about his (good) "passion" (*epithymia*) to be with Christ when he dies (Phil 1:23). To be human is to have passions and desires; it is simply the way humans are wired, and it can create all kinds of goodness: zeal for charity work, for training wise leaders, for spreading the gospel, for investing in family and healthy friendships. There tend to be two reasons why passion becomes a vice: it is *misdirected* or *out of control*. Having money can be very good and honorable (Prov 10:15); it is a vice and snare when it becomes an obsession: "The lover of money will not be satisfied with money; nor the lover of wealth, with gain. This is also vanity" (Eccl 5:10). Anger can be good and healthy, if it is a response to real injustice and is bridled and directed toward a good resolution. "Anger" (*thymos*) often appears in vice lists (Gal 5:20), but it is taken for granted this is unhealthy forms of anger, anger that holds onto hate and seeks vengeance and harm. Texts like Ephesians 4:26 imagine that a healthier form of anger can maintain its cool (cf. Rom 10:19).

A Caring Family as Paul's Master Image of Love

We have spent ample time on the specific *words* that Paul used that express love, but we would be missing out on understanding how Paul conceived of and communicated about love if we didn't attend to his key metaphor that shaped his understanding of love: *family*. This goes unnoticed often when studying Paul, because he uses family language so much (God as Father, Christ as Son; believers as sons/children); but it is worth flagging here because there is a sense of tenderness and nurturing that is involved in how Paul viewed the family of faith in the household of God, especially because of Jesus the Son.

I used to have a view of the Roman household that assumed families were purely utilitarian, focused on productivity, and more or less absent of sentiment. But as I have studied Roman texts related to family in more depth, it is clear that love and care were commonly expressed sentiments, between

11. Miller, *Ten Commandments*, 391.

CHAPTER 5

spouses, siblings, and parents and children. A good example of this is captured in the Roman inscription honoring a beloved daughter, Nymphe (*CIL* 1.2.1222).

> If any have a sorrow to compare to ours
> Let him draw near and weep freely.
> Here a grieving parent laid to rest
> Nymphe, his only daughter, whom he
> Cherished with a gentle love while yet he could.
> Now she who was so dear to her family
> Has been carried off from her home and is covered by earth.
> Her fair face and figure praised as fair
> Now are in insubstantial shadow,
> Her bones but a bit of ash.[12]

The bond and love between parents and children is certainly innate and natural, but we can also see the social values of familial love explicated in the foundational social and political ethics of Aristotle, who affirmed that parents love their children as a part of themselves, and children love their parents as those who brought them into the world. He goes on to also talk about a special bond between siblings, the sharing of blood and upbringing making them a special household community (Aristotle, *Nicomachean Ethics* 1161b28–1162a2).[13] Again, Greeks and Romans held a cultural conception of love and affection for family, not unlike how we view familial bonds today.

What made Paul's writings unique—and undoubtedly destabilizing to some Roman readers—is the way he transferred that sentiment of familial love to human relationships with the divine, a notion that might seem overly familiar, even dangerously intimate.[14] Most Romans believed that mutuality in love

---

12. Translation from Paul J. Shore, *Rest Lightly: An Anthology of Latin and Greek Tomb Inscriptions* (Wauconda, IL: Bolchazy-Carducci, 1997), 34.

13. See Jérôme Wilgaux, "Consubstantiality, Incest, and Kinship in Ancient Greece," in *A Companion to Families in the Greek and Roman Worlds*, ed. Beryl Rawson (Malden, MA: Wiley-Blackwell, 2011), 220.

14. See my extended discussion of this in *Strange Religion: How the First Christians Were Weird, Dangerous, and Compelling* (Grand Rapids: Brazos, 2024), 129–43.

106

Paul's Conception of Love

was normal in family relationships, but the gods are like celestial magistrates, and what mortals owe to them primarily is allegiance, service, and respect, not friendly affection. Therefore, it might seem flippant to pretend to have intimate association with the divine. But this is precisely how Paul expressed a *Christian* relationship with the Father through Jesus Christ, the Son: "But when the fullness of time had come, God sent his Son, born of a woman, born under the law, in order to redeem those who were under the law, so that we might receive adoption as children. And because you are children, God has sent the Spirit of his Son into our hearts, crying, 'Abba! Father!' So you are no longer a slave but a child, and if a child then also an heir, through God" (Gal 4:4–7). Paul's proclamation of the gospel to gentiles was not just a message about curtailing divine judgment; it was an invitation to become a part of the loving family of God. The Son, Jesus, welcomes outsiders inside to share in his unique privileges in the family, and the Spirit knits this family together. While the Aramaic *abba* doesn't refer to a little child's term for "daddy," it is a term of endearment and a sign of intimacy.[15] The Spirit makes it possible for strangers and enemies of God to call God "Abba," to call out to the Father as a child of God.

No doubt this affected Paul's understanding of the church. One of his favorite expressions for fellow Christians is "brothers/sisters" (*adelphoi*).[16] Paul tended to use the vocative form of *adelphos* when he made a serious point, as if reminding them of their responsibilities to one another and the whole family.[17] In other cases, even when a vocative was not used, it is clear that high expectations were set for love, care, and mutuality, as with the issue of tolerating difference of religious practice, as in Romans 14:15: "If your brother or sister is being injured by what you eat, you are no longer walking in love. Do not let what you eat cause the ruin of one for whom Christ died."

---

15. For a more detailed discussion of the early Jewish and Christian use of the term *abba*, see my "The Babylonian Talmud and Mark 14:26–52: Abba, Father!," in *Reading Mark in Context: Jesus and Second Temple Judaism*, ed. Ben C. Blackwell, John K. Goodrich, and Jason Maston (Grand Rapids: Zondervan, 2018), 224–30.

16. See the excellent study, Reidar Aasgaard, *My Beloved Brothers and Sisters! Christian Siblingship in Paul* (London: T&T Clark, 2004); Paul R. Trebilco, *Self-Designations and Group Identity in the New Testament* (Cambridge: Cambridge University Press, 2012), 16–46.

17. E.g., Romans 12:1; 15:30; 16:17; 1 Corinthians 1:10; 10:1; 14:20; 2 Corinthians 1:8; 8:1.

CHAPTER 5

And in Galatians, Paul explicitly refers to the church community as a "household of faith" (*tous oikeious tēs pisteōs*), a special family brought together by faith in Christ Jesus (Gal 6:10). They have a calling to love one another, specifically to seek the good for the other (*ergazōmetha to agathon*). Perhaps the intimacy of the Christian family should be taken for granted by readers even when the metaphor is not explicitly used, as might be the case with Paul's opening address in Romans: "to all God's beloved [*agapētois theou*] in Rome, who are called to be saints" (Rom 1:7). The belovedness of believers is an indication of a special relationship they have with God, specifically as cherished family.

INFLUENCES AND SOURCES OF PAUL'S LOVE LANGUAGE

In some cases when we read Paul's letters, it is assumed that his teaching on love comes from his own reflections on the nature of the gospel and the kind of people and communities it creates (e.g., Rom 5–8). But it is also possible that, in some cases, he was passing on specific phrases and teachings from an earlier era of Christianity. This may reveal some influences on his thinking and expression. We will not make much of this (i.e., attempting to detect pre-Pauline traditions), but it is valuable to spend a little bit of time considering sources and influences.

The holy kiss ritual. In four different letters, Paul exhorts his readers to greet one another with a "holy kiss."[18] First Peter has a similar exhortation ("kiss of love"; 1 Pet 5:14). There are no stated origins of this congregational ritual in the New Testament. Because Paul mentions it without explanation to the Roman churches (16:16), we can assume the tradition predates Paul.[19] But where did it come from, and what role did it have in the community's assembly? Justin Martyr mentions a mutual kiss as part of his explanation of sacramental traditions. After this exchange of affection, the bread and cup were served (*First Apology* 1.65).[20] Because Justin may have written this a century after the beginning of Christianity, we cannot presume this is how Pauline churches (or pre-Pauline churches) practiced this tradition.

---

18. *En philēmati hagiō*; 1 Thessalonians 5:26; 1 Corinthians 16:20; 2 Corinthians 13:12; Romans 16:16.

19. Anthony C. Thiselton, *The First Epistle to the Corinthians*, NIGTC (Grand Rapids: Eerdmans, 2000), 1344.

20. See Denis Minns and Paul Parvis, *Justin, Philosopher and Martyr: Apologies* (Oxford: Oxford University Press, 2009), 253.

108

Paul's Conception of Love

In the first-century Greco-Roman world, kissing was a token of affection often exchanged among relatives, but not exclusively so.[21] Friends could greet each other with a kiss, and it could also be a kind gesture between colleagues or neighbors. Ben Sira, for example, warns his readers that you should be wary of someone who kisses your hand while asking for a loan (Sir 29:5). In the Gospels, the so-called sinful woman kisses Jesus's feet (Luke 7:38). When Jesus's hosts cast the eye of suspicion on this inappropriate behavior, he rebukes them for not offering him hospitality, including anointing and kisses given to guests (Luke 7:45). Of course, the most infamous gesture in the gospel tradition is the betraying kiss of Judas (Matt 26:48; Mark 14:44; Luke 22:47). It is interesting to consider that the Christian holy kiss might have developed as a kind of undoing of the treachery of Judas. Stephen Benko argues that the holy kiss traces its origins to the risen Christ's breathing of peace on his disciples (John 20:21–23): "how did he breathe on them? . . . The answer that comes most readily to mind is that Jesus kissed the disciples."[22]

It could be that this ritual developed soon after the earliest churches formed as a symbol of love, affection, and a new family-like relationship.[23] This diverse group of Jews and gentiles, slaves and free, men and women, must come together not in competition or evaluation of social rank but as brothers and sisters in Christ.[24] The gesture of their greeting is a symbol of love, a kiss. What did it mean that it was a *holy* kiss? Some argue that this was to reinforce that this should not be sexual or erotic. The word "holy" (*hagios*) would certainly reinforce that notion, but I think the main reason for this adjective is the special social identity of this particular group of people, members of the family of the holy God.[25] Holiness here does not qualify the kiss with some

21. Edwin M. Yamauchi and Marvin R. Wilson, eds., *Dictionary of Daily Life in Biblical and Post-biblical Antiquity* (Peabody, MA: Hendrickson, 2017), 945–58.

22. Stephen Benko, *Pagan Rome and Early Christians* (Bloomington: Indiana University Press, 1984), 82.

23. On the power of kinship images and metaphors in early Christianity, see Stephen C. Barton, *Discipleship and Family Ties in Mark and Matthew*, SNTSMS (Cambridge: Cambridge University Press, 1994); Trebilco, *Self-Designations*, 16–67.

24. See Klaus Thraede, "Ursprünge und Formen des 'heiligen Kusses' im frühen Christentum," *Jahrbuch für Antike und Christentum* 11/12 (1967–1968): 124–80, esp. 144.

25. William Klassen, "The Sacred Kiss in the New Testament: An Example of Social Boundary Lines," *New Testament Studies* 39 (1993): 132–35.

CHAPTER 5

sense of distance, but the opposite: it reinforces unity and intimacy among God's special people, the saints.

Love in liturgical expressions. In Paul's postscripts, he tends to include some kind of liturgical expression, often in the form of a benediction. Perhaps Paul produced all of these out of his own imagination and wording. But there is some reason to think that he inherited some of these expressions from preexisting liturgy. One clue is the use of the Aramaic *Maranatha* ("Our Lord, come!") at the end of the love saying in 1 Cor 16:22 (see below). I am always hesitant to try to dig down beneath his wording to discover previously formed traditions. Nevertheless, if we are going to look for earlier traditions in his writings that have a generic and liturgical ring, the postscripts appear to me to be the best place.

Let anyone be accursed who has no love for the Lord. Our Lord, come! (1 Cor 16:22)

I appeal to you, brothers and sisters, by our Lord Jesus Christ and by the love of the Spirit, to join me in earnest prayer to God on my behalf. (Rom 15:30)

Agree with one another, live in peace; and the God of love and peace will be with you. (2 Cor 13:11)

The grace of the Lord Jesus Christ, the love of God, and the communion of the Holy Spirit be with all of you. (2 Cor 13:13)

May the Lord direct your hearts to the love of God and to the steadfastness of Christ. (2 Thess 3:5)

Peace be with the whole community, and love with faith, from God the Father and the Lord Jesus Christ. Grace be with all of you who have an undying love for our Lord Jesus Christ. (Eph 6:23)

All who are with me send greetings to you. Greet those who love us in the faith. (Titus 3:15)

Again, I don't want to assume Paul was passing on preformed liturgical quotations; perhaps they were original to him, perhaps not. But as possible

Paul's Conception of Love

evidence that Paul was passing on a Christian tradition of love blessings, we might look at other (non-Pauline) letters.

> Greet one another with a kiss of love. Peace to all of you who are in Christ. (1 Pet 5:14)

> Keep yourselves in the love of God. (Jude 21)[26]

If all these final benedictory texts attest to a wider early Christian tradition, then we can say a few things about the commonalities. First and most obviously, love is treated as the fingerprint identification of Christian faith and the truest form of Christian expression. To be a Christian is to be loved by God, to love God, and to love each other. Second, there is no consistency (even within Pauline texts) with regard to the divine object of love or divine giver of love. Sometimes it is God the Father (2 Cor 13:11), sometimes Christ (1 Cor 16:22), and sometimes the Spirit (Rom 15:30). Third, love is a unifying concept in all of these texts, bonding believers to God and one another. These benedictions seek peace, reconciliation, cooperation, and goodwill within the church and in relation to God. Finally, these love expressions end these letters with a spirit of grace and warmth.

In this chapter, our goal was to look at the big picture of how Paul used love language and consider possible sources of and influences on his thought and expression. In the next few chapters, we will argue that love is truly at the heart of Paul's theology, and this can be examined in terms of four areas: love at the heart of the gospel of God, love at the heart of religion, love at the heart of Christian community, and love at the heart of the Christian mission.

---

26. This appears not quite at but close to the end of the short letter.

6

Love at the Heart of Paul's Gospel of God

Paul was nothing if not someone overwhelmed by the love of God.

—Michael J. Gorman[1]

For Paul, the story of the gospel begins with love, God's love. Whatever specific system, method, or mechanism we might promote to explain Paul's conception of atonement and salvation, the starting point for any legitimate Pauline theology is the affectionate heart of God and the compassion-driven activity of God in Jesus Christ. While I don't think Paul himself thought in fully developed Trinitarian terms of love of God, love of Christ, and love of the Spirit, we can see in his writings that love language is used in relation to all three. However Paul imagined the interrelationship between them, it all begins with God the Father, and so we will start there as well.

The Extravagant Love of God the Father

Romans doesn't begin with an explanation of the doctrine of God's love, but it does begin with love in a way. Paul addresses the Romans as "all God's beloved in Rome" (Rom 1:7).[2] While this form of salutation prescript is unique to this letter, I hesitate to read too much into it; Paul often refers to his readers as

1. Michael J. Gorman, *Cruciformity: Paul's Narrative Spirituality of the Cross*, 20th anniversary ed. (Grand Rapids: Eerdmans, 2021), 141.
2. *pasin tois ousin en Rōmē agapētois theou.*

Love at the Heart of Paul's Gospel of God

beloved (of God). At the same time, this could be a subtle preview of love as a theme of this weighty letter as a whole.[3] Of course, the first four chapters dwell on the "righteousness of God" and the right-making gospel work of this God through Jesus Christ. But if you jump ahead to Romans 5:1–11, Paul offers an extended meditation on divine love at the heart of the gospel. The immediate link is probably the Abrahamic pattern of faith reckoned as righteousness, now in an ultimate way through Jesus Christ raised from the dead (4:22–24). Paul ends chapter 4 by associating Jesus's death with our trespasses and his resurrection with our *dikaiōsis*, "justification." He makes clear here that justification is not simply a legal status but a covenant reality that involves a dynamic relationship with God. This inspires Paul to go into further detail about "the fundamental reconstruction of our entire life, our very being, into the life of God" in Romans 5–8.[4] Along the same lines, a number of scholars have recognized that Romans 5 and 8 use a lot of experiential language or appeal to the lived reality of life with God.[5] Luke Timothy Johnson refers to Romans 5 as the heart of Paul's argument in the letter, which reveals the relationship between the love and grace of God and his righteous and right-making activity.[6] God does not act out of (mere) duty or obligation but genuine affection. When it comes to

3. Jewett is one of the only commentary writers on Romans who makes an explicit connection between Romans 1:7 ("God's beloved") and the love language that occurs later in the letter (like 5:5–8; 8:31–39; 9:13). See Robert Jewett, *Romans*, Hermeneia (Minneapolis: Fortress, 2006), 113.

4. Michael J. Gorman, *Romans: A Theological and Pastoral Commentary* (Grand Rapids: Eerdmans, 2022), 144.

5. "Christian experience speaks here," says Ernst Käsemann, *Commentary on Romans*, trans. Geoffrey W. Bromiley (Grand Rapids: Eerdmans, 1980), 134. See also James D. G. Dunn, *Romans 1–8*, WBC (Dallas: Word, 1988), 252; Frank Matera, *Romans*, PCNT (Grand Rapids: Baker, 2010), 16; Susan Eastman, "Christian Experience and Paul's Logic of Solidarity: The Spiral Structure of Romans 5–8," *Biblical Annals* 12 (2022): 233–53.

6. Luke Timothy Johnson, *Reading Romans: A Literary and Theological Commentary* (Macon, GA: Smyth & Helwys, 2001), 83, writes, "In a very real way, Romans 5 is the heart of Paul's argument, for it is where he brings to a climax the positive demonstration of his thesis concerning how 'God's righteousness' has worked to make humans righteous through faith." N. T. Wright believes that chapter 8 is the heart of the letter. See his *Into the Heart of Romans* (Grand Rapids: Zondervan, 2023).

CHAPTER 6

Paul's extended explication of God's love at the heart of the gospel, there is no richer text in his writings, so we will spend time looking at 5:1–11 in detail.

SECURE IN GOD'S EXTRAVAGANT LOVE

Paul begins with the reality of what is traditionally called justification. I hesitate to translate *dikaioō* using the English term "justify," because too often justification is treated as a doctrine or theological truth divorced from relational dimensions.[7] For Paul, being *dikaioō*-ed by God is a covenantal dynamic of reconciliation. This is demonstrated well by Romans 5:1–11 (especially 5:10).

> Therefore, since we have been made right by faith, let us have peace with God through our Lord Jesus Christ. Through him also we have obtained access by faith into this grace in which we stand, and let us boast on account of the hope of the glory of God. And not only this, but also let us boast in afflictions, in full knowledge that affliction produces endurance, and endurance builds character through testing, and this character becomes hope. Now this kind of hope is unashamed, because God's love has been poured into our hearts through the Holy Spirit given to us.
>
> While we were still weak, at the right time Christ died for the ungodly. Rarely would anyone let themselves die for even a civil person. Maybe someone might dare to die for a truly good person. But God shows his own love for us in this way: while we were still sinners, Christ died for us. So now having been made right by his blood, so all the more it must be true we will be saved from judgment by him! For while we were enemies, we were reconciled to God through the death of his son; having this reconciliation to begin with by his death, all the more it is true we will be saved by his life. Not only that, but also we can boast in God through our Lord Jesus Christ, through whom now we have obtained such reconciliation. (Rom 5:1–11, my translation)

7. For a more nuanced, covenantal perspective, see Michael Gorman, *Inhabiting the Cruciform God: Kenosis, Justification, and Theosis in Paul's Narrative Soteriology* (Grand Rapids: Eerdmans, 2009), especially 40–104; James B. Prothro, *A Pauline Theology of Justification: Forgiveness, Friendship, and Life in Christ* (Eugene, OR: Cascade Books, 2023).

Love at the Heart of Paul's Gospel of God

I prefer to translate *dikaioō* in 5:1 as "made right," which indicates a relationship restored by God, rather than "justified," which can sound like legal jargon. The result of God's work of right-making in covenant relationship is peace. Ancient people were constantly mindful of staying in the good graces of the gods; inviting and securing peace and prosperity, and curtailing wrath, they worked hard to maintain the *pax deorum*, "peace with the gods."[8] This involved many sacrifices, prayers, rituals, and oaths. Mortals saw themselves as clients appeasing a divine patron. The story with Paul's God is different. Here is a God who offers peace freely and graciously. As Paul will go on to explain, instead of waiting for mortals to come to *him*, this deity willingly and eagerly goes to *them* to secure reconciliation and peace.

Paul continues in Romans 5:2 to reframe the result of justification as a standing of grace (*charis*). This is a position of favor, the way a parent naturally favors their own child. A child doesn't usually have to plead to be treated well by the parent. Mothers and fathers have a natural affection for their children; they stand in a place of grace. This grace location is the grounds for Christian hope. Hope in what? Paul writes, *tēs doxēs tou theou*, "the glory of God." This is a bit of a laconic phrase, but I take it to mean that Christians can confidently look forward to sharing in the honor and glory of God. At the beginning of this letter, Paul referred to not being ashamed of the gospel (Rom 1:16). We see this theme of honor and shame appear throughout, and it is present in 5:1–11. Paul makes it clear that those who identify with the crucified one will experience persecutions and sufferings in their identification with him. That is the bad news, but the good news is that Christ's people will also share his glorification in the end.

If we look ahead to Romans 8 briefly, we can see that same theme in 8:12–25; Paul identifies two paths, the way of the flesh and the way of the Spirit. The flesh's way is enticing but deadly. The Spirit's way is a quieter beckoning, but it is the sturdy route to life. Those who are made right with God by Christ—by faith, by the Spirit—are true brothers and sisters of Christ and joint heirs, "if, in fact, we suffer with him so that we may also be glorified with him. I consider that the sufferings of this present time are not worth comparing with the glory about to

---

8. See my extensive discussion of this dynamic in Greco-Roman religion in *Strange Religion: How the First Christians Were Weird, Dangerous, and Compelling* (Grand Rapids: Brazos, 2024).

CHAPTER 6

be revealed to us" (8:17–18). Paul's point in these later verses is that hope is true and secure but invisible and must be held onto by faith and trust.

Going back to Romans 5:2, we see that the hope of the glory of God comes from a sense of peace and security in God's right-making activity that enables the believer to endure sufferings and hardships while still clinging to the promise of final vindication and relief. I would paraphrase Paul's point in this way: Your reputation may go through the gutter, your life may get worse in some ways because of your commitment to Christ and Christ's way, but you have a sure hope of glory in the end—your dignity and honor will be restored.

Boasting here does not mean bragging, certainly not bragging about one's achievements. The language of boasting (*kauchaomai*) was the way someone talked about broadcasting what they identify with, what values, people, and entities they want to be associated with. Think about the modern T-shirts or sweatshirts we wear and their logos or designs—sports symbols, brand-name clothes, rock bands. Or another example is our posters and bumper stickers, even our phone background images. This would be our way of "boasting." Not that we are a part of that band, or directly responsible for that sports team winning, but we are broadcasting who we are, connecting our identity to a certain thing, person, team, or idea. Paul says here to the Romans (again, paraphrasing broadly): We ought not to tie our souls to anything we can see or touch here and now (like an idol) but to the promise of the God who has made things right through Jesus Christ.

In Romans 5:3, Paul takes his argument to another level—Christians boast not just in a hope of vindication, basking in the triumphant glory of God, but they can even boast in *sufferings* here and now. Paul wasn't talking about every single kind of suffering (e.g., health problems, broken relationships, bereavement). He was talking about the resultative tensions and difficulties that occur when Christians boast in—that is, identify themselves with and tether their lives to—Christ and not some other god or group or value system. I think Paul was trying to give his readers perspective on persecution and counting the cost of really following Christ. Suffering is not merely an unfortunate reality of life, Paul argues, but part and parcel of choosing the good in a world that isn't always good. There is a way to process suffering as a Christian that transforms these experiences into hope. (And I think when Paul talks about hope in 5:3, he means hope *and joy*, the kind of hope that propels us forward knowing good things are ahead.) I like Michael Bird's labeling of 5:3–4 as a "factory of virtue,"

Love at the Heart of Paul's Gospel of God

but I would phrase it slightly differently as a "factory of formation in Christ." Paul's progression of argument looks like this:

suffering → endurance → (tested) character → hope

There is a particular way to process suffering that converts that energy into *endurance*; this is a kind of spiritual sublimation. Suffering can make you weaker or stronger. If persecution leads you to question and wonder what you really believe, and then your faith and trust become deeper and stronger, that produces endurance. The pounding on your spirit from challenges and pushback can create a resilience barrier. You become fortified by pressure, and your life builds up a protective shield and barrier. And as that process continues, the barrier becomes harder and harder like the metal forging of armor, and that becomes *character*, tested by long-term endurance and resilience. As all of that becomes innate to who you are, and you are entirely focused on the things of Christ (Phil 2:20–21), you start to live by hope.

Paul adds that hope is *unashamed* (Rom 5:5; cf. 1:16–17), because it is not an empty wish that things might change, but that character of trusting Christ has so enveloped your person that you can live in the reality of that future hope *now*. The reason he brings up being unashamed is that having faith in the Lord Jesus Christ is not an easy path. There are many "enemies of the cross of Christ" (as Paul tells the Philippians [Phil 3:18]), and those who become friends of the cross of Christ will find themselves at odds with many in the dominant Roman culture. I don't think Paul suffered from a persecution complex; I think he was realistic about the cost of throwing one's lot in with Christ. But in those very moments when it is difficult to endure the suffering, to accept the testing, to have hope, Paul wanted the Roman Christians to go back to one key truth: God has willingly and enthusiastically poured out his love and filled up our hearts, which we experience through the Spirit (Rom 5:4–5).[9] This is deeply experiential language; this is not a dry and dull doctrinal statement. Jimmy

---

9. Gaventa notes that the language of pouring may allude to Christ's pouring out of his blood: "God's love is no abstraction, not a characteristic of God that can be isolated from what God does. . . . God's love is demonstrated in [Christ's] death. God's love looks like this death on behalf of the enemy." Beverly Gaventa, *Romans*, NTL (Louisville: Westminster John Knox, 2024), 145.

CHAPTER 6

Dunn describes Paul's language of God's poured-out love as "a cloud-burst on a parched countryside."[10] Refreshment, nourishment, new life. Karl Barth ties Paul's climactic statement here about God's affection to the movement from suffering to hope. Mortals, all by themselves, are not fit to endure and hope and await glory. Only God can help, and only God's love is the ground for reconciliation, transformation, and true hope. "[God's] Love is that which endures in our endurance, which is proved in our probation: it is the hope in our hope. By its power, hope is not put to shame; by its power, we glory in hope; glory even in tribulation; by its power we have peace with God; and by it we are what we are not—new men."[11]

The next section (Rom 5:6–11) is an extended proof of this love and what it means to live with God through Christ, as we know God's deep affection. In these verses, Paul looks at the God-human relationship from three perspectives: humans as weak and ungodly (5:6), humans as sinners (5:8), and humans as enemies of God (5:10). Equally, in all these vantage points, God loves his creatures and takes initiative in rescuing them. I hesitate to parse out the differences between these perspectives (to some degree they overlap), but perhaps we might look at it this way:

Weak and ungodly. In what was meant to be a reciprocal relationship, humans have failed to acknowledge, love, and trust God. And yet, Christ died and gave himself for these antiworshipers out of his love and concern.

Sinners. "Sinners" (*hamartōlōn*) here I take to mean those who have broken God's commandments. They have proven in their actions a failure to love and obey God in their hearts and their behavior—Paul's "us" (*hēmas*) means he includes himself in that accusation! During the human act of transgression, God enacted his own plan for his Son Jesus to die to redeem sinners.

Enemies. Paul's examples build to a climax: humans were not just failed worshipers or just "sinners" but even *enemies* of God, hostile to God, his pur-

---

10. Dunn, *Romans 1–8*, 252. Similarly, Charles Cranfield explains that this imagery reflects the "unstinting lavishness" of divine love, in *A Critical and Exegetical Commentary on the Epistle to the Romans*, ICC (Edinburgh: T&T Clark, 1975), 1:262.

11. Karl Barth, *The Epistle to the Romans*, 6th ed. (London: Oxford University Press, 1933), 148.

118

Love at the Heart of Paul's Gospel of God

poses, and his ways; even with all of that, God sought reconciliation. While we were pushing God away, he was pulling us closer.

What these three perspectives have in common is the message that God loved his people, not just or primarily what he could gain from his people. More than that, he loved them in spite of their animosity toward him. On top of that, he showed the fullest extent of love through sacrifice.[12] As Paul explains, it makes sense to die for a good person, because of what benefit they bring in their life. But who in their right mind would save the weak? Sinners? Enemies?

Paul's point behind all of this (going back to the experienced reality of God's right-making activity in Rom 5:1–2) is that Christians can stand confident and secure—not because of their own ability to hold their ground but because they are held in the grace and love of God, proven in the death of Christ, known by the Spirit's presence, and energized anew by communion with the living Lord Jesus.[13] John Barclay explains that self-worth is determined not by personal worth but by God's investment and love: *"as a divine gift, given to all in the death of Christ, as act of love for the wholly unworthy, Paul figures the Christ-gift as the ultimate incongruous gift."*[14]

THE SACRIFICIAL LOVE OF CHRIST

The story of the gospel begins with the extravagant love of God, but at the same time, it is the story of the Son of God, Jesus Christ.[15] This is clear in Romans 5:6–11: God's love is demonstrated in the death of his Son. The climax of God's love is the handing over of Christ unto death. In order to explore this in more depth, we will jump ahead from Romans 5:1–11 to Romans 8:31–39, where the theme of divine love is picked up again with the spotlight now on Christ:

12. See A. Katherine Grieb, *The Story of Romans: A Narrative Defense of God's Righteousness* (Louisville: Westminster John Knox, 2002), 62–63.

13. See Richard B. Hays, "Christ Died for the Ungodly: Narrative Soteriology in Paul?," *Horizons in Biblical Theology* 26 (2004): 58.

14. John M. G. Barclay, *Paul and the Gift* (Grand Rapids: Eerdmans, 2017), 479; similarly, see Gaventa, *Romans*, 147.

15. Credit to Grieb, *Story of Romans*, 63, for the language of "extravagant" for God's love in the gospel.

CHAPTER 6

So then, what do we say about these things? If God is dedicated to us, who dares to stand against us? Indeed, he did not spare his very own Son, but instead gave him up for all of us; so why would he not also graciously give us everything else? Who would dare to bring a charge against those whom God has chosen as his special possession? God alone decides who is innocent. Who has the right to condemn? No one but Christ Jesus, the one who died, and more than that, who was raised from the dead, who is at the right hand of God, who also intercedes for us.

Who can separate us from the love of Christ? Hardship or distress or persecution or famine or nakedness or danger or the sword? As it is written: "For your sake we are being killed all day long; we are accounted as sheep to be slaughtered."

But in all these things, we are conquerors through the one who loved us. For I am convinced that neither death nor life, angels, rulers, present or future, powers, heights, depths, anything in creation can separate us from the love of God in Christ Jesus our Lord. (Rom 8:31–39, my translation)

Similar to chapter 5, Romans 8 reflects on the reality of human suffering. And much of the same point is being made about standing secure in the care of God. What we see in Romans 8 is a broadening of the perspective to a *cosmological scale*—enemies, opponents, rivals; some of them are more than mere human persecutors. By the end of this section, Paul mentions angels, rulers, and all manner of powers and forces. There are a lot of malevolent beings out there, Paul believed, but the whole point is that none can stand against the God who has reconciled this people and made them his own. He has vowed to protect his people from any harm.

I am reminded of a perspective and ritual from the Roman world called *evocatio*.[16] When Rome would stand at a distance ready to attack a city, they would invite the gods of the city to abandon it and join the Roman pantheon before their siege. Roman myths sometimes attest to gods withdrawing their protection from the city and leaving the inhabitants vulnerable to harm with-

16. Clifford Ando, *The Matter of the Gods: Religion and the Roman Empire* (Los Angeles: University of California Press, 2008), 128–35.

Love at the Heart of Paul's Gospel of God

out their patronage. We have record of one city tying down the statue of a patron deity to prevent it from fleeing in view of a raiding enemy.[17] All that to say, there might be reason for the Roman Christians to fear worshiping this foreign God of Israel and the Lord Jesus Christ. *How can we be sure we won't be abandoned in our hour of need?* Paul's reassurance is simple: God has proven his love by giving up the one thing he holds most dear, the life of his Son.[18] So he fears nothing else; he withholds nothing else. And moreover, Christ rose from the dead in victory over death, stands in power in heaven, and even now intercedes on behalf of believers.

Starting in 8:34, Paul's attention turns entirely to Christ: Can anyone or anything separate Christ from the people that he loves? Nothing. And no happenings should be taken as signs of divine displeasure or cursing. In Paul's time, it was natural to associate suffering and misfortune with divine curses. For example, some Romans prayed to the god Fever, presuming that illness was a result of offending this deity (Valerius Maximus 2.5.6). Paul grounds the Roman Christians' security and well-being, not in the whims of a volatile being, but in the consistent, constant, and generous love of Christ.

To support this argument, Paul quotes Scripture: "For your sake we are being killed all day long; we are accounted as sheep to be slaughtered" (Rom 8:36, quoting Ps 44:22). This verse is about suffering, but the keywords here are "for your sake" (*heneken sou*). The persecutions that believers endure are not a sign of wrath or divine abandonment but the natural consequences of aligning with *this* God against other beings, powers, and entities. While Paul quotes only a small snippet of Psalm 44, this happens to be a fitting text for the Roman Christians to meditate on.

The psalm begins with a confession of the great works and deeds of the God of Israel: repelling and destroying Israel's enemies and preserving his own people (Ps 44:1–2). Israel's war victories were not their own, but their God fought for them (44:3). Then the psalmist moves into worship, professing the

---

17. The Tyrians, out of fear Apollo would abandon them to be sieged by Alexander the Great, chained the main cult statue to the ground; see Diodorus Siculus 17.41.7–8; Plutarch, *Alexander* 24.5–8; Quintius Curtius Rufus 4.3.21–22.

18. The notion of giving up one's son could have resonances with the Akedah; see Arland Hultgren, *Paul's Letter to the Romans: A Commentary* (Grand Rapids: Eerdmans, 2011), 337.

CHAPTER 6

glory of God the King, who continues to have victory over the enemy and has earned Israel's trust (44:4–8).

Starting in v. 9, the psalm takes a turn to lament; the psalmist cries out in anguish because he and his people feel rejected and humiliated, like sheep left to slaughter (Ps 44:11), like captives taken into slavery (44:12)—a laughing-stock of neighbors and objects of scorn (44:13–16). The psalmist clings on to hope—barely (44:19). Surely God knows that his own people are being killed all day and will soon be butchered (44:22). The final section of the psalm is a call to action for God: "Rouse yourself! Why do you sleep, O Lord? Awake, do not cast us off forever! . . . Rise up, come to our help. Redeem us for the sake of your steadfast love" (44:23, 26).

There is a gritty rawness to this psalm, as it moves back and forth from hope to despair, worship to lament, praise to accusation. I would paraphrase the upshot of the psalm in this way: We have stood by you, O Lord, and we are standing aligned with you against your enemies. We know your fidelity in times past, but we need you now, we are dying because of you (for your sake), and we call out to you in our gravest hour of need.

We don't know the exact situation of Paul's Roman readers, but he expected this message to resonate with them. They must not interpret their sufferings as curses or bad omens. These sufferings reinforce their identification with Christ. As Jewett sums up, "Christ died for their sake, and they die for his. No one can therefore claim that their suffering divorces them from Christ and his cross."[19]

But ultimately the confidence believers have is not that they have been faithful to Christ but that Christ's love is pure and perfect; his devotion is true. And in *that* love, Christians are *supervictors* (*hypernikōmen*), able to resist and conquer all enemies, even one's own doubt and fears. What truly prevails in the end is the love of God demonstrated in the death of Christ.

I want to address questions about atonement since the death of Christ is prominent in this section of Romans. I chose to title Romans 8:31–39 "The Sacrificial Love of Christ" because twice Paul mentions Christ's death (8:32, 34). But when I use the word "sacrificial," I don't assume Paul is thinking of Christ's death in terms of appeasement of divine wrath. Rather, the references to Christ's death are analyzed here not cultically but in terms of the *fullness* of

19. Jewett, *Romans*, 548.

Love at the Heart of Paul's Gospel of God

God's love. The Song of Songs says, "Love is as strong as death" (Song 8:6). Paul is saying here that death proves the strength of love. Christ's death should not be interpreted theologically as God's begrudging sacrifice of his Son, as if sinful humans have messed the world up and God has to resolve this pesky problem. On the contrary, in spite of humans messing things up, God still loves them *so much* that Father and Son agreed to this sacrifice of love. Two words at the beginning of this passage are prominent and frame the rest of the passage: *hyper hēmōn*—"for us." "If God is *for us*, who can be against us?"[20] Charles Cranfield proposes that "for us" is a "concise summary of the gospel."[21] The essence of God's good news in Jesus Christ is that God loves us and wants goodness and blessing for us, even as we are sinners and enemies.

Augustine's theological exposition of Romans 8:32 is illuminating. He contrasts the differences between the actions of Father and Son, on the one hand, and that of Judas, on the other. Father handed Son over to death, Son gave himself over to death, and Judas gave Christ up (i.e., betrayed him) as well.[22] Same action but very different purposes—and that makes all the difference.

> The Father and Son acted in love; Judas acted in treachery. You understand that we have to take into consideration not just what a person does but the disposition and intention in which the person acts. We find God the Father doing the same thing that Judas does; we bless the Father but we detest Judas. . . . God's objective was the saving action by which we were redeemed; Judas' objective was the price for which he sold the Lord. The Son himself considered the price he paid for us; Judas considered the price he received in the sale. A different intention makes for a different action. . . .

20. Craig Keener, *Romans*, NCCS (Eugene, OR: Cascade Books, 2009), 110, draws a conceptual connection between Romans 8:31 and Psalm 118:6: "With the Lord on my side, I do not fear. What can mortals do to me?"

21. Cranfield, *Romans*, 1:435; affirmed by Gaventa, "Neither Height nor Depth: Discerning the Cosmology of Romans," *Scottish Journal of Theology* 64 (2011): 273. See similarly N. T. Wright, "The Letter to the Romans," *NIB* 10:612.

22. *Paradidōmi* (passive form) is regularly used in the Gospels in reference to the betrayal of Jesus, especially by Judas (Matt 17:22; 20:18; 26:2, 15, 21, 23, 45, 48; Mark 9:31; 10:33; 14:10, 18, 21, 41, 44; Luke 9:44; 18:32; 22:4, 6, 21, 48; 24:7, 20; John 6:64, 71; 12:4; 13:2, 11, 21; 18:2, 5; 21:20).

CHAPTER 6

This is the great value of charity. Notice that it alone distinguishes; by itself it separates one person's action from another's.[23]

To conclude our discussion of Romans 5 and 8, we can say Paul clearly underscores the point that at the center of the gospel is the right-making work of God (justification), which is driven by the righteousness of God. God's righteousness is not a cold commitment to doing right but comes from deep, unreserved love. Scot McKnight presents a comprehensive list of all of the gifts and blessings graciously bestowed by God on his beloved people according to Romans:

1. Grace (5:2; 6:1)
2. Justification, righteousness (of God), justice (5:1; 8:30, 31, 32, 33, 34)
3. Peace with God (5:1) and reconciliation (5:10, 11)
4. Sharing in God's glory (5:2–3; 8:17, 18)
5. Hope (5:4)
6. Life (5:10, 17–18, 21; 6:4, 10, 13, 22–23; 7:10; 8:2, 6, 10, 13)
7. Love (5:8; 8:31–39)
8. The Spirit (5:5; 7:6)
9. Salvation (5:9, 10; 8:24)
10. Liberation (6:18, 22; 8:2, 21)
11. Community and belonging in Christ (7:4)
12. Adoption as children of God (8:16, 19, 23)
13. Redemption of the body (8:23)
14. Called unto glorification (8:28–30)
15. Christoformity (8:29)
16. Christ's intercession (8:34)
17. Secure relationship (8:31–39)
18. Conquerors in life (8:37)[24]

All these things are given for the sake of saving and redeeming sinners, and all of these are bestowed according to the love of God in Jesus Christ.

23. As cited in J. Patout Burns Jr., *Romans: Interpreted by Early Christian Commentators* (Grand Rapids: Eerdmans, 2012), 214.

24. Scot McKnight, *Reading Romans Backwards: A Gospel of Peace in the Midst of Empire* (Waco, TX: Baylor University Press, 2019), 163.

Love at the Heart of Paul's Gospel of God

THE SPIRIT AS GOD'S LOVING PRESENCE

Famously, Gordon Fee titled his massive tome on the Holy Spirit in Paul *God's Empowering Presence*.[25] In the person and work of the Holy Spirit, Paul believed that the one God was uniquely present; and, of course, the Spirit *is* God's power that he shares with his people. But I think Fee would agree that it is equally appropriate to describe the Spirit as God's *loving* presence.[26] At the risk of oversimplification, we might say that Paul understood God the Father as the *author* of divine love, Jesus the Son as the incarnate *agent* of divine love, and the Spirit as the conduit of the *experience* of divine love. The Spirit is the living presence of God with his people, and their experience of God—and God's love—is known through the Spirit God has put within them. We see this clearly in Romans 5:5 (discussed at the beginning of this chapter): "Now this kind of hope is unashamed, because God's love has been poured into our hearts through the Holy Spirit given to us" (Rom 5:5, my translation). God's love is not a theoretical feeling of God, whereby he sends positive energy from heaven. It is a known reality expressed by God and experienced by believers in the gift of the Spirit that resides in the being of the believer. Later in Romans, Paul invites the Romans to pray for the mission he must undertake. He makes a solemn request to the Romans: "I appeal to you, brothers and sisters, by our Lord Jesus Christ and by the love of the Spirit, to join me in earnest prayer to God on my behalf, that I may be rescued from the unbelievers in Judea, and that my ministry to Jerusalem may be acceptable to the saints, so that by God's will I may come to you with joy and be refreshed in your company" (Rom 15:30–32). Here Paul identifies a unique bond and connection between the Roman churches and himself, forged by the one lordship and new shared family of Jesus Christ (Rom 8:15, 29); and Paul also points to the "love of the Spirit." In Greek, the phrase *tēs agapēs tou pneumatos* could be taken as the "love shown by the Spirit" (subjective genitive), or the "love shown toward the Spirit" (objective genitive). But there are other options for how this could be understood. It could refer to the love that believers have for one another

---

25. Gordon D. Fee, *God's Empowering Presence* (Peabody, MA: Hendrickson, 1994).

26. This point is made well by Susan Eastman, "Oneself in Another: Participation and the Spirit in Romans 8," in *"In Christ" in Paul: Explorations in Paul's Theology of Union and Participation*, ed. Michael J. Thate, Kevin Vanhoozer, and Constantine R. Campbell (Tübingen: Mohr Siebeck, 2014), 103–25.

CHAPTER 6

that is inspired by the Spirit's own investment of love in the person. If we connect Romans 5:5 to 15:30, we might imagine that God pours his love into believers through the indwelling of the Spirit, and that Spirit generates a fullness of love that overflows in their hearts such that they love others out of that deluge. The Spirit, then, is not only a confirmation and witness to God's love in human hearts but also a factory of love, transforming believers into people of compassion, service, and generosity. Paul's appeal here is that the Roman believers would stand with him in prayer for the flourishing of his apostolic ministry that is under threat. For Paul, this is not a one-way street. He was not just inviting them to love him; he too longed to be in their company and enjoy mutuality.[27] The Spirit's love was the web that connected these strangers and made them family through Jesus Christ.

We have spent most of this chapter focusing on Paul's Letter to the Romans—for good reason, we find strategic places where Paul proclaims the extravagant, sacrificial, and life-giving love of God. Rarely does Paul mention the Holy Spirit in relation to divine love, though Romans 15:30 is a prominent occurrence.

Divine Love	References
God's Love	Rom 5:8; 8:39; 2 Cor 13:11 ("God of love and peace"); 13:13; 2 Thess 2:16; 3:5
Christ's Love	Rom 8:35, 39; Rom 14:15 (presumed); Gal 2:20; Eph 3:17 (implied), 19; 5:2, 25; 2 Cor 5:14? ("love of Christ urges us on"); 2 Thess 2:16; 1 Tim 1:14
Spirit's Love	Rom 5:5 (agency); 15:30 ("love of the Spirit"); Eph 2:4; association: 2 Cor 13:13; Phil 2:1–2

But another key text outside of Romans involving the Spirit and love is worth discussing briefly as it reinforces our proposed interpretation of Romans 15:30. We turn now to Philippians 2:1–2: "If then there is any encouragement in Christ, any consolation from love, any sharing in the Spirit, any compassion and sympathy, make my joy complete: be of the same mind, having the same love,

27. See Douglas J. Moo, *The Epistle to the Romans*, NICNT (Grand Rapids: Eerdmans, 1996), 925.

Love at the Heart of Paul's Gospel of God

being in full accord and of one mind." Paul wrote his Letter to the Philippians in the midst of great distress. Paul was in prison facing an unknown future, Epaphroditus (the Philippians' own messenger to Paul) had experienced a life-threatening situation, and the Philippian believers as a whole were wrestling with persecution from without and major disagreements within. Overall, Paul's message is one of encouragement toward joy and hope and exhortation toward unity through humility. The beginning of chapter 2 offers the crestfallen Philippians an opportunity to remember the most vivid moments of love and joy they experienced in the gospel of Christ. Paul lists a variety of terms that revolve around feelings of deep affection (*paraklēsis, paramythion, splanchnon, oiktirmos*); all of these point to personal knowledge of God's love in Jesus Christ. Precisely in those low moments of their faith, Paul was reminding the Philippians of the palpable love of God, the warm envelope of the gospel's embrace. Such experiences are "in Christ," as Paul often states, but he also adds to this *koinōnia pneumatos*, which we might paraphrase "sharing in one Spirit," and in the context of these affectionate descriptors, we might add, "sharing in the one Spirit (of love)." Paul told the Corinthians, "where the Spirit of the Lord is, there is freedom" (2 Cor 3:17); here he was practically reminding the Philippians, where the Spirit of the Lord is, there is *love*. And Paul's point was not just that the Philippians are loved but that God's indwelling Spirit fills the lives of believers such that they can care for each other with that same kind of generous love.[28] While the term "love" doesn't appear in the following verses, the features of love are clearly expressed: "Do nothing from selfish ambition or conceit, but in humility regard others as better than yourselves. Let each of you look not to your own interests, but to the interests of others" (2:3–4)—humility, attentiveness, preoccupation with the other, investment in their needs. And this comes to a climax in the model of Christ's own story of self-lowering and self-sacrifice out of obedience to the Father and grace toward sinners (2:6–11).

The Good News of God's Love in Jesus Christ

In this chapter, we have examined the nature and expression of divine love. What we have found is that love is at the heart of the gospel Paul preached.

---

28. See Jeannine Brown, *Philippians*, TNTC (Downers Grove, IL: IVP Academic, 2022), 100–101.

CHAPTER 6

Paul's gospel is not simply the message that sinners need saved. It is not just that God justifies the ungodly, or that the death of Christ brings life. Those things are true, but the deep center of Paul's gospel is the love of God: *ho theos hyper hēmōn*: "God is for us" (Rom 8:31). This short statement captures Paul's belief and personal understanding that God is turned toward us in love, is attentive with care and compassion, acts with concern and personal responsibility, puts everything at his disposal to nurture and protect, and holds nothing back so as to bless and bring prosperity to his creation.

The depth and urgency of that divine love is shown in the incarnation, but the fullest extent is demonstrated in the crucifixion of the Son of God, Jesus Christ (Rom 5:10). We see a more autobiographical reflection of this in Galatians where Paul refers to Christ as the Son of God who "loved me and gave himself for me" (Gal 2:20). This is probably a hendiadys, as the loving is expressed in that self-sacrifice of Christ. Love gives; love spends of self to protect and bless the other. Self-preservation is a powerful instinct, and when it becomes an overriding factor, it short-circuits love and intimacy. Only the deepest love would cause someone to hand themselves over to death willingly for another person. But this is how Paul viewed Christ, the one who expressed his love on the cross.[29]

In the next chapter, we will look at Paul's understanding of religion as love for God, a concept founded in the Jewish Shema and further exemplified in the life of Jesus; Paul preferred to talk about religion in terms of faith (*pistis*), but love language sometimes appears, and we will see how love and faith are closely connected.

---

29. Susan Eastman refers to the "sacrificial, proactive, and boundary-crossing love" of Christ that Paul promotes and embodies in his own lifestyle and care for the Galatians. See *Recovering Paul's Mother Tongue: Language and Theology in Galatians*, 2nd ed. (Eugene, OR: Cascade Books, 2021), 119.

7

Love at the Heart of Paul's Religion

Grace be with all who have an undying love
for our Lord Jesus Christ.

—Ephesians 6:24

In the previous chapter, the focus was on how Paul talks about love and the heart of God, the compassion and care of the triune God as the foundation for God's right-making activity in the world. That is the foundation of the gospel Paul preached. Yes, God sent his Son to redeem humanity because of sin, but there is a truth that comes before that: God saved sinners because he loves them. God's saving love is not tit for tat, a divine act that leaves the redeemed with a debt they cannot possibly repay. That doesn't mean God's love doesn't have relational expectations and assumption of reciprocity. Ancient people, both Jews and gentiles, understood that the divine and the human live in a circle of giving and receiving, mutuality, even if not on equal terms.[1] So a reaction from believers is expected and, according to Jewish religion and tradition, that response is love. We have already given ample attention to the Shema, the core creed, command, and prayer that guided Jews in their covenantal orientation: love of the one God with the whole self; that is the essence of Jewish piety.

1. See John M. G. Barclay, *Paul and the Gift* (Grand Rapids: Eerdmans, 2017).

CHAPTER 7

Love and Covenantal Piety

It is worthwhile, before looking at Paul, to examine which texts and to what degree Old Testament, early Jewish, and early Christian texts reflect this investment in love as the center of covenantal piety. Of course, it is thoroughly woven into the whole book of Deuteronomy, as we have already discussed (Deut 11:1; 13:3; 30:6), and sections of the book of Joshua that affirm the law, especially as warnings as Israel fights their way into the land of Canaan. God's people were commanded to "love the Lord your God, to walk in all his ways, to keep his commandments, and to hold fast to him, and to serve him with all your heart and with all your soul" (Josh 22:5; also 23:11).

This is further reinforced in texts like Nehemiah (1:5), Daniel (9:4), Hosea (6:6; 12:6), and the Psalms—for example, "Love the Lord, all you his saints, the Lord preserves the faithful" (Ps 31:23; cf. Ps 116:1). Again, love here is not primarily an emotion, nor is it strictly an act (of duty, for example), but it is conceived of as a commitment of the entire self to this God, the entire being of each covenant member wrapping their whole self and identity around YHWH.

Many Second Temple Jewish texts also echo the love command of the Shema; Tobit acknowledges that joy and blessing will come to those who "love God" (Tob 14:7). Ben Sira offers a hymn-like teaching about wisdom bestowed upon those who love God, fear him, follow his law, and respect Israel's leaders (Sir 1:9, 16; 2:30; 7:27–30). The story of the prophets presented in Bel and the Dragon includes professions of faith that hold onto God's promise of salvation for those who love him (37).

In the Jewish Psalms of Solomon, divine mercy is expected for those who love God (Psalms of Solomon 4.25); those who love God in truth can put their hope in God (6.6; also 14.1, 10).[2] Love of God is thematically woven into the Testaments of the Twelve Patriarchs[3] and the Jewish Sibylline Oracles (5.360; 8.482). And loving God is affirmed almost a dozen times in the Dead Sea Scrolls.[4]

And, of course, the Shema's love command is affirmed and repeated by Jesus as well, according to the Gospels, where Jesus explicitly and extensively

---

2. These are found in recension textual readings.

3. See Testament of Issachar 5.2; Testament of Dan 5.3; Testament of Benjamin 3.1.

4. See 1QHa VI, 26; 4Q393 III, 2; 4Q525 frag. V, 13; 11Q11 VI, 12; 11Q19 LIV, 12–13; 11Q22; 1QH VII, 12–14.

130

Love at the Heart of Paul's Religion

quotes Deuteronomy 6:5 (Matt 22:37; Mark 12:30; Luke 10:27; see our earlier discussion in chapter 4). When we look at the New Testament epistles (aside from Paul), we find love toward God explicitly mentioned only in 1 John: love for God is the ultimate virtue, and love for fellow Christian brothers and sisters follows and flows from love for God (1 John 4:20–21; 5:2).

When we look at the Apostolic Fathers, again the Shema's love command appears on occasion, though it is not pervasive. Ignatius commends the Christian Magnesians for their love for God (*To the Magnesians* 1.1); he writes to Polycarp asking that wives love the Lord and respect their husbands and that husbands likewise love their wives as the Lord loves the church (*To Polycarp* 5.1). In the Epistle to Diognetus, we find the promise of flourishing and abundance for those who love God (12.1).

Two things are noticeable when we look at these scattered references to love for God in ancient Jewish and Christian texts: clearly they point back to the Deuteronomic love commandment as *the* core expression of covenantal devotion, fidelity, worship, and obedience; these are signs that Jews and Christians recognize the essential virtue and attitude of love as the soul of piety and religion. But, second, because such formal expressions of love for God are so few and far between—even sometimes absent from several texts of Scripture and highly influential early Jewish literature—it must be the case that other terms and concepts offer alternative language and expression of the same devotion to God. That is certainly the case with Paul, and we will explore all these matters in this chapter.

THE SHEMA AND THE COVENANTAL LOVE COMMAND IN PAUL

While it is clear that the Synoptic Gospels all attest that Jesus quoted the Shema's love commandment in his teaching, this is not the case with Paul; at least Paul did not cite it verbatim. However, scholars have looked to 1 Corinthians 8 for some signs of the influence of the Shema on his teaching on idols.[5] That is a good place to start our discussion. Paul's *peri de* ("now concerning [the topic of...]") language signals a key matter he feels the need to address, in this case food sacrificed to idols (1 Cor 8:1). There appear to be two attitudes in the Corinthian

---

5. See the detailed study by Erik Waaler, *The Shema and the First Commandment in First Corinthians: An Intertextual Approach to Paul's Re-reading of Deuteronomy*, WUNT 2/253 (Tübingen: Mohr Siebeck, 2008).

CHAPTER 7

church toward this matter. On the one hand, you have those who have such confidence in their faith in Christ that they boldly profess that "no idol in the world really exists" (8:4), and they feel free to eat meat dedicated to false gods because they do not worship these illusory deities. Therefore, they find liberty to eat any such food because of their enlightened perspective. We can call these people who have a robust Christian conscience "the strong" (see Rom 15:1).

But then there are other believers who cannot stand the thought of eating meat that has been dedicated to an idol. They believe that somehow that meat has been tainted by its association with a wicked god, and ingesting it is a form of idolatry and sin. For them, it is not just food, but it is participation in idol worship.[6] Because these believers have a weaker understanding of freedom from such entanglements and the neutrality of food itself, we can call them "the weak."[7]

It is clear Paul aligns with the strong in terms of his own understanding of food, purity, and worship; believers can feel free to eat any meat, because no matter how many statues and myths proclaim a massive pantheon of gods, there is only one God of creation that has real power (1 Cor 8:5–6). However, there is a place to show restraint in one's own choices, not because of the fear of idolatry per se through food consumption but because a fellow believer might actually be led into sin, tempted to worship or fear the gods they once revered (8:9–13). Knowledge is important, but it isn't everything. In fact, pride in one's own knowledge can lead to serious harm in the community. There is a place for limiting one's own freedoms to protect the faith of a brother or sister.

Paul draws on parts of the Shema in his discussion of this subject in 1 Corinthians 8:1–13. First, he clearly affirms Deuteronomy 6:4 when he acknowledges the nonexistence of idols and that "there is no God but one."[8] In 1 Corinthians 8:6, Paul christologically exposits the Shema's monotheistic creed by explaining that the word *theos* (God) refers to God the Father, the origin and purpose of life, and the word *kyrios* (Lord) refers to Jesus Christ, the supreme agent of life. Somehow these two beings are part of the oneness of Israel's God, but the key point Paul makes in this passage is that mental knowledge is not the only

6. Gordon D. Fee, *The First Epistle to the Corinthians*, NICNT (Grand Rapids: Eerdmans, 1987), 428, explains, "What is in view is a former idolater falling back into the grips of idolatry."

7. My interpretation follows Richard B. Hays, *First Corinthians*, IBC (Louisville: Westminster John Knox, 1997), 136–37.

8. Greek: *oudeis theos ei mē heis.*

Love at the Heart of Paul's Religion

thing one needs for healthy faith. In fact, knowledge can inflate the ego of the individual, and taking pride in having all the answers without regard for the other ends up hurting, not helping. Personal knowledge makes for a bigger ego, not a better community; or, in Paul's words, "knowledge puffs up, but love builds up" (1 Cor 8:1).[9] He goes on, "Anyone who claims to know something does not yet have the necessary knowledge; but anyone who loves God is known by him" (8:2). The combination in this passage of Paul's reference to the oneness of God (8:4, 6) and to those who love God (8:3) has led some scholars to believe that Paul was teaching from the Shema (especially Deut 6:4–5).[10]

The Shema begins with a confession of a fact—God is one—but then calls for love of God, and attentiveness to the community as they pass on the law's teachings and love God together. Paul talks about basic knowledge (i.e., facts) but also a deeper relational knowledge that requires intimacy where one's full self is known to the other and vice versa. Those who love God and dare to draw close to him will find themselves in close communion with God; they open their inner being up to God, and he can know them in a deeper way through that relationship, just as the psalmist exclaims, "The LORD is near to all who call on him, to all who call on him in truth" (Ps 145:18). The point of the Shema prayer and confession is not the power of human knowledge but acknowledgment of the need for this one God, and the necessity of love to bind themselves to the God who has chosen to make himself known to them and to know them through and through.

OTHER PAULINE TEXTS ABOUT LOVE FOR GOD

1 Corinthians 2:9. Staying within 1 Corinthians, we can turn back to chapter 2 to see another occasion where Paul mentions love for God, seemingly in passing, as if it is taken for granted as a key expression of Christian piety and religion.

---

9. Again, Fee writes, "Christian behavior is not predicated on the way of knowledge, which can lead to pride and destroy others, but on the way of love, which is in fact the true way of knowledge" (*First Epistle to the Corinthians*, 407); see similarly, David E. Garland, *1 Corinthians*, BECNT (Grand Rapids: Baker, 2003), 368.

10. See N. T. Wright, "Monotheism, Christology, and Ethics: 1 Corinthians 8," in *The Climax of the Covenant* (London: T&T Clark, 1991), 120–36; Brian S. Rosner, "Deuteronomy in 1 and 2 Corinthians," in *Deuteronomy in the New Testament: The New Testament and the Scriptures of Israel*, ed. Maarten J. J. Menken and Steve Moyise (London: T&T Clark, 2007), 126–27.

CHAPTER 7

Paul attempts to quote some text of Scripture—it's unclear which text because his wording does not match any Old Testament text exactly, whether from the Hebrew version(s) known to us or the Greek. Here is Paul's wording:

> What no eye has seen, nor ear heard,
> Nor the human heart conceived,
> what God has prepared for those who love him. (1 Cor 2:9)

The context of this quotation in 1 Corinthians is Paul's proclamation of the power and wisdom of God in the seeming weakness and folly of the cross of Christ. In 2:6–16, he admits that this requires secret wisdom that is not reflected in the philosophies of the popular sages of the day (2:6–8). Only Spirit-given insight opens the eyes to these deep truths about God and his workings (2:10–13).

The scriptural quotation is often compared to similar (though not identical) wording in Isaiah 64 where the unexpected and awe-inspiring work of God is extolled.

Isaiah 64:1–4 NRSV (based on the Hebrew)	**Isaiah 64:1–4 NETS (translation of Greek LXX)**
O that you would tear open the heavens and come down, so that the mountains would quake at your presence— as when fire kindles brushwood and the fire causes water to boil— to make your name known to your adversaries, so that the nations might tremble at your presence! When you did awesome deeds that we did not expect, you came down, the mountains quaked at your presence.	If you should open heaven, trembling from you would seize the mountains, and they would melt as wax melts from the fire. And fire shall burn up your adversaries, and the name of the Lord shall be manifest among your adversaries; nations shall be confused at your presence! When you do your glorious deeds, trembling from you will seize the mountains.

134

Love at the Heart of Paul's Religion

Isaiah 64:1–4 NRSV
(based on the Hebrew)

From ages past no one has heard,
   no ear has perceived,
no eye has seen any God besides you,
who works for those who wait for him.

Isaiah 64:1–4 NETS
(translation of Greek LXX)

From ages past we have not heard,
   nor have our eyes seen any God
      besides
   you,
and your works, which you will do to
those who
wait for mercy.

This text is the most likely inspiration for Paul's quotation, even if the wording is not an exact match. Clearly, Paul's mention of the heart (*kardia*) is not from Isaiah 64:4, so some have wondered whether Paul was also thinking of Isaiah 65:17: "For heaven will be new, and the earth will be new, and they shall not remember the former things, nor shall they come upon their heart [*kardia*]" (NETS).[11] But Isaiah 65:17 is about letting go of the former ways and structures, and does not really correspond to what Paul is referring to here, that is, the heart's inability to take in the full mystery of God's work.[12] Jerome comments that the wording Paul uses in his quotation matches a line from the Latin version of the Apocalypse of Isaiah 11.34.[13] This could mean that, in the words of Gordon Fee, the citation is in fact "an amalgamation of OT texts that had already been joined and reflected on in apocalyptic Judaism, which Paul knew either directly or indirectly."[14] Or it is also possible that Paul was

11. See H. H. Drake Williams, *The Wisdom of the Wise: The Presence and Function of Scripture within 1 Cor. 1:18–3:23* (Leiden: Brill, 2001), 164–65.

12. See the discussion in Roy E. Ciampa and Brian S. Rosner, "1 Corinthians," in *Commentary on the New Testament Use of the Old Testament*, ed. G. K. Beale and D. A. Carson (Grand Rapids: Baker, 2007), 701.

13. Jerome, *Commentary on Isaiah* 64.4; see discussion in Roy E. Ciampa, "Composite Citations in 1–2 Corinthians and Galatians," in *Composite Citations in Antiquity*, vol. 2, ed. Sean A. Adams and Seth M. Ehorn, LNTS 593 (London: T&T Clark, 2018), 186.

14. Fee, *First Epistle to the Corinthians*, 116. Pheme Perkins, *First Corinthians*, PCNT (Grand Rapids: Baker, 2012), 60, proposes that three Septuagintal texts influenced Paul's wording: Isaiah 64:3; Isaiah 52:15; and Psalm 31:19.

CHAPTER 7

paraphrasing a text or a combination of texts from Isaiah and adding heart and love language as part of his theological interpretation.

What can we say, then, about the inclusion here of love for God in 1 Corinthians 2:9? Either a Jewish writer before Paul, or Paul himself, was using "those who love God" as a recognizable covenantal expression for God's people. Richard Hays makes an important point about this: the Corinthians, as we know, were obsessed with knowledge and spiritual insight, and it would have been convenient for Paul to say, "those who *know* God." But here, as with 1 Corinthians 8:1–3, he underscores *love*, a commitment of the whole person, in humility and generosity, to the covenant God and the whole covenant community.[15] There is a deeper understanding of the nature and ways of God that can only be obtained through loving God.

1 Corinthians 16:22. At the very end of Paul's lengthy letter to the Corinthians, he offers a set of final directives and a closing blessing. Most of Paul's letters end on a warm and positive note, as we find in 1 Thessalonians 5:23–28, where Paul prays for their purity, reminds them of God's faithfulness, asks for prayer from them, sends greetings, and closes with a word of grace. Occasionally Paul ends with a sterner tone, as we find in Galatians:

> See what large letters I make when I am writing in my own hand! It is those who want to make a good showing in the flesh that try to compel you to be circumcised—only that they may not be persecuted for the cross of Christ. Even the circumcised do not themselves obey the law, but they want you to be circumcised so that they may boast about your flesh. May I never boast of anything except the cross of our Lord Jesus Christ, by which the world has been crucified to me, and I to the world. For neither circumcision nor uncircumcision is anything; but a new creation is everything! As for those who will follow this rule—peace be upon them, and mercy, and upon the Israel of God.
>
> From now on, let no one make trouble for me; for I carry the marks of Jesus branded on my body.
>
> May the grace of our Lord Jesus Christ be with your spirit, brothers and sisters. Amen. (Gal 6:11–18)

15. Hays, *First Corinthians*, 45.

Love at the Heart of Paul's Religion

When he should be wrapping up his message, he can't help but slip back into a little admonishment, his mind still preoccupied with the problems besetting this community. A similar dynamic appears to be happening with the closing of Paul's First Letter to the Corinthians: "I, Paul, write this greeting with my own hand. Let anyone be accursed who has no love for the Lord. Our Lord, come! The grace of the Lord Jesus be with you. My love be with all of you in Christ Jesus" (1 Cor 16:21–23).

On the rarest of occasions does Paul explicitly mention his personal autograph in the final section of his letters (2 Thess 3:17; Phlm 19; Col 4:18; Gal 6:11), and he does so here in 1 Corinthians. In part it could be an authentication mark, but based on Galatians, there is something to say about Paul underscoring the seriousness of the letter as a whole, and especially of the closing statements and commands, as if he is emphasizing his point in this way: *make no mistake, what I am about to say is very serious, and you need to know this comes directly from my heart into this pen!*

I wouldn't go quite so far as to say it is an act of desperation, but certainly a statement of grave concern. Immediately after the autograph remark, he writes to the Corinthians: "Let anyone be accursed who has no love [*phileō*] for the Lord" (16:22). This statement is striking and almost uncharacteristic of Paul for a few reasons. First, very seldomly does Paul make a curse warning (malediction).[16] He references curses elsewhere in 1 Corinthians 12:3, Romans 9:3, and Galatians 3:10 and 3:13. The most similar malediction to 1 Corinthians 16:22 appears in the first chapter of Galatians, where Paul announces, "if we or an angel from heaven should proclaim to you a gospel contrary to what we proclaimed to you, let that one be accursed! As we have said before, so now I repeat, if anyone proclaims to you a gospel contrary to what you received, let that one be accursed" (Gal 1:8–9). Curse maledictions were a religious phenomenon known more widely in the Greco-Roman world, and curses as we find in 1 Corinthians 16:22 attempt to affect human behavior by invoking harmful action from the divine realm.[17] But this version from Paul reflects a

---

16. See Garland, *1 Corinthians*, 773.

17. See the excellent contextualizing study of John Fotopoulos, "Paul's Curse of Corinthians: Restraining Rivals with Fear and *Voces Mysticae* (1 Cor 16:22)," *Novum Testamentum* 56 (2014): 275–309.

CHAPTER 7

distinctly *Jewish* conception of covenantal curses and blessings.[18] Just as Deuteronomy promotes love of YHWH and curses for those who turn away from YHWH, so Paul reminds the Corinthians of what is at stake. If this is the case, the Aramaic *Maranatha* ("Our Lord, come!") could be an invitation for the Lord to dispense judgment on his people, to reward the faithful and punish the disloyal.[19]

Some scholars have wondered whether Paul may be quoting a piece of early Christian liturgy or tradition in this malediction to the Corinthians.[20] It has a ring of formality to it, and, on top of that, the verb "love" in 16:22 is *phileō* and not the expected verb *agapaō*.[21] *Phileō* is an extraordinarily rare verb in Paul's letters, found only here (1 Cor 16:22) and Titus 3:15 (for believers loving one another). My inclination is to see Paul drawing from Christian liturgy here, not as a random insertion but as very fitting to the wider purposes of his messages to the Corinthians. Gordon Fee, for example, urges that loving Christ is not just about loving the person of Christ but also everything that Christ stands for. "To insist on human wisdom over against the gospel of the Crucified One is to 'not love the Lord'; so with living in incest, attendance at idol feasts, and so forth. The ultimate issue for Paul, therefore, is not their obedience to his word, but their love, or lack thereof, for the Lord himself. Failure to obey Christ is lack of love for him; to reject him in this way is to place oneself under the *anathema*."[22]

The whole of 1 Corinthians is about Christ and his culture and way, and also about love. And of course, the theme of love is present in several final statements in this letter: "Let all that you do be done in love" (16:13); "My love be with all of you in Christ Jesus" (16:23). For Paul, love is not just a warm sentiment or a fleeting feeling of affection. Love, of course, includes the emotions

18. This approach is favored by Anthony Thiselton, *The First Epistle to the Corinthians*, NIGTC (Grand Rapids: Eerdmans, 2000), 1350–52, who points to the work of Anders Eriksson, *Traditions as Rhetorical Proof: Pauline Argumentation in First Corinthians*, ConBNT (Stockholm: Almqvist & Wiksell, 1998).

19. See Thiselton, *First Epistle to the Corinthians*, 1351.

20. See Joseph Fitzmyer, *First Corinthians*, AB (New Haven: Yale University Press, 2008), 629.

21. *Agapē* and *agapaō* appear frequently throughout 1 Corinthians: 2:9; 4:14, 17, 21; 8:1, 3; 13:1–4, 8, 13; 16:14, 24.

22. Fee, *First Epistle to the Corinthians*, 926.

138

Love at the Heart of Paul's Religion

(longing, desiring, appreciating), but the core of Christian love is complete devotion to another, in this case Christ—and a full apprehension of Christ, which includes caring deeply about the things of Christ and the people of Christ.

Romans 8:28. In Romans chapter 8, Paul offers hope in the midst of suffering (Rom 8:18–30). While present suffering might be acute and overwhelming, the new life in God's glorious future will provide relief and joy beyond one's wildest dreams. This hope lies beyond what is known and seen in the moment. The Spirit fills the gap, as it were, between the now and the not yet, ministering to the believer's soul in its anguish and pain in this broken age. But believers who are filled with the Spirit rely on God's promise, trusting that "all things work together for good for those who love God [*agapōsin ton theon*]" (Rom 8:28). Much like with 1 Corinthians 2:9, here in Romans it seems as though the reference to those who "love God" is said in passing as a reference to believers. It would have been a comfortable—though not natural—way for Jews (and later on, Christians) to talk about the covenantal dynamic that binds God and his people in a love relationship. It is certainly a vestige of the impact of the Shema, the confession of the unique oneness of God, and the essential covenantal command to love God exclusively, genuinely, and wholeheartedly.

When Paul says that all things will work for the good of those who love God, we need to be attentive to two popular misreadings here. First, Paul is not saying God will bless only those who love him. In Romans 5, Paul already stated that Christ died for the ungodly, demonstrated love toward sinners, and pursued reconciliation toward his enemies (Rom 5:6–10). God is not waiting on human initiative, and it is not a quid-pro-quo dynamic. He loves and blesses according to his own goodwill. The second thing to clarify is this: Paul is also not saying that believers will not have bad experiences or hard times. In fact, the purpose of Romans 8 is precisely to prepare believers for suffering in the present. What Paul is saying is that these present difficulties may seem to carry no meaning or even set one back from moving forward in life, but in God's wider work, he will bring good out of these experiences toward his good gospel end. This section of Romans ends with the emphasis on believers' membership in God's family, a family he is intent upon taking care of (8:29–30). Again, the language of loving God is not especially distinctive in this passage; in fact, throughout Romans 5–8, time and again Paul puts the emphasis on God's own initiative, love, will, plan, and purpose, not that of the believer. But when we compare Romans 8:28 to 1 Corinthians 2:9 and 16:22, it is a reminder that

CHAPTER 7

God's people are expected to reciprocate love and show genuine commitment and faith in this God of love and generosity.

PAUL'S PREFERRED EXPRESSIONS OF CHRISTIAN DEVOTION TO GOD

There is no getting around the fact that, while a few texts indicate Paul's awareness of and attentiveness to the Shema's foundational conception of covenantal love of God, these phrases are simply too sporadic to reflect his dominant way of talking about devotion to God. But it would be a mistake to assume that just because the word "love" is not present the idea is absent. I would propose that Paul takes the love of God with the utmost seriousness but has other language he prefers to express such commitment and devotion. We will explore these below.

Devotion and pleasing God (*areskō*). Sometimes Paul uses the language of "pleasing God" to indicate piety and devotion. This is related to loving God, because those who love God want to please him by valuing what God values. This connection between loving and pleasing the loved is drawn out well in this proverb by Ben Sira: "Those who fear the Lord seek to please him, and those who love him are filled with his law" (Sir 2:16). Ben Sira is affirming here that Shema-obedient love for God involves reverence (fear) and devotion to the law, all to the end of pleasing him.

When we turn to Paul, we can easily see that he makes it a priority to teach believers that their ultimate aim is to please God. In 1 Thessalonians 2:4, Paul uses the apostles as examples of those who seek to please God rather than please mortals (see also Gal 1:10). Later in the same letter, he urges the Thessalonians to live to please God and to grow in passion for that action evermore (1 Thess 4:1; cf. 1 Cor 7:32; 2 Cor 5:6; Eph 5:8–10). In his Letter to the Romans, Paul also repeats the commitment of pleasing God, which cannot happen when one is focused on the flesh (Rom 8:8). In fact, there is a tension between pleasing God and serving neighbor, on the one hand, and pleasing self, on the other. Christ is the ultimate example of the one who did not seek his own comfort, glorification, or pleasure but cared for others as of first priority (Rom 15:1).

Holy devotion (*hagios*). Another distinctive of Paul's expression of religion is holiness. Believers are called to be holy and blameless before the Lord (1 Thess 3:13; 4:3–8; 5:23; 1 Cor 6:11; Rom 12:1–2). Holiness is often conceived of in

140

scholarship as a form of strict and dutiful piety, and moral purity is certainly a part of what it means to be holy, but the core Jewish concept regarding holiness is about wholeness of devotion and all that is entailed with close proximity and intimacy with God. Jewish holiness necessitates separation or removal from certain spheres, things, and activities, but of first importance it is about dedication to the one God. We see that clearly in the repeated statement in the Pentateuch, "Holy to the Lord."[23] Most readers of the Bible nowadays would not connect love for God and holiness directly. The former seems like a heart matter and the latter about moral and spiritual conduct. But when we look at the foundational statements about holiness in the Old Testament, love of God and holiness are two ways of expressing singleness of devotion.

Let's look at Deuteronomy 6–7. As we have discussed already, Deuteronomy 6:4–9 introduces the covenantal expectation that Israel shall love God with a pure love and devotion. The Lord rescued Israel from slavery in Egypt and then gave them the law for their flourishing and well-being (Deut 6:20–25). In the next chapter, Deuteronomy 7:1–26, the focus is on Israel's holiness as they enter into the land of Canaan. Deuteronomy offers sober warnings that Israel must not flirt with idolatry and intermix in marriage with the Canaanites. Their temples and altars must be entirely demolished, idols purged by fire, "For you are a people holy to the Lord your God; the Lord your God has chosen you out of all the peoples on earth to be his people, his treasured possession" (7:6). The discussion goes on to affirm YHWH's love for Israel (7:8) and his covenant loyalty for a thousand generations (7:9). Later in Deuteronomy, it is repeated again that Israel is a people "holy to the Lord" and that they are YHWH's "treasured possession" (14:2; cf. 26:19). A Deuteronomic view of holiness is not a cold and sterile ritualistic piety; quite the opposite, holiness is Israel's embodiment of total commitment to and undying love for YHWH, Israel's covenant partner.

When Paul teaches the Thessalonians about the will of God regarding their consecration (*hagiasmos*), he mentions control of the body and sexual purity (1 Thess 4:3). He reminds them that the calling of God is unto holiness and not impurity. There are certainly dos and don'ts when it comes to embodied holiness. But holiness *itself* is not about a certain prescribed set of actions. It is the

23. See, for example, Exodus 28:36; 30:10; 30:10; Leviticus 19:8; 23:20; Numbers 6:8; Deuteronomy 7:6.

141

CHAPTER 7

necessary entailments and outworkings of belonging to God in covenant, love, and devotion that is exclusive and therefore special (see 1 Cor 6:11, 12–20).

Faithful devotion (*pistis, pistos*). While it is true that Paul occasionally uses love to refer to devotion to God, it is rare enough that it is certainly not his preferred or default language. Paul was very comfortable commanding his churches to love *each other*, but he used other terminology for direct devotion to God. We have mentioned a couple of related terms and language (pleasing God, holiness), but when reading Paul's letters, it is clear that the dominant term he used in relation to God is "faith" (*pistis*).[24] For example, Paul used "faith" as a summary term for the whole of the gospel (Gal 1:23; 3:23, 25). To the Romans, he explained that the gospel reveals the righteousness of God "from faith to faith," and then Paul quotes Habakkuk 2:4, "The one who is righteous will live by faith" (Rom 1:16–17; cf. 3:22). It is apparent for Paul that this "faith" is especially in Jesus Christ (Gal 2:16–17; 2:20; 3:22; Phil 3:9). Sometimes Paul can express this as faith in *God* (1 Thess 1:8). Faith language is the natural lexicon of devotion toward Father and Son.

This preference for faith language, though, does not mean that Paul didn't want his readers to love God. On the contrary, he expected them to love God, as is right and good according to Scripture. In fact, the way Paul uses faith language can be understood to express love-like devotion *in other words*. "Love" (*agapē*) and "faith" (*pistis*) are certainly not identical and not synonyms, but if we are thinking of a Venn diagram, we can say that for Paul, the circles would overlap considerably. Paul exhorts the Galatians, "For in Christ Jesus neither circumcision nor uncircumcision counts for anything; the only thing that counts is faith [*pistis*] working through love [*agapē*]" (Gal 5:6). We know who is expected to be showing faith and expressing love here—believers. But who are they meant to be loving according to this verse? God? Each other? The aphoristic quality of this second clause points in the direction of *all of the above*. Christians are expected to show faith *and* love, or loving fidelity, toward God and others; that is the real mark of being in Christ.[25] If that is the right

---

24. See my *Paul and the Language of Faith* (Grand Rapids: Eerdmans, 2020); see also Michael J. Gorman, *Cruciformity: Paul's Narrative Spirituality of the Cross*, 20th anniversary ed. (Grand Rapids: Eerdmans, 2021), 216.

25. See James D. G. Dunn, *The Epistle to the Galatians*, BNTC (Peabody, MA: Hendrickson, 1993), 271–72, who writes, "the first Christians seized [*agapē*] and made

Love at the Heart of Paul's Religion

interpretation, then love and faith, *agapē* and *pistis*, belong together, "faithful and dynamic love," as Lou Martyn states.[26]

Related to this, scholars have had energetic conversation about Paul's introductory thanksgiving statement in Philemon: "I thank my God always, making mention of you in my prayers, because I hear of *your love* [*agapē*] *and of the faith* [*pistis*] *which you have toward the Lord Jesus and toward all the saints*" (Phlm 4–5 NASB). I have cited the NASB translation because it reflects well the Greek word order of the italicized section.[27] A simple reading of this verse might suggest that Paul knows of Philemon's love and faith toward Jesus and toward the saints (i.e., other Christians). But Paul is not normally in the habit of talking about Christian love for Jesus, and even less likely to praise faith (*pistis*) toward other believers. Because of these perceived peculiarities, some translations partition this verse by pairing faith with Jesus and love with the saints, as we find in the NRSV: "When I remember you in my prayers, I always thank my God because I hear of *your love for all the saints* and *your faith toward the Lord Jesus*." There is some sensibility to these pairings, because in Colossians 1:4, Paul makes a similar statement: "In our prayers for you we always thank God, the Father of our Lord Jesus Christ, for we have heard of *your faith in Christ Jesus* and of the *love that you have for all the saints*" (Col 1:3–4). Here the Greek phrases *are* separated, *tēn pistin hymōn en Christo Iēsou* ("your faith in Christ Jesus"), and *tēn agapēn . . . eis pantas tous hagious* ("the love . . . for all the saints").

But back to Philemon, some scholars think that there is no need to parcel out faith and love as if one needs to draw a thick line of distinction between the two in Paul's thought. Markus Barth, for example, argues that in Philemon 4–5, not only should "faith" and "love" be kept together, but they function sensibly

---

it their own, particularly Paul. This must be because for them it expressed with exceptional fitness their sense of the wholly generous, sacrificial and actively outreaching concern on their behalf shown by God in Christ. The love which was the basis of their acceptance by God should also be its expressions."

26. J. Louis Martyn, *Galatians: A New Translation with Introduction and Commentary*, AB (New Haven: Yale University Press, 2008), 473.

27. Philemon 5: *akouōn sou tēn agapēn kai tēn pistin hēn echeis pros ton kyrion iēsoun kai eis pantas tous hagious*. Ann L. Jervis, *Galatians*, NIBCNT (Peabody, MA: Hendrickson, 1999), 132, sums this up well: "Paul states that faith is not abstract but a way of life that is made effective, visibly and daily, through love."

CHAPTER 7

here as a hendiadys, two words coming together to form one concept. "The Greek diction makes evident that at this place love and faith are treated almost as one single thing, one single way, attitude, and act. . . . Faith is then not related to love as theory is to practice, or dogmatics is to ethics; and the two ought not be carefully set apart. . . . When he wants to praise a Christian such as Philemon, he mentions his love *and* his faith."[28]

Similarly, Dunn refers to faith and love *together* here in Philemon as "the sum of the Christian lifestyle,"[29] and likewise Fitzmyer talks about them as "the sum of Christian conduct."[30] This complementary relationship between faith and love is proven throughout the Pauline corpus; it is especially prominent in 1 Thessalonians.

> We always give thanks to God for all of you and mention you in our prayers, constantly remembering before our God and Father your work of *faith* [*pistis*] and labor of *love* [*agapē*] and steadfastness of hope in our Lord Jesus Christ. (1 Thess 1:2)

> But Timothy has just now come to us from you, and has brought us the good news of your *faith and love* [*tēn pistin kai tēn agapēn hymōn*]. He has told us also that you always remember us kindly and long to see us—just as we long to see you. (1 Thess 3:6)

> But since we belong to the day, let us be sober, and put on the breastplate of *faith and love* [*pisteōs kai agapēs*], and for a helmet the hope of salvation. (1 Thess 5:8)

Given this natural pairing for Paul, we can see that he saw them as sibling virtues and activities. Faith and love are not identical, but they do appear to function in 1 Thessalonians 3:6 and 5:8 as a hendiadys, something like "faithful devotion" or

28. Markus Barth, *Colossians: A New Translation with Introduction and Commentary*, AB (New Haven: Yale University Press, 1994), 272.

29. James D. G. Dunn, *The Epistles to the Colossians and to Philemon*, NIGTC (Grand Rapids: Eerdmans, 1996), 317.

30. Joseph A. Fitzmyer, *The Letter to Philemon: A New Translation with Introduction and Commentary*, AB (New Haven: Yale University Press, 2008), 96.

Love at the Heart of Paul's Religion

"loyal love." We can add to these statements to the Thessalonians a brief comment from Ephesians: "Peace be with the whole community, and love with faith [*agapē meta pisteōs*], from God the Father and the Lord Jesus Christ" (Eph 6:23). Notice what kind of statement this is—a blessing from God the Father and the Lord Jesus. Paul is praying that God would bestow peace upon their community, as well as divine love and divine *pistis*, faith (or faithfulness). In a sense, he is saying, may you have and know the peace of God, and God's love that is marked by his faithfulness and devotion to you.[31] This is not an isolated occurrence in Ephesians. The virtues of peace, love, and faith are also expectations and ideals for the Christian community as laid out clearly and extensively in Ephesians.[32] To reiterate, Ephesians teaches that *love* is ultimately modeled by God, God loves his people, and his bestowal of love is meant to energize their love for one another and for God; and the same goes for faith. Believers are saved by grace and through faith (Gal 2:8–9), but in 6:23, we learn that God's love includes God's own fidelity and devotion to his people, an inspiration for the virtue of fidelity.

The question is left for us to ask—*If "faith" is not so different theologically from "love," why does Paul seem to prefer the former (in terms of default vocabulary) and not the latter in relation to God?* I can offer two speculations here. First, Paul's preference for the divine title of "Lord" (*kyrios*) for Jesus had a political texture to it in the Greco-Roman world, and it would have been easily understandable for Paul to preach *pistis* (faith, trust, loyalty, allegiance) in a heavenly Sovereign called Jesus. The Jewish priority of love for God (Deut 6:5) would require some explaining since Greeks and Romans did not typically think about love as the most natural action toward a deity or ruler. So one issue may be that *pistis* simply fit well with the relationship between subject (believers) and ruler (Christ Jesus) going in both directions—human belief in Jesus, and Jesus's own commitment to his people.

Second, Paul may have been picking up the distinctiveness of faith language that goes back to the Jesus tradition itself. While we don't find Paul quoting

31. I am in agreement with and following here the reading of Ernest Best, where peace, love, and faith are divine attributes and blessings on the people (*A Critical and Exegetical Commentary on Ephesians*, ICC [Edinburgh: T&T Clark, 1998], 618).

32. See Ephesians 1:4, 15; 2:4, 14–17; 3:17; 4:2, 3, 4–5, 13, 15; 5:2; 6:15, 16; and Lynn H. Cohick, *The Letter to the Ephesians*, NICNT (Grand Rapids: Eerdmans, 2020), 435–36. In the final chapter of this book, we look at love language as a whole in Ephesians.

CHAPTER 7

the teachings of Jesus very often, it is no coincidence that Paul focused on *pistis* (and the verbal form *pisteuō*), and so did Jesus according to the Gospels. Jesus preached faith (Mark 1:15; 11:22; Luke 18:8; John 3:36; 5:38), he affirmed faith (Matt 8:10; Luke 7:9), he healed in response to faith (Matt 8:13; 9:22, 28; 15:28; Mark 5:43; 10:52; Luke 7:50), he criticized lack of faith (Matt 17:20; Mark 4:40; Luke 8:25), and he prayed for his disciples' faith (Luke 22:32). In fact, this appears to be Jesus's dominant message: belief in the good news and faith and trust in his own message about the coming kingdom of God. Oddly, we have the same mystery in the Gospels' account of Jesus's teaching that we do in Paul. While there are signs that Jesus and Paul both affirmed the Shema's command to love God (see earlier, chapter 4), both Jesus and Paul focus more on faith. The most logical explanation is that the faith teaching is meant to be an urgent call for devotion through acceptance of this new good news and trust in the person of Jesus as he is God's Messiah.

Despite Paul's preference for faith language in relation to devotion to God in terms of frequency of word usage, there is a case to be made that Paul put a priority on loving God as the heart of Christian religion and piety—love as the ultimate virtue. In 1 Corinthians 13, Paul discusses love between brothers and sisters in Christ at length, precisely because these Christian Corinthians were *not* doing a good job loving each other. Paul does not address love for God or love from God explicitly, but what we do learn from this text is Paul's conception of love as the master of all values, virtues, and commitments. No value or gift is valuable without love; no act of service is meaningful without love (1 Cor 13:1–10). He uses an analogy about growing up, setting aside immature and childish ways, and knowing and behaving in a more perfect way, and that centers on love. If love is the ultimate action and orientation from one believer toward another, how can it not also be the highest and best expression of devotion to God? This is confirmed by Paul's own climactic expression: "And now faith, hope and love abide, these three; and the greatest of these is love" (13:13).

Is Hate a Christian Virtue for Paul?

Before we conclude this chapter, I want to touch briefly on the notion of hatred as a religious virtue. On a few difficult occasions, Paul repudiates hatred as a vice (Rom 1:29; 3:14; 1 Cor 5:8; Col 3:8; Eph 4:31). Human hatred toward other people tends to come from a place of disgust and resentment, and giving in to

Love at the Heart of Paul's Religion

feelings of injustice, anger, or resentment. In Jewish tradition, hatred and love are opposites; love heals and unites, and human hatred destroys and divides (Prov 10:12). But sometimes hatred language is used as a virtue—not hating *people*, of course, but hating certain evils or activities. For example, Proverbs mentions six things the Lord hates: "haughty eyes, a lying tongue, and hands that shed innocent blood, a heart that devises wicked plans, feet that hurry to run to evil, a lying witness who testifies falsely, and one who sows discord in a family" (Prov 6:16–18). When hatred language is used in this sense, it is not a feeling of resentment toward a person but a line drawn in the sand regarding good and evil, righteousness and wickedness. It is a statement about values and one's orientation to those values, whether attraction (love) or repulsion (hate). Israel is enjoined in Proverbs to align with YHWH's values and to reject what YHWH considers harmful and wrong. Similarly, Ben Sira advises, "Return to the Most High and turn away from iniquity, and hate intensely what he abhors" (Sir 17:26).

Likewise, Jesus used hatred language in formative ways when it came to piety and devotion. "No one can serve two masters; for a slave will either hate the one and love the other, or be devoted to the one and despise the other. You cannot serve God and wealth" (Matt 6:24). This statement is not really about love and hate in an exclusively emotional sense. Does any slave, after all, love his master (in a sentimental sense)? Also, in this hypothetical two-master scenario (a nonsensical situation, which is the whole point), you don't automatically hate what you don't love. In fact, Jesus's statement is not about hatred with resentment and spite, but his teaching reflects the sage's use of this binary to talk about what one holds close and what one rejects or stands against. In the Gospel of Luke, Jesus teaches his disciples that to truly follow him, they must hate their father and mother, wife and children, brothers and sisters, and even their own life (Luke 14:26; cf. John 12:25). Jesus did not call for self-hatred in a literal sense. What he was getting at is that their priority must be Jesus himself and the kingdom of God, and no other person (including themselves) must interfere with that commitment. Hatred language represents an absolute in moral discourse—rejection, not acceptance.

On one occasion, Paul explicitly makes reference to the virtue of hatred: "Let love be genuine; hate what is evil, hold fast to what is good" (Rom 12:9). We might get some clarity on Paul's meaning by looking at a parallel statement he makes to the Thessalonians: "test everything; hold fast to what is good,

CHAPTER 7

abstain from every form of evil" (1 Thess 5:21–22). This love-hate moral binary is part of traditional Jewish moral teaching.

> The LORD loves those who hate evil; he guards the lives of his faithful. (Ps 97:10)[33]

> Hate evil and love good. (Amos 5:15)

When Paul calls for abhorrence of evil, he means an absolute turning away from evil, and a strong embrace of what is good. Hatred should never be toward a person, and not even a group. The enemy is evil, but people deserve love. Evil people cannot be changed through more evil (Rom 12:17); they must be loved with the love of Christ. But believers must reject, abhor, and *hate* evil itself, run away from it, and put all of one's energy into destroying it. In that sense, hatred is good and part of the gospel's good news that Paul preached.

In this chapter, our attention has been on whether or to what degree Paul understood the primary form of religion and devotion to God as love. None of the early Christian writers extensively affirmed the Shema's command to love God with the whole self. Paul occasionally refers to believers as those who love God, but he clearly preferred other vocabulary, like being holy before the Lord and seeking to please God. Faith language is dominant in Paul's expression of devotion to God, but we have tried to demonstrate that Paul thought of faith and love together, sometimes as a hendiadys, as the sum of Christian religion, loyal love, singular devotion, and passionate trust.

In the next chapter, we will address the subject where Paul uses love language the most: love for fellow believers. It is apparent that love is meant to be at the heart of Christian community.

33. The Septuagint offers this English translation: "You who love the Lord, hate evil! He guards the souls of his devout" (Ps 96:10 LXX).

8

Love at the Heart of the Christian Community

For Paul, the ultimate denial of the gospel of the Cross is the refusal
to live according to the pattern of self-emptying love which it
proclaims: the gospel demands conformity to Christ's death.

—Morna Hooker[1]

How did Paul expect Christians to live *as Christians*? What did it mean to
live in the way of Christ? What did it mean to imitate Christ? What did
Paul look for as signs of maturity in the life of the believer? It should be clear
by now that love is the answer.

LOVE AS THE MASTER VIRTUE OF THE CHRISTIAN LIFE IN COMMUNITY

In Romans 14:15, Paul uses an important phrase (which we have already mentioned) that clues us in to how he thought about love as a lifestyle and virtue: "If your brother or sister is being injured by what you eat, you are no
longer *walking* in love." The verb *peripateō* here refers to the physical action
of walking and is a Jewish expression for lifestyle, including core virtues and
habits.[2] Theoretically, you could walk in hate, or walk in pride. The qualifier
kata agapēn, "according to love," sets up a certain standard for how one lives.

1. Morna D. Hooker, *From Adam to Christ* (Eugene, OR: Wipf & Stock, 2008), 65.
2. See J. Paul Sampley, *Walking in Love: Moral Progress and Spiritual Growth with
the Apostle Paul* (Minneapolis: Fortress, 2016), 100–101.

CHAPTER 8

For the Christian, Paul assumes, the dominant theme of one's life and activity ought to be love. The upshot of Romans 14:15 is that if the believer is not paying attention to how their behavior might harm others (even inadvertently), they have forgotten how to live Christianly, to live in the way of Christ, which involves marching to the tune and drumbeat of love.

But Paul believed that love wasn't just something that people muster up, or produce and increase it out of sheer willpower. It is inspired by the love of God the Father, embodied in the life and death of Jesus the Son, and empowered by the Holy Spirit. In his Letter to the Philippians, Paul reminds them of the palpable experience of the love, compassion, and sympathy of God that enveloped their community and brought them great joy (Phil 2:1–2), and in their low points they needed to remember that divine embrace of love. Only with such a deluge of God's affection on them in mind could Paul pray that their love for one another would overflow (Phil 1:9).

This is even clearer in the latter chapters of Paul's Letter to the Galatians. Throughout the letter, he hinted to the Galatians that the way of the flesh is selfish, enslaving, and doomed to death and decay. The way of the Spirit is freedom and life and opens the believer up to care for others. The "fruit of the Spirit" stands in contrast to the "works of the flesh." These are two different and diametrically opposed ways of being in the world. The latter spoils relationships and poisons community; the former inspires gentleness, compassion, positivity, and peace, knitting the community together in love.[3]

John Painter has made the argument that the fruit of the Spirit list for Paul is really about love (*agapē*), and the rest of the items that Paul mentions (joy, peace, goodness, etc.) are different aspects of the one great virtue and Spirit-product of love.[4] He likens this to 1 Corinthians 13, where Paul says "love is patient, love is kind. . . ." If that is true, Paul was telling the Galatians, "the Spirit produces love, which then inspires kindness, faithfulness, gentleness, and so forth."[5] Painter probably makes too much of the singular form of the word "fruit" (*karpos*; as in, love is *the* fruit of the Spirit), but what his reading has in its favor is Paul's overall emphasis on love in Galatians. Early in the letter, Paul

3. John M. G. Barclay, *Paul and the Gift* (Grand Rapids: Eerdmans, 2017), 426, describes flesh as "the environment of human agency untransformed by the Spirit."

4. John Painter, "The Fruit of the Spirit Is Love," *Journal of Theology for Southern Africa* 5 (1973): 57–59.

5. See Painter, "Fruit of the Spirit," 59.

Love at the Heart of the Christian Community

had mentioned the love of Christ, the Son of God (Gal 2:20). But Paul's call for Christians to love another is a repeated exhortation and theme in chapter 5. In his list of the fruit of the Holy Spirit, as we already mentioned, love is the focus. In Galatians 5:6, Paul makes it clear that circumcision (or uncircumcision for that matter) ought not to be the Galatian believers' preoccupation but rather "faith working through love." While Paul had focused his attention on the language of faith (*pistis, pisteuō*) earlier in the letter, now in chapter 5, the focus shifts to love (*agapē*); but, ultimately, these twin virtues belong together, and it makes sense for this shift of emphasis, because—as Pieter de Villiers puts it—"love is the face of faith," that is, the life expression of commitment to God and conformity to the way of the gospel of Jesus Christ.[6]

One of the issues Paul addresses in Galatians involves the meaning and nature of freedom. It seems likely that the rival teachers in Galatians were presenting to the Galatian Christians some notion that obedience to the law (and circumcision as an initiatory ritual) would protect them from outside dangers. But Paul was worried about what was going on *inside* the community, the selfishness and rivalries that were harming their unity (Gal 5:15). Paul affirms their freedom (5:1) but warns them not to confuse freedom *from sin* for a license to be selfish. Rather, "through love [*agapē*] become slaves to one another" (5:13). Paul did not mean this in any literal way, because slaves are not agents free to choose whom they serve. Paul was offering an image of devotion to the other (and not to self alone). And, in fact, this was a kind of paraphrase of Leviticus 19:18b, "You shall love your neighbor as yourself" (Gal 5:14). Paul's conception of Christian freedom was not *pure* freedom to do whatever you want but freedom from sin and death, from the law, from flesh, in order to function in a human way as God intended, in obedience to God and love of neighbor, stranger, and enemy. John Barclay poignantly describes Paul's thinking here: "'freedom' is not autonomy but the product of an allegiance that breaks the power of previously taken-for-granted (and now 'alien') norms. He is dead to the regime of the Law, since his life is derived from and governed by the Christ-event: 'it is no longer I who live, but Christ who lives in me' (2:19–20). All other criteria of value have been discounted by the superordinate worth of belonging to Christ."[7]

---

6. Pieter G. R. de Villiers, "Transformation in Love in Paul's Letter to the Galatians," *Acta Theologica* (supplement) 19 (2014): 155.

7. Barclay, *Paul and the Gift*, 428–29.

CHAPTER 8

Frances Taylor Gench is quick to explain that when Paul promotes the master virtue of love to the Galatians, this is life or death stuff, not mushy sentimentalism. "The exhortation to 'love' . . . is so familiar to Christian congregations that it is liable to slide right by. It is therefore important to note that the love of which Paul speaks is more than the warm feeling one has toward another. It is more than that emotion extolled in greeting cards as 'the feeling you feel when you feel you're going to feel a feeling you never felt before.'"[8] Rather, Gench continues, Christian love starts with a deep feeling of concern and affection for the other but turns into action for the sake of one's neighbor, costly service modeled by Jesus himself. Paul's image of offering ourselves as slaves to one another is extreme, but it represents love's inclination to treat others as another self and do whatever is necessary to preserve, protect, care for, and seek the best for them.[9]

This spirit and work of love does not come about through sheer grit or human determination. It is work wrought by the God who loves. The Spirit produces the fruit of love as a natural result or by-product of believers abiding in God and living in cooperation with the Spirit.[10] We see this also in 1 Thessalonians 4:9–10. Again, we have a troubled community (for different reasons), and Paul became worried about their well-being. One of the key considerations is the state of their communal grace and unity. Earlier in chapter 4, he calls out impropriety, especially sexual immorality and exploitation (1 Thess 4:3–8). In a state of disarray, they failed to walk in love and instead succumbed to primitive behaviors of selfishness and harm toward the other. So Paul reminded them of *philadelphia*, the generous and steadfast love that is expected of siblings (4:9). This is not moral training that one learns from a book or a philosophical school. Rather, Paul commends the Thessalonians, because they have already proven they are "God-taught" (*theodidaktoi*). It is not exactly clear what Paul means by this, but I find it reasonable to interpret this as the idea that they have seen and experienced the love of God through the gospel and immediately assimilated and embodied that same love in their relationship with fellow believers. In fact, Paul credits the Thessalonian believers with loving all the brothers

8. Frances Taylor Gench, "Galatians 5:1, 13–25," *Interpretation* 46 (1992): 292.

9. Gench, "Galatians 5:1, 13–25," 293.

10. Gordon D. Fee, "Freedom and the Life of Obedience (Galatians 5:1–6:18)," *Review and Expositor* 91 (1994): 209: "the Spirit effectively produces in them the very character of God."

152

Love at the Heart of the Christian Community

and sisters throughout Macedonia. How? Perhaps they have sent gifts and aid where it was needed, or expressed concern and compassion through letters or representatives traveling from them to meet a need or give comfort elsewhere. Paul's Letter to Philemon points out that Philemon himself loves all the saints (*hagioi*), especially through his gifts and generosity that refresh the hearts of believers (Phlm 7). This could mean a number of things, but I wonder whether it is the gift of encouragement, a word of affirmation and blessing that lifts up the spirits of the downtrodden. Perhaps that is what these gifted and loving Thessalonian Christians offered to Macedonians near and far (who knows?). In any case, once upon a time, they were loving not only each other well but also many other brothers and sisters in their geographic network; but certain signs of problems in their community pointed to backsliding in their walk of love. We can say again that Paul treated love as a key indicator of maturity, and not only that but that a community wasn't experiencing its intended life unless it was walking in mutual love, respect, generosity, and care.

LOVE AS THE GOAL OF DIVINE INSTRUCTION

In two different letters, Paul refers to love as the focus of God's covenantal instruction to his people for the good of their life together (Gal 5:13–15; Rom 13:8–10). We will give a brief summary of each text and then probe deeper into Paul's love hermeneutic that establishes love as the fulfillment of the divine law. We have already spent some time in Galatians 5, so we can pick up where we left off, then turn to Romans 13.

The freedom that believers are granted through the gospel of Jesus Christ is pointed in a particular direction, namely, service to others (Gal 5:13). Paul backs this up with an appeal to the law. Earlier in Galatians, he was reluctant to press the Galatians to obey specific laws, but here he points to a single commandment, "You shall love your neighbor as yourself" (5:14). We have already discussed at length the meaning and use of Leviticus 19:18b in Jewish and early Christian tradition (see chapter 4). Paul quotes this supertext twice (Gal 5:14; Rom 13:9). The NRSV uses the language of "summed up" for the Greek verb *plēroō*, but the classic and more straightforward translation is "fulfilled." What does Paul mean by "fulfill" (or "sum up")? In the context of his arguments and exhortations about freedom to serve others in love and not dwell on selfish desires, fulfillment involves the essence or goal of the covenantal instruction

153

CHAPTER 8

given to Israel.[11] Paul reveals that the law has always been about love.[12] Therefore, if the Galatians bicker and "bite and devour one another," they are doing
the exact opposite of what God desires (5:15). If we skip ahead a little bit to
the beginning of chapter 6, Paul returns again to service-oriented love and
calls the Galatians to "bear one another's burdens, and in this way you will
fulfill the law of Christ" (Gal 6:2).[13] The phrase "law of Christ" (*ton nomon
tou Christou*) is the subject of much debate. What exactly does this refer to?
Some advocate for this referring to the teachings of Jesus (like the Sermon on
the Mount); others think it means the Old Testament read through a christological lens. Others still take *nomos* not as "law" (as in rule/regulation) but
"pattern" or "lifestyle," Christ's own way of being.[14] I find the last of these the
most persuasive, because all along in Galatians Paul has pointed to the person
of Jesus Christ. But notice here again the language of "fulfillment" (*anaplēroō*).
It would be natural for the reader to think back to Gal 5:14 and make a connection between graciously caring for and carrying one another's burdens and
responding to the expectation of love of neighbor. What I think Paul is trying
to express is something like this:

> You, Galatians, want to be attentive to the law, right? Then focus on the
> "law of Christ," that is, the law of love, which is the whole point of God's

11. I think David A. deSilva is spot on when he shows that at the end of Paul's Letter to the Galatians (which included critique of strict law obedience), Paul believed
and affirmed that "Torah still bears witness to God's purposes, God's plan, and God's
standards of righteousness" (*The Letter to the Galatians*, NICNT [Grand Rapids: Eerdmans, 2018], 450).

12. See the discussion by James D. G. Dunn in *Theology of Paul the Apostle* (Grand
Rapids: Eerdmans, 1998), 656–57.

13. Kengo Akiyama, *The Love of Neighbour in Ancient Judaism: The Reception of Leviticus 19:18 in the Hebrew Bible, the Septuagint, the Book of Jubilees, the Dead Sea Scrolls,
and the New Testament* (Boston: Brill, 2018), 145, makes the interesting observation
that "carrying the burden" would have been a task especially designated for slaves in
the Greco-Roman world. This reinforces the connection between 6:2 and 5:13.

14. See the extended discussion in Gupta, *Galatians*, SGBC (Grand Rapids:
Zondervan, 2023), 244–246. See also Michael J. Gorman, *Cruciformity: Paul's Narrative Spirituality of the Cross*, 20th anniversary ed. (Grand Rapids: Eerdmans, 2021),
176, where he defines "law of Christ" as "*the narrative pattern of faith expressing itself in
self-giving, others-regarding love of the crucified Messiah Jesus.*"

Love at the Heart of the Christian Community

covenantal instruction. Don't worry about the *stoicheia tou kosmou* ("elements of the world"), or how to get into the good graces of a particular club or onto a special team with these other teachers. Pour all of your energy into one thing: compassionate and caring service where you love each and every person in your community. The gospel is freedom, but not the kind of freedom that cuts all bands and ties and lets you indulge in gratifying your flesh like a spoiled child. Real gospel freedom is cutting you loose from whatever might hinder you from living the way God intended, to liberate you to the end of generous support of one another, imitating Christ himself. (my paraphrase)

Romans 13:8–10 is noticeably parallel to Paul's Galatians message about love. In Romans 13:1–7, Paul addressed the Christian obligation of showing respect to civil leaders and giving the government what they are owed in taxes (Rom 13:6–7). In 13:8, Paul picks up on the word "debt" (*opheilō*) from 13:7 and transitions to talking about the internal culture of the church, as if to say, What debts do we have toward one another, what do we owe to each other? Paul dispels any notion that we ought to charge bills to one another like an IOU from the government. There is only one obligation that fellow Christians have toward one another: love. There are two ways to read the Greek text of Romans 13:8b. The most common translation is this: "the one who loves the other has fulfilled the law." This takes *ton hereton* (the other) as the object of love. But another way would be to take the whole phrase *ton heteron nomon* as one and translate, "the one who loves has fulfilled the *other law*." What *other law*? In Romans 13:1–7, Paul is taking for granted the civic law of Rome, what Rome binds the people to obey, the law of Caesar. Paul here might be saying, acknowledge and adhere to Caesar's law insofar as you are able. In Romans 13:8–10, Paul then could be adding, God's law (the *other* law) has one key expectation: love. I am not sure which of the two readings of Romans 13:8b is more likely (I lean toward "the other law," the second option), but what is clear in either case is that Paul affirms here what he wrote to the Galatians: expressing and embodying love is the summation and fulfillment of the essence of God's law.

In Romans 13:9–10, Paul is even more explicit about the neighbor-love command as the summative virtue than he was in Galatians 5:14. In Romans 13:9, Paul gives a representative list from the Ten Commandments (no adultery, murder, theft, coveting, etc.) and then explains that "love your neighbor as yourself" is the summation or "unifying principle" of such moral imperatives

155

CHAPTER 8

for holy community life.[15] In Romans 13:10, Paul explicitly expresses that love is the fulfillment (*plērōma*) of the law, and to put a fine point on the matter, he explains this is inverse: "love does no harm to neighbor" (my translation; 13:10a). I think the implications would have been clear to the readers. Christians are obligated to love, not as a box to check but as the whole goal of God's guidance and instruction. By mentioning "love does no harm," Paul is giving the Romans a lens through which to view the venerable Ten Commandments. Some of God's law is structured as prohibitions, but the moral philosophy is simple: love your neighbor, and love knows not to do things that are hurtful. Love does much more than avoid harm, but love cannot do less.

One of the key takeaways from these related passages in Galatians and Romans is this: Paul sensed that many believers desire to obey God and respond to God's instruction. Paul taught very clearly that there is a fundamental value that all Christ followers should focus on, namely, love of neighbor. This love is meant to be practical, persistent, and pervasive. It begins with seeing and valuing the other (as another self) and is expected to grow into concern and practical care, service and burden-carrying, support and advocacy, and generosity and sacrificial involvement.

Love and Unity

One of the most detailed and extensive teachings on love in the Bible appears in the well-known passage 1 Corinthians 13:1–13, but this is no wedding homily in the original context of Paul's correspondence with the Corinthian church. This text is part of a larger section of this letter offering serious instruction on the work of the Spirit in the church for the sake of unity and mutual benefit, beginning in 1 Corinthians 12:1. Each person is blessed with a gift to share with the community, one Spirit bestowing a variety of unique skills and contributions, Paul explains. In 12:12–26, he portrays this Spirit-blessing like one body made up of individual and unique parts working as a whole. The parts work together, they struggle together, and they benefit from good things together. But there can be dysfunction as well. Paul warns the Corinthians about real threats to

---

15. J. P. Louw and Eugene A. Nida, *Greek-English Lexicon of the New Testament: Based on Semantic Domains* (New York: United Bible Societies, 1989), 1:613 (*anakephalaioō*). See also Ceslas Spicq, *Agape in the New Testament* (Saint Louis: Herder, 1966), 2:59.

Love at the Heart of the Christian Community

their communal body and social well-being, especially when pride and arrogance lead to jealousy over what might seem like the most powerful or praiseworthy gifts of the Spirit. The path to *greatness* (*hyperbolē*, the "more excellent" way) is not acquiring glory for oneself but rather modeling service to others in love. As Richard Hays puts it, love is the sine qua non of the Christian life.[16]

That is the background for Paul's eloquent love message. Far from being a mere reminder of the beauty of love, it is more of a corrective teaching meant to repair a broken and unhealthy Christian community. Instead of fighting over who gets the fancy leadership titles, or more time in the spotlight, or more impressive roles, what really matters to *God* is love.

Before getting into the specifics of 1 Corinthians 13:1–3, I think it is helpful to point to Pheme Perkins's comparison of this passage and the meditation on love in Plato's *Symposium*. Plato extols the virtues and benefits of love in community in ways similar to what Paul wrote hundreds of years later. Plato wrote, "Love fills us with togetherness and rains all our divisiveness away.... Love moves us to mildness, removes from us wildness. He is giver of kindness, never of meanness ... father of elegance, luxury, delicacy, grace, yearning, desire. Love cares well for good men, cares not for bad ones. In pain, in fear, in desire, or speech, Love is our best guide and guard; he is our comrade and our savior. Ornament of all gods and men. Every man should follow Love, sing beautifully his hymns."[17]

There are striking similarities between Plato and Paul, including unity, grace, excellence, and preeminence. One of the major differences that Perkins points out is that Plato focused on the term *eros*, not *agapē*. The former includes sexual desire and fulfillment; the latter does not. And the context of the symposium itself gives the air of high society. Paul may have been framing his discourse on love as a critique of high society gatherings. Perkins writes, "One can imagine the city's wealthy elite charmed by poetic celebrations of Eros. It has no place for the ugly, unsophisticated, lowborn, or impoverished—in short, for those members of Christ's body whom Paul has endowed with greater honor (12:24). By adopting a little-used noun, *agapē*, Christians could reorchestrate

16. Richard B. Hays, *First Corinthians*, IBC (Louisville: Westminster John Knox, 1997), 221.

17. Plato, *Symposium* 197d–e, trans. Alexander Nehamas and Paul Woodruff (Indianapolis: Hackett, 1989), 37; as cited in Pheme Perkins, *First Corinthians*, PCNT (Grand Rapids: Baker), 154.

CHAPTER 8

the cultural discourse about love as a divine gift. This small passage . . . replaces the praises of love familiar to his audience from their childhood."[18]

With this background in mind, we can now take a closer look at Paul's text. First Corinthians 13:1–3 is a comparison illustration. The supposed glorious gifts of the Spirit are empty and meaningless without love: sonorous and heavenly tongues, spell-binding prophetic insight, grandiose gestures of sacrifice, even heroic self-sacrifice are nothing if love is not the core of one's being in the world and default orientation toward others. The Corinthians had drifted so far from the path of goodness that they needed an extended reminder of what love actually *is*. Here is an exposition in brief.

Love is patient (*makrothymeō*). It is openhearted and long-suffering. A loving spirit does not have a short fuse; it has a long fuse. A short fuse leads to anger, fighting, and bickering. Love knows not to reject the other impulsively, and love never gives up on the other (see 1 Thess 5:14).

Love is kind (*chrēsteuomai*). Love cares; love is gracious and munificent. The French biblical scholar and lexicographer Ceslas Spicq explains Paul's appeal to love's benevolence this way: "The point is brotherly love, a loving attitude that includes a willingness to serve one's neighbor. This virtue is possessed only by magnanimous and unselfish souls who are characterized by kindness, friendliness, and liberality."[19] Kindness, in many ways, is a hallmark of the Christian faith. Roman historian Suetonius makes mention of a disturber of the peace named Chrestus (*Claudius* 25.4). Many scholars think he was confusing the common slave name Chrestus with *Christos* (Christ). Later on, second- and third-century Christians testified that opponents of Christianity would mock their faith by calling them *Chrestiani* to connect this people with a lowly slave name, which reflected the slave's base nature (Greek *Chrēstos* can mean "useful," as in utilitarian).[20] Tertullian turned this around, recognizing that the root word of *Chrestiani* (*Chrēstos*) can also mean "good" or "kind." Tertullian

18. Perkins, *First Corinthians*, 154.

19. Ceslas Spicq, *Theological Lexicon of the New Testament*, trans. James D. Ernest (Peabody, MA: Hendrickson, 1994), 3:515.

20. See Justin, *First Apology* 4.5; Tertullian, *Apology* 3; *To the Heathen* 1.3.9; Lactantius, *Divine Institutes* 4.7. See the discussion in A. Andrew Das, *Solving the Romans Debate* (Minneapolis: Fortress, 2007), 150–51; Margaret H. Williams, *Early Classical Authors on Jesus* (London: Bloomsbury, 2023), 67–68; Martin Hengel, *Paul between*

Love at the Heart of the Christian Community

writes, "Christian, so far as the meaning of the word is concerned, is derived from anointing. Yes, and even when it is wrongly pronounced by you 'Chrestianus' (for you do not even know accurately the name you hate), it comes from sweetness and benignity" (*Apology* 3). Here is the point: Paul clearly wanted Christians to be known for their love, their sweetness and kindness, generosity of spirit, and a benevolent disposition that is even winsome and charming.

Love is not envious (*zēloō*). The Greek noun *zēlos* simply refers to an overwhelming passion. Passion is not an inherently good or bad thing. It depends on what that passion is directed at. *Zēlos* is often translated in the Bible as "zeal," an intense desire for something. In fact, Paul tells the Corinthians to "be zealous" (*zēloō*) for the greater gifts of the Spirit (1 Cor 12:31), and later he again says, "Pursue love and *be zealous for* gifts of the Spirit" (14:1, my translation). "Zeal," as a good and healthy expression, is love let loose toward healthy and positive ends. Imagine seeing a family member or close friend for the first time after many years—you instinctively want to run to them and give them a big hug. That's *zēlos*, that's passionate love, and in that case it is a good and right thing. But when Paul warns the Corinthians not to be *zealous*, he is talking about the vice we call envy. This is an extreme form of passion for a person or thing that is overly protective. Paul's main point is that the Corinthians should not be jealous of the gifts that others are given by the Spirit. They should focus their passion not on how to one-up the other but on how to love each other well.

Love is not self-centered (*perpereuomai, physioō, aschēmoneō, zēteō ta heautēs*). Paul adds four more terms that reinforce his point about selfish passions not reflecting Christian love. The verb *perpereuomai* refers to boasting and drawing attention to self. The verb *physioō* adds a word image to the discussion; it literally means "blowing up" (like a bubble), in this case referring to inflating one's own ego. Love is not preoccupied with getting one's own way. Paul was not saying individuals can't advocate for their own needs or rights. The problem, rather, is an unhealthy obsession with self-glory.

The next verb in this thought unit is *aschēmoneō*, which indicates shameful activity, appropriately translated in many English translations as "rude." With a fragile ego, it is easy to fight so hard to draw attention to oneself that any sense of patience, courtesy, or politeness is thrown out the window. Imagine a cus-

---

Damascus and Antioch: The Unknown Years (Louisville: Westminster John Knox, 1997), 230–31; Martin Hengel, *Studies in Early Christology* (Edinburgh: T&T Clark, 1995), 2.

CHAPTER 8

tomer yelling at a cashier. Or a belligerent traveler bullying a flight attendant. Or a restaurant patron leaving a nasty comment on the bill rather than a tip. It's rude, plain and simple—the opposite of generous and kind. It's selfish, shallow, and petty; it's all about ego.

The last thing Paul adds to this series on selfishness is *ou zētei ta heautēs*, love "does not dwell on mine, mine, mine" (my paraphrase). Paul puts his finger here on the root issue, juvenile selfishness. When there is no love in the midst of disagreement or difficulty, the relationship turns into a battle of power, each one obsessed with what they have lost or don't have. Paul insists, love is fundamentally open to caring for the other.

Love is not hot and bothered (*paroxynō, ou logizetai to kakon*). This goes back to the virtue of patience. Often the verb *paroxynō* is translated "to be provoked," which is about an extreme reaction of anger and hurt, with a hint of the desire for retaliation. That is where the second statement comes in (*ou logizetai to kakon*, "does not keep count of wrongdoing"). The word *paroxynō* refers to resentment, plotting revenge, wishing and wanting harm for the other who has offended you, casting aspersions, and harboring resentment. But love is the opposite. Love doesn't keep score of how much the other has done wrong to me (*logizetai to kakon*); love wishes good things for the other (*logizestai to agathon*, theoretically).

Love does not take pleasure in wrong but in what is good and true and right (*adikia, alētheia*). Let's say your enemy is wrongly accused and convicted of wrongdoing. It is in our baser nature to relish such happenings. We might say, "One way or another, they got what they deserved!" But Paul says that love shares in the joy of those who are vindicated by the truth (*synchairō tē alētheia*). To continue our hypothetical scenario, let's say one's enemy is wrongly convicted, but then the truth comes out and they are vindicated. Paul says, "Celebrate with them!" That is a hard teaching, even counterintuitive. *Who would celebrate good things going the way of the enemy?* Paul's point is that love doesn't look at people through the lens of spite and bitterness. Everyone deserves a fair trial, even our enemies. Love wants that for everyone, even the people we don't like.

First Corinthians 13:1–13 is divided into four parts:

The Necessity of Love (13:1–3)
The Graciousness of Love (13:4–6)
The Expansiveness of Love (13:7)
The Finality of Love (13:8–13)

Love at the Heart of the Christian Community

We have already addressed the first two sections. Let's look now at the third, the expansiveness of love (13:7). This is a staccato-style list of the expansiveness, openness, and breadth of love. *Agapē* carries all, believes all, hopes all, and endures all. Such a grandiose expression of love is hard to contemplate. It is easier, perhaps, to consider the opposite. Paul's list has to do with commitment; love is fiercely committed to the other. The opposite is giving up when things get rough or ugly. *Love doesn't give up!* Perhaps there is a subtext of Christ as the model of love. It is as if Paul is hinting this: Christ didn't drop you. Christ didn't lose faith in you. Christ didn't lose heart. Christ didn't give up.

The last section (13:8–13) is an eschatological reflection. Love is not a temporary or fleeting virtue. It outlasts all the other spiritual gifts because of the power God has vested in it. We learn from the letter that the Corinthians craved the most ostentatious spiritual gifts that would attract attention and perhaps even increase someone's social status. Paul was not interested in the optics of the spiritual gifts, but the impact, the way these gifts do what they were meant to do, fortify the community. Spiritual gifts are not a tool for personal success; at their best, they operate as means to bless others. That is why love is the greatest resource of all and will outlast anything else.

First Corinthians 13:1–13 is probably not a preformed hymn or pre-Pauline ancient Christian liturgy (as some scholars have thought in previous generations); I read it as a situationally inspired ode to love. We find a similar tribute to love in 1 Clement 49, which bears evidence of influence from Paul's language and imagery:

> Love unites us with God; love covers a multitude of sins; love endures all things, is patient in all things. There is nothing coarse, nothing arrogant in love. Love knows nothing of schisms, love leads no rebellions, love does everything in harmony. In love all the elect of God were made perfect; without love nothing is pleasing to God. In love the Master received us. Because of the love that he had for us, Jesus Christ our Lord, in accordance with God's will, gave his blood for us, and his flesh for our flesh, and his life for our lives. (1 Clement 49.5–6)[21]

---

21. See Robert M. Grant, *Paul in the Roman World: The Conflict at Corinth* (Louisville: Westminster John Knox, 2001), 41–42.

CHAPTER 8

Clement captured well Paul's dream of unity in community in the church. If there is no love among Christians, there is no Christ. If there is no spirit of kindness and grace, there is no Spirit. If there is no generous service and self-sacrifice for one another, there is no respect for the sacrifice of Christ.

LOVE, COMPASSION, AND GENEROSITY

In 2 Corinthians 8–9, Paul makes an extended appeal for the Corinthians to fully participate in the provision collection for the saints (see 1 Cor 16:1; Rom 15:22–29), which he later calls the "gift" (*charis*) and "ministry" (*diakonia*; 2 Cor 8:1–7). We can piece together that some churches had fallen on hard times and needed support. Paul was helping to organize and distribute gifts from the churches in his network, along with help from other leaders like Titus.[22] What does this have to do with love? Paul frames the Corinthians' participation in this endeavor as a demonstration of love and compassion (2 Cor 8:8). Apparently, the Corinthians had originally pledged their participation but for one reason or another appeared to need a word of encouragement to follow through. In these two chapters, we get insight into Paul's theological thinking about practical expressions of compassion and love through this exigency.

First, Paul points to a variety of churches throughout Macedonia (probably Philippi, Thessalonica, and Berea) who are model examples for the Corinthians.[23] They were experiencing hard times financially themselves but had a deep desire, even joy, for supporting their struggling brothers and sisters (2 Cor 8:2). Not only did these churches give, but they went far beyond in their generosity (8:3). Paul repeatedly points to the necessity of this being not a command or requirement (*epitagē*; 8:8) but a choice (*authairetos*; 8:3; see 9:7). These Corinthians had already shown passion and concern (*prothymia*; 8:11; 9:2), but this needed to be proven in action. Passion is good, but it must translate into action to carry out its intended effect of giving care. As Garland writes, "genuine love will show up in the checkbook."[24]

---

22. For a detailed study, see David J. Downs, *The Offering of the Gentiles: Paul's Collection for Jerusalem in Its Chronological, Cultural, and Cultic Contexts* (Grand Rapids: Eerdmans, 2016).

23. David Garland, *2 Corinthians*, NAC (Nashville: Broadman & Holman, 1999), 365.

24. Garland, *2 Corinthians*, 376.

Love at the Heart of the Christian Community

Love is mentioned explicitly only once in these two chapters on the collection for the saints, but Paul uses other terms and expressions that amount to the same thing, or they color a picture of tangible love. The most important key term in these chapters is "grace" (*charis*). Paul uses this term variously in reference to God's own grace (2 Cor 8:1, 9), blessing (8:4), thanksgiving (9:15), and the collection itself (8:7).[25] John Barclay makes clear that Paul thinks in terms of grace being showered down from on high, which leads to a cascading waterfall of gift-giving: "Paul figures human gift-giving as the product of divine gift-giving, a flow of divine *charis* into human *charis*, as if the human agents were conduits or channels.... [This] encourages the Corinthians to think of the world as a rich resource of open-ended possibility in which God is able to multiply resources, provided they are not hoarded but given."[26] But why does God give so graciously and empower his people to support each other so generously? The answer must be *love* (see Rom 5:6–11). This is reinforced in 2 Corinthians by Paul's christological statement: "For you know the generous act of our Lord Jesus Christ, that though he was rich, for your sakes he became poor, so that by his poverty you might become rich." Paul's reference to the wealth and poverty of Christ are not literally about money; I take Paul to mean something like he writes in Philippians 2:6–11, that the Son of God left his glory-filled station on high to humble himself in the incarnation and die a slave's death on a cross.[27] Augustine explains it this way: "He received our poverty, when He was clothed in the form of servant, emptying himself; lest thou shouldst dread His riches, and in thy beggarly state shouldst not dare approach Him. There, I say, He put on the form of a servant, there He was clothed with our poverty; there He made Himself poor, and us rich."[28] Fred Craddock reasons that Christ's poverty involves "the essence of ultimate reality coming under the conditions of human existence, the Eternal in time, the noncontingent being made subject

---

25. See John Barclay, *Paul and the Power of Grace* (Grand Rapids: Eerdmans, 2020), 133.

26. Barclay, *Paul and the Power of Grace*, 133; see also Barclay, "2 Corinthians," in *Eerdmans Commentary on the Bible*, ed. James D. G. Dunn (Grand Rapids: Eerdmans, 2003), 1365.

27. See the excellent discussion of this in Fred B. Craddock, "The Poverty of Christ: An Investigation of II Corinthians 8:9," *Interpretation* 22 (1968): 158–70.

28. Augustine, *Expositions on the Psalms* (*NPNF*[1] 8:495). See also Craddock, "Poverty of Christ," 166.

CHAPTER 8

to all the contingencies of our common experience."[29] This is different from contributing generously to a benevolence effort with money, but this is not just about money. Paul saw participation in this endeavor as an act of compassion aimed at changing lives for the better. The phrase *di' hymas* is crucial in 2 Corinthians 8:9: "for your sake, for your benefit." Christ gave up his glory and riches *for us*. This means *love*. No one gives up blessing and wealth for no reason. Christ did something difficult, stretching, hard, even unexpected, to bless and care for those in a state of *ptōcheia*, "poverty, emptiness." Again, this is love; this is how Paul defines *agapē*, compassion and care that gives and serves, proven as genuine and unyielding when it is at great cost and sacrifice.

And Paul uses this short and poetic christological narrative to serve as a model to inspire the Corinthians to make good on their pledge of support. God's great grace should inspire a spirit of abundance of generosity in the church. As Barclay sums up, "God's selfgiving in Christ rebounds in Christian devotion and creates multiple ripples of generosity in a wide pool of human relationships."[30]

In this chapter, we examined several texts from Paul that demonstrate his conviction that love is the ultimate mark of virtue, the goal of the Christian life. Occasionally, Paul pointed to loving God, but even more so he exhorted believers to love each other deeply, as a response to God's love for them in Jesus Christ. It is clear from the material we have covered that love is meant to be at the heart of the Christian community, the sign of Christ's lordship and the Spirit's transformative presence. In the next chapter, we will consider a bit of a hypothetical question but one that is crucial for rounding out our discussion of Paul and love. While we have ample evidence that Paul expected Christians to love one another, what did Paul think about the Christian posture toward the outsider, the unbeliever? From Paul's writings, we catch very few glimpses of his perspective on relationships with people outside of the church. And yet, this question is important for processing how Paul viewed humanity in general and the nature of the Christian mission.

---

29. Craddock, "Poverty of Christ," 166.
30. Barclay, "2 Corinthians," 1365.

9

Paul on Love of the Outsider

> The love "God poured into our hearts" (Rom 5:5) is precisely the love for those who are weak, ungodly, sinners at enmity with God (5:6–10). Given the reach of God's own love, it is difficult to imagine that Paul regards love "for one another" to end at the proverbial church door.
>
> —Beverly Gaventa[1]

So far in the book, we have discussed Paul's perspective on God's love for believers, believers' love for God, and believers' love for each other. But what about the outsider? Is the Christian priority of love an internal phenomenon, within the confines of the believing community, or does it pulsate outward beyond the walls of the church? Did Paul embody and teach the importance of loving *everyone*, believers and unbelievers alike? Another way to approach this subject is to put Paul to the good Samaritan test. Imagine Paul was on a short journey, for example from Lystra to Iconium, a distance of about sixty kilometers, and let's say he happened upon a traveler on the side of the road, who was bloodied and in clothes torn to rags, barely alive. Would Paul stop and check on the poor soul? And how would we know Paul's attitude toward such circumstances? In Paul's writings, we are privy to only a glimpse into his communication with churches or to leaders, texts primarily about challenges and disputes within Christian communities. We have precious little

---

1. Beverly Gaventa, *Romans*, NTL (Louisville: Westminster John Knox, 2024), 373.

CHAPTER 9

information about his interactions with unbelievers, let alone his thoughts about wider society. Therefore, if we are being honest, it is hard to answer the good Samaritan test. However, we have some clues in his writings that might point us toward his views and commitments in relation to the world based on his understanding of the gospel and the ways of God especially revealed in Jesus Christ. Before we investigate these clues, it is helpful in the first place to examine how Paul looked at the church as a bounded community.

Paul and the Church Community

It is clear from Paul's letters that his map of spiritual geography had defined borders; the church was a space unto itself where one was either inside or outside.[2] For example, Paul makes it clear to the Corinthian Christians that they should be invested in the spiritual and moral well-being of each other, but it is not their business to condemn or stand in judgment over those who are outside the church community (*tous exō*; 1 Cor 5:12).[3] That does not mean that Christians should be cut off from outsiders. Paul repeatedly affirms the importance of churches carrying a positive reputation in the wider society. To the Colossian Christians, he advises, "Conduct yourselves wisely toward outsiders [*tous exō*], making the most of the time. Let your speech always be gracious, seasoned with salt, so that you may know how you ought to answer everyone" (Col 4:5). The language of "conduct" (*peripateō*; lit., "walk") assumes ongoing, direct interaction with unbelievers. Most Christians did not have the choice to avoid non-Christians. There were so few Christians in the first century that most believers lived beside and worked with unbelievers on a constant basis. Paul wanted to ensure that Christians would be viewed by outsiders as women and men of integrity, goodness, and even charm. What Paul teaches the Thessalonian believers is also telling in terms of his assumption of Christians being

---

2. See Paul Trebilco, *Outsider Designations and Boundary Construction in the New Testament: Early Christian Communities and the Formation of Group Identity* (Cambridge: Cambridge University Press, 2017); and *Self-Designations and Group Identity in the New Testament* (Cambridge: Cambridge University Press, 2011); see also Wayne Meeks, *The First Urban Christians: The Social World of the Apostle Paul*, 2nd ed. (New Haven: Yale University Press, 2003), 94–96.

3. David E. Garland, *1 Corinthians*, BECNT (Grand Rapids: Baker, 2003), 190.

observed by outsiders and the crucial importance of respectable behavior for the common good in society: "we urge you, beloved, to do so more and more [in loving one another], to aspire to live quietly, to mind your own affairs, and to work with your hands, as we directed you, so that you may behave properly toward outsiders and be dependent on no one" (1 Thess 4:10–11). Again, this reinforces inside-outside boundaries but also attests to insiders (Christians) representing the faith in their life in society. Most scholars presume that 1 Thessalonians is one of Paul's earliest extant texts; if that is the case, it is fascinating to recognize that Christians could be associated in the minds of outsiders with their church community as a distinctive group in some way.

Now these boundaries are important for social identity formation for Paul within the believing communities he ministered to, but there are also signs that these boundary walls were permeable; that is, *outsiders* were sometimes *inside* the church, unbelievers *as unbelievers* intermixing with believers. We catch glimpses of this in Corinth when Paul addresses appropriate behavior of Christians in recognition of unbelievers in their midst. In chapter 14, in particular, Paul repeatedly insists that Christian behavior in worship and communal mutual edification should make sense to visiting outsiders and even carry meaning for them.

> Therefore, one who speaks in a tongue should pray for the power to interpret. For if I pray in a tongue, my spirit prays but my mind is unproductive. What should I do then? I will pray with the spirit, but I will pray with the mind also; I will sing praise with the spirit, but I will sing praise with the mind also. Otherwise, if you say a blessing with the spirit, how can anyone in the position of an *outsider* [*idiōtēs*] say the "Amen" to your thanksgiving, since the *outsider* [*idiōtēs*] does not know what you are saying? (1 Cor 14:13–16)

> If, therefore, the whole church comes together and all speak in tongues, and *outsiders* [*idiōtēs*] or unbelievers enter, will they not say that you are out of your mind? But if all prophesy, an unbeliever or *outsider* [*idiōtēs*] who enters is reproved by all and called to account by all. (1 Cor 14:23–24)

The language that is used here in 1 Corinthians 14 of "outsiders" is not the same as above, where it was literally "those who are outside" (*tous exō*; 1 Cor 5:12; Col 4:5). Here in the later part of 1 Corinthians, the term is *idiōtēs*, which literally

CHAPTER 9

means "self-person," as in an isolated individual. At times it can mean "unskilled" or "untrained" (Acts 4:13; 2 Cor 11:6), signaling someone not formally trained by a community, ignorant without proper apprenticeship. But in 1 Corinthians 14:13–16, 23–24, it has a different shade of meaning; here it refers to those who are not official members of the Christian community but are present, interested, and in some way involved.[4] Some have referred to these Corinthian *idiōtai* as the "uninitiated," or even "seekers"; we might also call them "fringe participants." "Outsiders" is a fair rendering, as long as it is clear that here they are active participants, and this is welcomed by Paul with a view toward encouraging belief.[5] Imagine your relatives have a big family reunion every five years, an elaborate affair in an exotic location with rich traditions like pie-making contests, major birthday and anniversary celebrations, and a big flag football game. Now, imagine one of the younger relatives brings their steady significant other (where there is a good chance they will get married in the future). In one sense, the significant other is an outsider, feeling awkward and unfamiliar with the traditions and cultural dynamics of the reunion. At the same time, they might be encouraged to participate in some of the aspects of the happenings, standing in a liminal position of not family and of welcomed attendee. These Corinthian "outsiders" function in a similar way; not fully insiders, but unbelievers who are in fact inside, participating in some aspects of the gathering.

Why is this important? And what does all of this have to do with our interest in Paul and love? It is easy to see that in general, Paul's teachings on love were focused on the body of Christ, the family of faith. And certainly Paul held all followers of Jesus accountable to mutual love in imitation of and response to God's own love through Jesus Christ. And that preoccupation that Paul had with forming Christian communities means that we know very little from his letters about his public ethics, how he thought about and treated people he bumped into outside the doors of these house churches. And yet, what we learn from a few of these texts about insider-outsider dynamics in Corinth is that Paul had compassion for the learning experience and participation of

---

4. See Bradley S. Billings, "The *Apistoi* and *Idiotes* in 1 Corinthians 14:20–25: The Ancient Context and Missiological Meaning," *Expository Times* 127 (2016): 227–85.

5. Note that in 1 Cor 14:24, Paul uses *apistoi* (unbelievers) as a synonym for these outsiders; they are welcomed participants, but they are not full-fledged members of God's family.

idiōtai, and in many ways, they were meant to be treated with the same warm embrace as fellow brothers and sisters. Now, Paul was clear that the *idiōtai* were not technically Christian brothers and sisters (yet); they were "unbelievers" (1 Cor 14:23), but they were sometimes present, and their presence meant that they would naturally be beneficiaries of Paul's many love statements and commands: "love one another with mutual affection" (Rom 12:9), "love one another" (Rom 13:8), walk in love (Rom 14:15), love by building one another up (1 Cor 8:1), love is the greatest good for the other (1 Cor 13:1–13), pursue love (1 Cor 14:1), "let all that you do be done in love" (1 Cor 16:14), become slaves to each other in love (Gal 5:13), the Spirit produces in you love (Gal 5:22), put up with one another in love (Eph 4:2), live in love (Eph 5:2), overflow with love for each other (Phil 1:9), clothe yourselves with love (Col 3:14). Rubbing shoulders with these *idiōtai* on a regular basis would naturally mean that the commitment to love, while formally aimed at the "family of faith," could not help but be extended to inside outsiders, like a real family today caring for a fiancé or close partner of a relative.

That sets up a natural transition to bring into the conversation another key piece of information about Paul's perspective on love and its potential application to outsiders—his affirmation of the neighbor-love command.[6] Twice Paul quotes Leviticus 19:18b ("love your neighbor as yourself"). In Galatians, it is in a summation of the whole Jewish law (Gal 5:14). In the context of the Galatian situation, it is clear that Paul's main focus was on the intracommunal life of the church, that they should serve and care for one another out of love, not "bite and devour" each other according to the flesh (Gal 5:15). In Romans 13:8–10, Paul offers an extended meditation on the virtue of love, in fulfillment of the law, and again summing up all of the commandments in the call to neighbor love (Rom 13:9). Here the word "neighbor" (*plēsion*) is repeated ("Love does no wrong to a neighbor" [13:10]), emphasizing love within the physical community. But given Paul's clear attitude that love (*agapē*) is the queen of all virtues and the truest compass for the Christian life (1 Cor 13:8–13), it would seem that neighbor love could and should be extended to anyone, just as Paul writes earlier in Romans: "Bless those who persecute you; bless and do not curse them" (Rom 12:14).[7] This is precisely the kind of wisdom Jesus offered

---

6. We have already explored this exegetically and canonically on pp. 78–88.

7. Trebilco makes the case that the reference to neighbor love in Romans 13:9–10

CHAPTER 9

(Luke 6:28), and this Lukan Jesus saying follows his command to love enemies (6:27). If Paul's views on love were formed in the same tradition, then neighbor love, though set at a default to one's own primary in-group community, should be applied even to other kinds of neighbors (like one's apartment neighbors) and extended even beyond to strangers and enemies.

This notion, that Paul not only had a vision for practicing virtues within the insider community but also to all, is affirmed in a few hortatory statements in his letters that use the language of "everyone" or "all":

Do good to all: "So then, whenever we have an opportunity, let us work for the good of *all*, and especially for those of the family of faith." (Gal 6:10)

Live peacefully with all: "Do not repay anyone evil for evil, but take thought for what is noble in the sight of *all*. If it is possible, so far as it depends on you, live peaceably with all." (Rom 12:17–18)

Be publicly known for gentleness: "Rejoice in the Lord always; again I will say, Rejoice. Let your gentleness be known to *everyone*." (Phil 4:4–5)

In Romans 12:17 and Philippians 4:4, it is unclear whether Paul's exhortations toward peace and gentleness extend to *all* within the Christian community or *all* within the world. The fact that both of these texts refer to developing a positive reputation in these areas ("in the sight of all"; "known to everyone") implies the broadest audience possible—that is, life in society, public life. This is reinforced in Galatians 6:10, where clearly "all" means "all people everywhere," because Paul goes on to mention the narrower circle in the following clause ("those of the family of faith"). Now, love (*agapē*) is not explicitly mentioned in these three "all/everyone" texts, but if Paul expected believers to publicly

---

should be taken as applicable to outsiders as well as insiders because in the previous section (13:1–7), Paul was writing about Christian engagement with Roman authorities; see Trebilco, *Outsider Designations*, 128–30; see also Hugh Montefiore, "Thou Shalt Love Thy Neighbor as Thyself," *Novum Testamentum* (1962): 157–70; Christopher N. Chandler, "'Love Your Neighbor as Yourself' (Lev. 19.18b) in Early Jewish-Christian Exegetical Practice and Missional Formulation," in *"What Does the Scripture Say?": Studies in the Function of Scripture in Early Judaism and Christianity*, ed. Craig A. Evans and H. Daniel Zacharias (London: T&T Clark, 2013), 47–54.

demonstrate goodness, peace, and gentleness, surely he would also want them to show love. So I think we have our answer to Paul and the good Samaritan question. If God made the first move in loving the ungodly, sinner and enemies (Rom 5:6–11), surely he would expect the same from his children, to show compassion to anyone they encounter.[8]

Luke's Portrait of the Benevolent Paul in Acts

While we don't really catch glimpses of Paul's direct encounters with unbelievers in his letters, we are given a much wider perspective on Paul's life and public ministry in the book of Acts. Scholars have differing views on the degree to which Luke's testimony about the early church reflects real events and conversations; we will be using this material to look at Paul from another perspective.[9] We will look at three scenes involving Luke's Paul in the book of Acts.

Scene One: Healing of the Crippled Man (Acts 14:8–18)

In Lystra, Paul and Barnabas encountered a man who wasn't able to walk. Luke makes it appear that this was a sort of chance encounter, but this man was listening in as Paul spoke to a crowd. Paul's attention was drawn to him ("looking

---

8. Michael J. Gorman comes to a similar conclusion in his *Becoming the Gospel: Paul, Participation, Mission* (Grand Rapids: Eerdmans, 2015), 96–99.

9. For helpful discussions of responsible comparison between Paul's letters and the Paul of Acts, see Stanley Porter, *The Paul of Acts* (Peabody, MA: Hendrickson, 2001), 187–206. On the historical reliability of Acts, I find Luke Timothy Johnson's discussion in *The Acts of the Apostles*, SP 5 (Collegeville, MN: Liturgical Press, 1992), helpful in terms of balance and nuance; Johnson recognizes that Luke stylizes the portrayal of Paul ("a man filled with the Holy Spirit, speaking God's word with boldness, working signs and wonders, and creating division among the people" [5]), but there is no reason to believe Luke fabricated whole stories. What we find is a recounting of history through a particular literary-theological lens. Johnson writes, "All historical writing, after all, demands a selection and creative shaping of materials, and all great histories have a large component of imagination. It is unrealistic to hold Luke to a standard of 'perfect factual accuracy,' failing which he is dismissed as a novelist. Narrative can be significantly shaped by an author's imagination and still report substantial historical information.... Recognizing the *ways* in which Luke literarily shapes his narrative, in fact, is an important step toward recognizing the *kind* of history he was attempting to write" (7).

at him intently"), and he just knew he had faith to be healed (Acts 14:9). So Paul called out, "Stand upright on your feet" (14:10). In that moment, he was healed, he jumped up and started to walk, and this was interpreted by the crowds as a sign of a theophany from Zeus and Hermes, Greek gods who were known to visit the realm of mortals in disguise and perform wonders (14:11–13). This is a bit of an unusual story in Acts, because it disrupts a normal preaching event where Paul (typically) proclaims the gospel and the crowd responds positively, negatively, or with some mixture. But in Lystra, the story doesn't make it to that speech's end and decision point; it appears that before concluding, Paul is moved to heal this man, and things get derailed when the crowds identify Paul and Barnabas as disguised deities. Before Paul and Barnabas could clear up this instance of mistaken identity, certain Antiochene and Iconion Jews arrive to sour the crowds toward them. Paul and Barnabas are stoned and thrown out, so brutally beaten that they were considered dead (14:19).

From this Lukan story, I think we have plausible evidence regarding how Paul viewed outsiders; he looked at the people he encountered with compassion. The specific terminology of "compassion" (e.g., *splanchnizomai*) is not found in this passage, but this story in Lystra parallels Acts 3, where Peter healed a disabled man near the temple gate. While compassion or love are not explicitly mentioned in either of these stories, they are narrated as chance encounters where an apostle stops and *atenizō* (looks intently, gazes), and then the healing occurs. It doesn't take much to connect the dots and observe the Spirit's influence and impact on the apostolic mission, not only on spreading the good news in word but also radiating outward to all places and people for the sake of the love and compassion of God that is demonstrated in these spontaneous healings.

Scene Two: Amazing Miracles in Ephesus (Acts 19:11–20)

Luke recounts that, during Paul's lengthy stay in Ephesus, he performed many astounding miracles by the work of God. He was so full of the Spirit that even objects he had touched (like aprons and handkerchiefs) retained spiritual power that could bring healing to the sick and could cast out demons (Acts 19:11–12). Jewish miracle workers who observed this phenomenon tried to replicate Paul's wonders but failed (19:13–14). Luke shares this detail to draw out the uniqueness of Paul's miracle-working power through the Spirit and the name of Jesus. Immediately, Paul's reputation spread to all the people in Ephesus, Jews and gentiles, and they all revered this *kyrios* called Jesus (19:18). We don't know exactly who were the people healed by the apostolic talismans, but some scholars have suggested that the specific mention of Paul's apron and handkerchiefs implies his garments or accessories from his workshop trade, as if local Ephesians sought him out, knowing his wondrous powers, and took them to their sick and spirit-possessed.[10] As Paul's ministry and message permeated the area, many revered this Jesus, and those who became believers repented of their sins, many of them renouncing sorcery. Luke portrays Paul's Ephesian ministry as very successful in affecting the culture of the entire city with the gospel. Again, the undertone seems to be Paul's very outward-facing ministry of word and wonders that healed and blessed many, especially the needy and suffering in Ephesus. If an Ephesian were to come to Paul's workshop and ask for one of his handkerchiefs to heal a sick relative, Luke seems to encourage you to see Paul as filled with the compassion of Christ and motivated to let the goodness of the gospel touch lives as the kingdom of God expands throughout the world. God's love for the world appears to be the invisible force driving the gospel mission outward to the furthest reaches.

Scene Three: Paul's Prison Ship Community and His Ministry in Malta (Acts 27:1–28:10)

Acts 27 recounts Paul's adventures on the high seas as his prisoner transport ship attempts to sail to Rome. We find Paul, under the most trying circumstances, taking charge of the seafaring community (which Luke mentions totals 276 souls in all).[11] On this treacherous voyage, we can imagine there

---

10. See F. F. Bruce, *The Book of the Acts*, NICNT (Grand Rapids: Eerdmans, 1988), 375; Ben Witherington III, *The Acts of the Apostles: A Socio-rhetorical Commentary* (Grand Rapids: Eerdmans, 1998), 579–80; James D. G. Dunn, *The Acts of the Apostles* (Grand Rapids: Eerdmans, 2016), 259; Mikeal Parsons finds it more likely that the mention of these textiles reflects Luke's depiction of Paul in the outfit of an orator (*Acts*, PCNT [Grand Rapids: Baker, 2008], 270); for a thorough (basically neutral) discussion, see Craig S. Keener, *Acts: An Exegetical Commentary* (Grand Rapids: Baker, 2014), 3:2840–41.

11. Some early Greek manuscript variants put the number at seventy-six; see

are a mixture of sailors, prisoners, and Roman soldiers.[12] No doubt, at the commencement of the journey, Paul was not in charge; Luke names a centurion called Julius (Acts 27:2). Julius ignored Paul's warnings about dangers ahead that would be costly, and sadly his predictions came to pass—a tempest swirled out of control, and the crew threw the cargo and tackle overboard to save their lives. Paul stepped up again to give leadership, sympathetic toward the passengers and crew who were starved and desperate. Not only did Paul try to encourage them (*euthymeō*; 27:22, 25), but he gave clear and direct instructions that would lead to their safety. One might take away from these events that Paul was simply acting in self-preservation—that is, saving the ship only to save himself. And perhaps that was a factor, but the picture Luke paints is more of a man who took pity on his terrified and exhausted fellow travelers; they had become a community by fate, and Paul was like a pastor to these troubled and helpless sheep. This is best demonstrated in his encouragement to take bread, almost like an emergency Lord's Supper where food was blessed, broken, and distributed (27:33–35), except this was a prisoner transport, not a church assembly. In fact, one wonders where they got bread for over two hundred people! One can only guess that they were emergency provisions, but the lack of explanation from Luke almost makes it appear that the bread's appearance or multiplication was some kind of quiet miracle. In any case, this warm-hearted scene in Luke's storm narrative offers a sense of Paul's concern and compassion for all the people on the boat, even the ones that treated him as a criminal.[13] It would have been easy for someone in Paul's position to turn a blind eye to passengers slipping into despair and jumping overboard to a watery death or succumbing to starvation. But he took seriously the prophecy that whoever stuck close to him would survive. Even when some had tried to escape of their own volition, Paul warned them that they could be saved only if they stayed together on the vessel (27:31).

Bruce M. Metzger, *A Textual Commentary on the Greek New Testament*, 4th ed. (New York: United Bible Societies, 1994), 442.

12. Dunn makes the case that the centurion would have commandeered a supply ship, or it may have been an imperial vessel that could accommodate his group (*Acts*, 338). Craig S. Keener includes the observation that many ancient sailors were slaves trained in nautical skills (*Acts*, NCBC [Cambridge: Cambridge University Press, 2020], 606).

13. See Patrick Schreiner, *Acts*, CSC (Nashville: Broadman & Holman, 2022), 657.

Paul on Love of the Outsider

While Luke did not reveal Paul's heart explicitly in this narrative sequence, we cannot help but see his unrelenting concern for everyone's well-being on the ship, where he would have probably been the only Christ-believer.[14] And yet, he protected their bodies and encouraged their hearts just like he would a church community.[15] And that same attitude continued as he was shipwrecked onto the barbarian island of Malta. When he tried to start a fire, a viper bit his hand, but Paul shook it off without any harm (Acts 28:1–5). The Maltans then concluded that, since Paul did not die, he must be a god (28:6). They showered Paul (and the shipwrecked survivors with him) with hospitality. When Paul learned about the illness of the father of the chief of the people, Publius, Paul voluntarily visited him and cured him through prayer and touch (28:7–8). This one act of grace and mercy led to all the Maltans bringing their sick friends and relatives to be healed by this foreign miracle worker, and Paul obliged. After that, the Maltans helped arrange for Paul and his company to make their way to Rome with ample supplies (like food and gear).

Scholars have wondered why Luke gives such extensive and detailed attention to the final sea voyage to Rome.[16] There is a clear theological emphasis on divine preservation and rescue from disaster and illness. But there is also this fascinating story of a *corpus mixtum* (soldiers, slave workers/sailors, prisoners) bonded together by fate and bad fortune, and Paul becomes their emergency leader. For several months, Paul was separated from a community of believers as he traveled with a prison cohort. This was his community. And the clear sense we get from this time is that Paul treated his traveling companions with the same charity and care that he would have shown fellow believers. This confirms what we have seen in the earlier scenes of compassion in Acts recounting Paul's engagement with unbelievers. We might conclude our short study

---

14. If Luke was an eyewitness, it was possible he accompanied Paul on this journey.

15. Sin Pan Ho argues that while at the beginning of the voyage there is a clear line of distinction separating the centurion Julius (authority) from Paul (the prisoner), by the end of chapter 27, they are on the same team, as it were; see "Changes in the Centurion on Paul's Last Journey to Rome," *Biblical Theology Bulletin* 52 (2022): 99–110.

16. See Warren Carter, "Aquatic Display: Navigating the Roman Imperial World in Acts 27," *New Testament Studies* 62 (2016): 79–96; Troy M. Troftgruben, "Slow Sailing in Acts: Suspense in the Final Sea Journey (Acts 27:1–28:15)," *Journal of Biblical Literature* 136 (2017): 949–68.

CHAPTER 9

of Paul's public ministry in Acts with this: Paul made a distinction between Christian and non-Christian when it came to faith but made no distinction when it came to compassion and care.[17] While the word "love" (*agapē*) never appears in Acts, there is clear evidence that Paul abided by the commandment "love your neighbor as yourself," as Jesus defined neighbor as the needy who is nearby, whoever they may be.

LOVE AT THE HEART OF CHRISTIAN MISSION

In this chapter, we have been pondering how Paul saw Christian engagement with unbelievers; we have proposed that, while Paul does not address this directly in his writings, there are signs that his teachings on love extended to everyone the believer might encounter, whether inside or outside of the church community. A correlate of this matter relates to Paul's conception of the Christian gospel mission itself. What expectations did Paul have for how and why the gospel is sent out into the world?[18] When it comes to evidence from Paul's letters alone (as opposed to including Acts' portrayal of Paul), there has been a preoccupation with the question whether Paul taught individual believers to evangelize or whether this was a special commission for apostles and evangelists. Brian K. Peterson, for example, argues that Paul does not express a need for Christians to make converts of outsiders.[19] I think that Peterson makes an important key point in his article, namely, that Paul's theology of mission is ecclesiocentric; Paul did not conceive of attracting unbelievers to the gospel outside of and detached from the vibrant community of the church. While *apostles* were sent out to spread the gospel, what we might call "ordi-

---

17. Keener, *Acts* (NCBC), 608, compares Paul's fellowship with his fellow seafarers to Jesus's dining with sinners (Luke 5:29–30; 7:34; 15:2; 19:7).

18. Peter T. O'Brien looks at a number of relevant Pauline texts about Paul's conception of the gospel mission in his *Gospel and Mission in the Writings of Paul: An Exegetical and Theological Analysis* (Grand Rapids: Baker, 1995).

19. See Brian K. Peterson, "Being the Church in Philippi," *Horizons in Biblical Theology* 30 (2008): 163–78; see also the scholarship Peterson cites that reinforce his findings: Martin Goodman, *Mission and Conversion* (Oxford: Clarendon, 1994), 94; Luke Timothy Johnson, "Proselytism and Witness in Earliest Christianity," in *Sharing the Book*, ed. John Witte Jr. and Richard C. Martin (Maryknoll, NY: Orbis Books, 1999), 154.

Paul on Love of the Outsider

nary Christians" were more likely to invite relatives, neighbors, and friends to visit their Christian community, hence the presence of unbelievers in the Corinthian church. But while we don't have direct commands from Paul that exhort believers to proclaim the message about Jesus verbally, we have important clues that point in this direction. How could the early church face such persecution for their faith if no one ever knew anything about their religious beliefs? Michael Gorman articulates this well:

> It is counterintuitive, and indeed it stretches the limits of credulity, to imagine that the early Pauline communities simply did good to their neighbors and assembled to worship Jesus as Lord, practicing communal cruciformity in a kind of holy huddle, even a publicly visible holy huddle, without ever explaining either kind of behavior to their friends or inviting them to participate. If such silence was the norm in the Pauline communities, specifically at Philippi, why did they co-suffer for the gospel with their community founder and their community Lord? Such suffering can only be explained if verbal witness—with or without the goal of conversion, but probably with that goal—was an integral and indeed routine aspect of the life of those in these Pauline communities.[20]

One of the key debated texts that *might* mention Christian evangelism is Philippians 2:16, where Paul refers to believers shining like stars in a dark world as they *epechō* the word of life. Scholars disagree about the meaning and translation of *epechō* in this context. Is Paul talking about the Philippian Christians *holding forth* the gospel, as in sharing the message publicly? Or is he talking about *holding fast* the gospel, showing commitment and fidelity despite opposition? When it comes to this verb in particular, I prefer the latter interpretation, but the earlier reference to shining like *phōstēres* (luminaries)

---

20. Gorman, *Becoming the Gospel*, 105; see similarly Dean Flemming, *Recovering the Full Mission of God: A Biblical Perspective on Being, Doing, and Telling* (Downers Grove, IL: IVP Academic, 2013), 182–85; also Flemming, *Why Mission?* (Nashville: Abingdon, 2015), 84–85. "Cruciformity" is Gorman's way of expressing the unique Christian lifestyle and culture of service and love in imitation of Jesus and culminating in his death on a cross for human sin (*Cruciformity: Paul's Narrative Spirituality of the Cross*, 20th anniversary ed. [Grand Rapids: Eerdmans, 2021]).

CHAPTER 9

still points to outward witness. James Ware refers to this as the "missionary purpose" of the church's life in the world.[21]

We have made a tentative case for early Christians having some sense of participation in the gospel mission to the world; yes, there were professionals (e.g., apostles and evangelists) who were especially called and commissioned to carry the good news of Jesus to the unbelieving world near and far, but there are some clues that all Christians should have open and gracious engagement with outsiders, and if Christ is Lord of *all*, then it stands to reason all Christians would naturally want to share Christ with them. We have one more insightful text to examine along these lines, Paul's explication of the motivation of his own apostolic mission, the love of Christ (2 Cor 5:11–15).

The Love of Christ and the Ministry of Reconciliation

We have had occasion to talk about 2 Corinthians in an earlier chapter (pp. 162–64), but here we will focus especially on Paul's self-reflection on his calling and ministry as an apostle. On various occasions throughout his letter, we catch glimpses of his background and commission as an apostle (Gal 1:1, 13–24; 1 Thess 1:5–8), but 2 Corinthians offers a deeper look, though there is a distinct rawness and anguish in this letter as Paul is defending his ministry as sincere and true. Second Corinthians finds Paul deeply hurt by his own spiritual children and confirming his apostleship; it reminds me of situations today where we see a good surgeon get dragged into an exhausting malpractice lawsuit without legitimacy. There is unnecessary shame, and the physician, who is trying to do good in the world, must submit themselves to intense scrutiny of every area of their life as the accusers look for something to criticize. The majority of the first six chapters of 2 Corinthians contains just such self-defense from Paul, a weary apostle who probably has days where he was wondering whether it is all worth it.

One might call the first half of 2 Corinthians "apostolic woes," as Paul lays out his innocence, honesty, and commitment to the gospel (and churches, like the one in Corinth) even though he must endure great trials, suffering, and public shame. He begins with a certain dangerous event in Asia (2 Cor 1:8–11),

---

21. James P. Ware, *Paul and the Mission of the Church: Philippians in Ancient Jewish Context* (Grand Rapids: Baker, 2011), 254; see 251–56.

where his life was on the line; he defends himself against accusations of duplicity from the Corinthians (1:12, 15–22). He repudiates any question of pride and self-commendation (3:1–3, 4–6) and returns again to a more thorough self-defense in chapter 4. He has never engaged in shameful behavior or deceitful activity (4:2), Paul explains, and he does not preach about his own greatness (4:5). We will give chapter 5 special attention in a moment, but it is worth jumping ahead to note two texts where he provides catalogs of his trials and sufferings (6:3–10; 11:22–29). Paul had survived great troubles and obstacles and had done his best to endure with integrity and honor. Some accused him of being weak and unimpressive, the messenger (Paul) hardly reflecting the glory of the message (the gospel of God), the supposed preacher of life and light looking more like darkness and decay. This is where his famous "treasure in earthen vessels" discourse comes in (4:7–12). The glory of God's gospel in Jesus Christ is priceless, Paul argues, but carried within weak vessels, and it requires spiritual insight and intuition to look beyond the humble container to recognize the inner treasure.

With this epistolary context in mind, let's take a closer look at the driving force behind this difficult apostolic ministry to which Paul has been called.

> Therefore, knowing the fear of the Lord, we try to persuade others; but we ourselves are well known to God, and I hope that we are also well known to your consciences. We are not commending ourselves to you again, but giving you an opportunity to boast about us, so that you may be able to answer those who boast in outward appearance and not in the heart. For if we are beside ourselves, it is for God; if we are in our right mind, it is for you. For the love of Christ [*hē agapē tou Christou*] urges us on, because we are convinced that one has died for all; therefore all have died. And he died for all, so that those who live might live no longer for themselves, but for him who died and was raised for them. (2 Cor 5:11–15)

In the previous section of the letter, Paul had been talking about living in this world with a singular focus on pleasing God (and not mortals; 2 Cor 5:9), knowing the future judgment of Christ.[22] The whole of 5:11–15, then, is an

---

22. See Frank Matera, *II Corinthians*, NTL (Louisville: Westminster John Knox, 2013), 129.

explication of the motivational force that drives his apostolic ministry—not popularity, greed, or the ability to manipulate others but deep reverence for the Lord. Paul's heart and soul are laid bare before God, and he has a clean conscience before the Corinthians as well (5:11b). There is much debate and discussion in scholarship about v. 13; the view I find most persuasive is that *exestēmen* ("we are beside ourselves") refers to ecstatic trances, where Paul sees visions and has heavenly experiences in the Spirit; and *sōphronoumen* ("in right mind"), then, refers to his normal mode.[23] In the Greek world, trances were a sign of a direct connection to the divine realm, much prized and admired. In that case, Paul was not facing criticism for having such ecstatic experiences, but in fact the opposite—Paul was not showcasing his visions publicly to prove his divine commission. Furnish offers Paul's perspective on the matter: "Ecstasy is not a benefit for others. His apostleship is not fulfilled by displays of religious frenzy, but by his sober-minded *persuading people* of the gospel and by his service to those who receive it. Paul's concern in these verses—as it has been already a number of times in this letter—is to say that his apostolate is validated by nothing else but the congregation's own experience of having been established and nurtured by its preaching and its pastoral care."[24]

Throughout this passage, Paul claims that he has done everything above board, his actions innocent, his motives pure and transparent. This is taken to the next level in v. 14a: "For the love of Christ urges us on." The genitive phrase *hē agapē tou Christou* could mean Paul's love for Christ (Greek objective genitive) or Christ's own love (Greek subjective genitive). Most scholars prefer the second option, in part because immediately following v. 14a is Paul's mention of the self-sacrificial death of Christ (2 Cor 5:14b–15). Also, what Paul writes at the end of the letter focuses on divine love and care: "The grace of the Lord Jesus Christ, the love of God, and the communion of the Holy Spirit be with all of you" (13:13). The essence of the gospel is the saving work and message of God who loved these estranged and hostile creatures through the incarnation, death, and resurrection of his Son, Jesus Christ. When Paul talks about the apostolic engine of the "love of Christ," it is common for scholars to imagine this

---

23. For a complete discussion of the various views on this verse, see Margaret E. Thrall, *A Critical and Exegetical Commentary on the Second Epistle to the Corinthians*, ICC (Edinburgh: T&T Clark, 1994–2000), 1:405–7.

24. Victor P. Furnish, *II Corinthians*, AB (New Haven: Yale University Press, 2021), 325.

Paul on Love of the Outsider

in terms of Paul's own experience of being loved; so Raymond Collins writes, "The love that Christ has for the apostle overpowers him. It takes control of him and directs him to do what he does."[25] I think the subjective genitive reading is correct; that is, Paul *is* referring to Christ's love. But I take the object of that love in a broader sense, namely, Christ loves the world, and the true apostles are vessels of that ministry of divine love and reconciliation.[26] The main verb in 5:14a is *synechō*, referring to pressure or compulsion (see Acts 18:5). Paul was driven primarily and forcefully by Christ's love mission in the world, and thus his apostolic ministry has no room for his pride or ego. He makes clear that his gospel message entails the death of Christ that leads to the death of all those in Christ (2 Cor 5:14b). That means death to their selfish ways, what he calls elsewhere "the old self" (*ho palaios anthrōpos*; Rom 6:6; Col 3:9; Eph 4:22). And what comes after that is release from pursuit of self-glory and pleasure, and exclusive commitment only and always to the one who died and was raised for them (2 Cor 5:15). Paul is trying to say to his suspicious readers this: If I preached this death to self/life committed to Christ, how could I live such hypocrisy by veiling sinister motives in my relationship with you? He affirms in this passage, and throughout all of 2 Corinthians, that he has always tried to act out of love for them (even when hard decisions had to be made), and that love was a channel of Christ's love that seeks to transform all things into God's own goodness.[27]

Perhaps inadvertently, we catch in this passage a glimpse of Paul's apostolic ministry manifesto, the driving passion of his mission. When Paul preached the gospel throughout the Roman Empire to the gentiles, he was empowered by Christ's love for the world, which propelled him to preach good news for the salvation of all. In a sense, then, Paul was not simply called to deliver a message

---

25. Raymond F. Collins, *2 Corinthians*, PCNT (Grand Rapids: Baker, 2013), 118; see also Anthony Thiselton, *2 Corinthians: A Short Exegetical and Pastoral Commentary* (Eugene, OR: Cascade, 2019), 71; Thomas Stegman, *The Character of Jesus: The Linchpin to Paul's Argument in 2 Corinthians* (Rome: Pontifical Biblical Institute, 2005), 168–70.

26. See Furnish, *II Corinthians*, 325; Thrall, *Second Epistle to the Corinthians*, 408.

27. See George Guthrie, *2 Corinthians*, BECNT (Grand Rapids: Baker, 2015), 304; also W. Hulitt Gloer, "Ambassadors of Reconciliation: Paul's Genius in Applying the Gospel in a Multi-cultural World; 2 Corinthians 5:14–21," *Review and Expositor* (2007): 589–601.

CHAPTER 9

to the world but to *love* the world, and this message was the best way to do that. But it stands to reason that other acts of love would also be produced by this compelling power of Christ's love (like the good Samaritan test question we began this chapter with). Love, it appears, is not only at the heart of God's relationship with his people, and his people's relationship with God, and the actions and virtues between believing brothers and sisters but also the driving force for engagement, mission, and ministry in the wider world, whether encountering neighbor, stranger, friend, or enemy.

10

Ephesians and Paul's Theology of Love

> God, who is rich in mercy, because of the generous love that he has for us, brought us back to life with Christ, even though we were dead in our transgression.
>
> —Ephesians 2:4–5, my translation

As we bring this book on Paul and love to a close, I find it fitting to end with the teachings on love in Ephesians for a few reasons. First, Ephesians is rightly labeled the "quintessence of Paulinism."[1] Whether one believes it is a genuine Pauline letter (which I am inclined to conclude), or the work of a student or disciple of the apostle, it captures in one place several key themes of Paul's teachings. It functions as a kind of greatest hits of his apostolic proclamation, reflecting and expanding on themes especially prominent in Romans, Galatians, and Colossians, such as divine supremacy and victory over death, perseverance in suffering, the transformed life under the lordship of Christ through the Spirit, unity of Jews and gentiles in the church, and holiness and purity in daily living in Christ. In some ways, Ephesians jumps from one topic to another (e.g., 2:11; 3:14; 4:1, 17, 25; 6:10). But if there is a case to be made for a thematic strand running throughout the whole of Ephesians, it would be

---

1. A. S. Peake, "The Quintessence of Paulinism," *Bulletin of the John Rylands University Library of Manchester* 4 (1917–1918): 285–311; later taken up by F. F. Bruce, *Paul: Apostle of the Heart Set Free* (Grand Rapids: Eerdmans, 1977), 424.

Paul's appeal to love (especially forms of *agapē*).[2] Here is a quick summary of the love language in the letter:

Believers are chosen through God's love (1:4).
Christ is God's Beloved (1:6).
God has deep love for sinners (2:4).
The indwelling Christ helps believers grow through his love (3:17).
The love of Christ fills believers with God's own fullness (3:19).
Believers ought to be patient with one another out of love (4:2).
Believers ought to speak the truth to one another with love (4:15).
The members of the church body promote growth together through love (4:16).
Believers are beloved children of God (5:1).
Believers imitate God by living in a loving way, following the example of Christ's love and self-giving (5:2).
Christian husbands must love their wives, just as Christ loved the church in his self-giving (5:25, 28, 33).
Tychicus is a beloved ministry partner (6:21).
Paul offers a final blessing of love and peace and exhorts the readers toward an undying love for Christ (6:23).

This is by far the most love-saturated Pauline letter; references to love appear in every chapter, and love is certainly a guiding element of almost every section of the letter. But it would be shortsighted to factor only uses of *agapē* (and cognates) into this picture. Paul uses varied vocabulary to affirm the same ideas, namely, the care of God and the need to care for one another. We will be presenting an exposition of Ephesians in this chapter, making the case that Paul came to see the

---

2. We will not engage in this chapter with Ephesians scholarship in depth; it serves more as my own running exposition. But for more scholarship on the subject of love in Ephesians, I recommend Michael J. Gorman, *Cruciformity: Paul's Narrative Spirituality of the Cross*, 20th anniversary ed. (Grand Rapids: Eerdmans, 2021), 261–66; Oda Wischmeyer, *Love as* Agape: *The Early Christian Concept and Modern Discourse* (Waco, TX: Baylor University Press, 2021), 100–107; on the related topic of grace in Ephesians, see John K. Goodrich, "According to the Riches of His Grace," in *The New Perspective on Grace: Paul and the Gospel after* Paul and the Gift, ed. Edward Adams et al. (Grand Rapids: Eerdmans, 2023), 105–28.

gospel itself and its implications and goals in terms of love, divine and human. Here are some of the other key terms that we will note in relationship to love as we walk through Ephesians: "grace/favor/gift" (*charis, charitaō, charizomai, dōron, didōmi*), "blood [of self-offering]" (*haima*), "lavishness/abundance [of blessing]" (*ploutos/plousios, perisseuō, ekperissou, hyperballō, megethos*), "mercy" (*eleos*), "kindness" (*chrēstotēs*), "peace" (*eirēnē*), "direct access [to the Father]" (*prosagōgē*), "fullness [in God]" (*plērōma*), "support" (*oikodomē* and cognates, *thalpō*), "nourishment" (*ektrephō*), "benevolence" (*eunoia*), and "fidelity" (*pistis*).

Another important aspect of Ephesians is kinship language, which is closely associated with being a part of a new loving family through Christ. To be called child/son/heir, to have a home with God, and to hold a deposit of a future inheritance are all ways of underscoring God's commitment and care for the lost and abandoned; in the gospel of Jesus Christ, God turns enemies and strangers into precious children who share the same belovedness the Father extends only to his Son.

I want to say a quick word about the possible situation behind Ephesians before turning to the text in detail. Unlike many of Paul's other letters, it is not clear from reading Ephesians that there is an urgent situation in Ephesus that he needed to address. There do not appear to be false teachers plaguing the community, or fatal schisms, or a need for Paul to defend himself or clear the air. Aside from the letter carrier, Tychicus, there are no specific people mentioned; the letter has a timeless quality. That is to say, it does not appear to be an occasional letter, which sets it apart from his other extant letters.

Another feature that stands out in Ephesians is the liturgical style of writing, making it a sort of epistolary homily on love. There are too few details that clue the modern reader into any kind of exigency that sparked this text. If it is authentic, we have to use some imagination and guesswork to hypothesize a scenario. I imagine that Paul, in prison shackles, is inevitably thinking about his life, his apostolic ministry, and—given the possibility of his demise—his legacy. Ephesians strikes me as an all-in-one of Paul's most common and most important preaching messages relevant to virtually all gentiles; perhaps he sent versions of this "greatest hits" compilation to several churches and slightly tailored each one to the audience, possibly modifying the only extant version to the Ephesians to engage a bit more with fear of spiritual powers in the heavens. Whatever the exact case, one thing is clear: if this is a gospel homily in epistolary form, the main message of Paul's kerygmatic preaching dwells on *love*: love from God in Jesus Christ, love expected for God from believers, and love for one another as the family of God is built up into an organic temple home in praise of the Lord.

Below, we will go through Ephesians section by section and note what Paul has to say about the gospel of love: its origins in the loving God, its demonstration in Jesus Christ, its efficacy through the Holy Spirit, and its expression and exercise in the church. The translation that is used in this chapter is my own.

A Secure Hope by the Grace of God (1:1–14)

> Paul, apostle of Christ Jesus through the will of God—to the holy people in Ephesus, the faithful believers[3] in Christ Jesus.
> Grace to you and peace from God our Father and the Lord Jesus Christ.
> Blessed be the God and Father of our Lord Jesus Christ, the one who blessed us with every spiritual blessing in the heavens in Christ. Similarly, he chose us through Christ[4] before the foundation of the world, that we should be holy and blameless before him, shaped by his love.[5] And he set our future for being adopted into his family through Jesus Christ to be like him, all this to fulfill what is pleasing to his will, and to bring praise to his glorious grace, which he bestowed on us in the Beloved One.
> In him we have redemption through his blood, the forgiveness of transgressions, according to his lavish grace given abundantly to us.
> With all wisdom and insight, he has made known to us the secret plan of his will, according to his good intention, which he established in advance

---

3. *pistois*. While it is conventional to translate this as "believers," I think Paul would use a participial form of *pisteuō* if that was his primary intent. Here I think he means those believers who are clinging on to Christ, hence "faithful believers." These Ephesian Christians are part of the holy family, committed to Christ and Christ's community.

4. *en autō*. Ephesians frequently includes a lot of "in him/in it" statements, and the referent and the meaning are sometimes unclear. Here I take it as a reference marking agency, which points back to Christ at the end of v. 3.

5. *en agapē*. This could refer to God's intention for believers to live in love, or God's own love that is formative and guides his plan for these chosen people. I slightly prefer the latter.

Ephesians and Paul's Theology of Love

for us, set according to the master plan regarding the fulfillment of the seasons of time. This plan is to gather up all things in Christ, both heavenly things and earthly things.

And in Christ also we stand to inherit, destined according to the purpose of he who works [these things out] according to the counsel of his will. And this is so that we may become, according to the praise of his glory, those who experienced hope in advance in Christ.

In him also you were sealed by the Holy Spirit who was promised, after you heard the word of truth, the gospel of your salvation, and also when you believed in him. The Spirit is a deposit of our inheritance, with a view toward the redemption of [God's own] possession [which is us], to the praise of his glory.

The letter begins with a basic prescript, which reminds the Ephesians of their status as holy and Paul's encouragement that they have been faithful believers. Typically, Paul then moves into a thanksgiving statement, but in this case he transitions to a benediction, blessing the God who himself blesses humble mortals. Paul reassures the Ephesians that they have been chosen, *hand picked*, by God. Because of God's love (*agapē*), he has crafted a plan to redeem them as holy and blameless (Eph 1:4). All of this happens through adoption into God's family through Christ the Son.

Note, too, the emphasis on grace. A more literal rendering of v. 6 would look something like this: "to the praise of the glory of his grace [*charis*], which he graced [*charitoō*] to us in the Beloved." This heavenly adoption also involves being released from the debts and penalties of transgression, through Christ's self-given blood (Eph 1:7). As Paul ponders this, he is again reminded of divine grace, lavishly given (*ploutos*) and in abundance (*perisseuō*).

These early verses set the tone and indicate key themes in Ephesians related to confidence in the plan of God to bless and redeem humanity, both Jews and gentiles. Over and over again, Paul makes clear God's interest and motivation, namely, his love. God does not act begrudgingly, and he is not stingy with support; rather, he gives lavishly, he loves deeply, and he blesses abundantly. The keyword *huiothesia* (1:5) refers to adoption and establishes a clear context for this divine blessing. God's plan is to make outsiders and even enemies into beloved family.

CHAPTER 10

The Story of the Cosmos (1:15–23)

> On account of this—after I heard about the faith you have in the Lord Jesus and your love[6] toward all the holy people—I have not stopped giving thanks [to God] for you, as I remember you in my prayers, [and here is the focus on my petition for you:] that the God of our Lord Jesus Christ, the Father of glory, would give you a spirit[7] of wisdom and revelation in [deeper] knowledge of him. [I pray that] the eyes of your heart may be filled with light so that you know exactly what the hope is to which he has called you, [keenly aware] of the abundance of his glorious inheritance among [his] holy people, what is the unfathomable grandeur of his power for the sake of us, believers, and the movement of his mighty strength.
>
> He has put this [same] power to work in the Messiah, when he raised him from the realm of the dead, and gave him a ruling seat at his right hand in the heavens. [And Christ] reigns far above every ruler and authority and power and sovereign and every other name that could be named, not only in this age but also in the age to come. And [God] has subordinated all things under [Christ's] feet and appointed him to be head over all things for the sake of the church, which is his body, the fullness of the one who fills up all things in all.

Here Paul presents his more traditional word of thanksgiving, showing appreciation for the spiritual maturity of the Ephesian believers (cf. Col 1:4). His prayer is for their continual insight into the riches they have by God's hand. We need not assume that Paul was responding to any severe deficiencies or problems in terms of situation, certainly not on the level we see in 1 Corinthians. One can imagine that Paul knows the kinds of things most believers struggle with—trust and hope—and he can assume as much for the Ephesians. Again, the focus is on a strong hope—that is, knowing the glorious inheritance that awaits these children of God.

---

6. *tēn agapēn*. Some ancient manuscripts have *agapēn* (love), but other early Greek witnesses to Ephesians do not. Because it is preferred in NA[28], we have included it here. For a text-critical discussion, see Andrew T. Lincoln, *Ephesians*, WBC (Dallas: Word, 1990), 46–47.

7. *pneuma sophias kai apokalypseōs*. It is unclear whether this refers to the Holy Spirit or the human spirit; this may be a both-and: the Spirit is the one who enables believers to grow in wisdom and insight.

Ephesians and Paul's Theology of Love

There is a clear liturgical ring in 1:18–19, with the repetition of *tis/ti* ("what is . . .") and the piling up of synonyms (also known as pleonasm): "energy" (*energeia*), "strength" (*kratos*), "might" (*ischys*). And similar to the earlier section of Ephesians, Paul uses grandiose language in relation to the work of God: *ploutos* (wealth), *hyperballon* (superior), *megethos* (greatness).

The last part of this section (vv. 20–23) focuses on Christ and the church. The power with which God is securing the future of the Ephesian believers has already been demonstrated in the resurrection of Christ. And Christ now rules on a seat of power higher than any imaginable being on earth or in heaven. Paul ends by drawing attention to the church, the body of Christ. The church has the privilege of being filled up with Christ's own fullness; there is no safer and more secure place to be than in that beloved community under Christ's attentive protection.

THE CHRISTIAN STORY: FROM SIN AND DEATH TO GOODNESS AND LIFE (2:1–10)

> And as for you—formerly you were dead because of your transgressions and sins, as you used to live your lives according to the way[8] of this world, according to the prince of the air realm,[9] that spirit now at work among the sons of disobedience. Back then all of us lived our lives driven by the desires of our flesh, carrying out the wishes of the flesh and [such wicked] thoughts;[10] we were then by nature[11] children destined for condemnation, just like everyone else. But God, who is rich in mercy, because of the generous love that he has for us, brought us back to life with Christ, even

---

8. *ton aiōna tou kosmou toutou*. Lit., "the age of this world," which appears to mean the state or nature of this world in a particular era.

9. *ton archonta tēs exousias tou aeros*. Lit., "the ruler of the authority of the air." The reference to air is unclear. It could be a synonym for heavens, but that would attribute to this figure powers rivaling Christ (which would contradict Eph 1:22–23). Another possibility is that *aer* here indicates the unseen realm of spiritual powers, much like the invisible wind that blows and affects visible objects. See this interpretation by Theodore of Mopsuestia (*Theodore of Mopsuestia: The Commentaries on the Minor Epistles of Paul*, trans. Rowan A. Greer [Atlanta: Society of Biblical Literature, 2010], 215).

10. *tōn dianoiōn*. Lit., "the thoughts." This phrase is elliptical, and given the reference to the flesh, it seems appropriate to assume wicked thoughts.

11. *Physei*. The reference here to "nature" doesn't mean biology or birth but the state of being "in Adam" (1 Cor 15:22).

though we were dead in our transgressions—remember: you are saved by grace—and he raised you along with him and gave you a seat with him in the heavens through Christ Jesus. He did this to demonstrate in the coming ages the incomparable wealth of his grace [manifesting] in his kindness for us through Christ Jesus. Again, by grace you are saved through faith. And this salvation is not something you had coming to you; it is a gift from God. It is not deserved because of what you have done, so there can be no boasting. In fact, we are the product of what God has done, created in Christ Jesus for good works, which God has prepared ahead of time so we can live a fruitful[12] lifestyle.

If Ephesians 1 ended with divine grace on the cosmological level, and then also the ecclesiological level, then chapter 2 transitions to focus on the individual. Paul here tells a before-and-after story. Previously, believers were dead in their sin, following the way of the world, driven by flesh and under the threat of judgment. Paul paints a bleak picture; without intervention, the situation is completely hopeless. But v. 4 signals the great reversal: *But God!* God is generously merciful and full of love (lit., "loved us with great love") and brought us back to life through Christ. And at the end of v. 5, we find an outburst that interrupts the flow of the sentence: "you are saved by grace"! There is a clear wow moment; Paul is rotting in prison in chains but has a big grin on his face as he ponders the limitless love and favor of God, the relentless rescuer.

Paul offers a series of Greek *syn-* verbs to show the extent of God's salvific work: *syzōopoieō* (make alive together with), *synegeirō* (raised up together with), *synkathizō* (granted a seat together with). God not only brought believers back to life with his resurrection power but exalted them with Christ and gave them seats of honor and authority—these are immense privileges undeserving of mere mortals, let alone sinners and transgressors. But again, Paul points out the abundant graciousness and kindness of God. It is not earned. It is not a right. It is simply the way of God to love and bless. There is a clear implication that believers, in response to this grace and kindness, ought to live in the ways of God, imitating him in doing what is good, not to pay God back but to fulfill human destiny of being good in the world as God is good.

12. *en autois*. This refers back to the "good works," hence a fruitful or productive lifestyle.

Gentiles Brought Near, Made One, and Given a Home in Christ (2:11–22)

Therefore, remember that back then you were gentiles in your flesh, called the uncircumcised by those called the circumcision, in respect to a bodily procedure performed by human hands. And you were without Christ back then, considered outsiders by the commonwealth of Israel, strangers to the covenants of promise, people [living] in the world without hope and without God.

But now in Christ Jesus you, formerly far away, were brought close by the blood of Christ. And he is our peace, the one who has made both groups into one [people], removing the dividing wall, and removing hostility [between the two] by his flesh [in death]. [In his death] he also abolished the law of commandments and decrees, so he could create in himself one new humanity in place of the two, establishing peace. And he reconciled both to God in one body through the cross, having killed the hostility in his work.

When Christ came, he preached the good news of peace to you who were far away [i.e., gentiles] and also the good news of peace to those who were near [i.e., Jews]. And through Christ we have special access—that is, both groups—to the Father through one Spirit. So then, you are no longer strangers and foreigners; on the contrary, you are equal fellow citizens[13] of all the holy people, and [you are] all fully family members of the household of God. And this household has been built on the foundation of the apostles and prophets, with Christ Jesus as the cornerstone, and in relationship to him the whole structure is joined together and grows into a holy temple for the Lord; in it also you are formed together as a house for God to dwell in the Spirit.

Paul engages in another before-and-after discourse, this time the status of the gentile Ephesian believers, once outsiders in terms of the covenantal promises and blessings of God, now made full participants through Christ. Paul paints a vivid picture of life outside of the commonwealth of Israel as no-man's-land, no hope, no relationship with God. But God himself invited these outsiders

---

13. *sympolitai*. The *sym-* part of this term, in context here, implies equality.

CHAPTER 10

in. The mechanism for this change is the blood of Christ. No exact concept of atonement is explicated here. The reference to the flesh of Christ associates this blood with his death, further reinforced by the mention of the cross. This is a self-sacrifice with a mission and purpose, namely, to kill hostility and division and bring peace and unity. The end goal is that this new single family of Jews and gentiles come together as one to become an organic temple, a household community knit together by the Spirit.

Love is not mentioned in this passage explicitly, but the reference to blood would take the reader back to Ephesians 1:7: redemption comes through Christ's *blood* according to the riches of his *grace* (see similarly Rev 1:5). The giving of one's own precious blood, especially unto death, is never done lightly; such self-sacrifice indicates preserving something or someone precious and valuable. Christ secured peace and brought unity and flourishing on account of deep love.

The ultimate purpose of this passage is to underscore not only the gracious self-giving of Christ but the final goal of reconciling Jew and gentile toward the end of building one big family, composed of equal siblings who together become a special dwelling place for God in the Spirit.

Paul's Mission to Preach the Good News of God's Love to Gentiles (3:1–19, 20)

> For this reason, I, Paul, prisoner of Christ Jesus for the sake of you gentiles—surely you have heard of the plan and grace of God given to me in relationship to you—according to a revelation made known to me, the secret,[14] as I already mentioned briefly [2:11–22]. I want you to read and learn from my understanding of the secret of Christ; in former generations it was unknown to mortals,[15] and now at last revealed to his holy apostles and prophets through the Spirit: the gentiles have become full participants in the inheritance and full[16] participants in the body and can fully embrace

---

14. *to mystērion*. While we do get the English "mystery" from this Greek word, Paul's usage is about a divine redemption plan involving gentiles that was hidden or kept secret until it was revealed; thus, I prefer the translation "the secret."

15. Greek: *tois huiois tōn anthrōpōn* (lit., "the sons of man").

16. My use of "full/fully" in this verse is meant to capture Paul's repeated use of

the promise in Christ Jesus through the gospel. For this gospel I became a servant according to the gift of God's grace given to me according to the operation of his power—to even me, least of all the saints, this grace was given, that I should preach the good news to the gentiles about the unfathomable wealth of Christ, and to shed light on what is the unfolding of the secret once hidden for many ages by God, the creator of all things, and now the manifold wisdom of God might be made known to all rulers and powers in the heavens. All this in accordance with an eternal purpose that he established in Christ Jesus our Lord, in whom we have open access with confidence through faith in him. So I ask in prayer that you not be discouraged by my afflictions, which I endure for your sake—this is your glory.

For this reason, I bow my knees to the Father, from whom every type of fatherhood takes its name in the heavens or on earth, praying[17] that he would give you, according to his rich glory, the power to be strengthened through his Spirit in your inner being,[18] making a home by faith for Christ to live in your hearts in love, rooted and grounded in that love so that you grow stronger and can comprehend with all the saints what is the breadth and length and height and depth, indeed to know the love of Christ—so abundant you will never fully comprehend—but the goal is that you become filled with all the fullness of God.

Now to the one who is able to go above and beyond what we ask in prayer or even imagine according to his power at work in us, to him be the glory in the church and in Christ Jesus for all generations for ever and ever. Amen.

In chapter 3, Paul continues with his focus on the good news for gentiles, but now with more of a personal reminiscence. Paul reflects on his own commission to reveal "the secret of Christ," welcoming gentiles as full members of the family of God through Jesus Christ. The gospel he preaches is ultimately about "the unfathomable wealth of Christ" (*anexichniaston ploutos tou Christou*; 3:8). As far as the gentiles are concerned, they have been fully integrated into the family of God through Jesus Christ (3:6). As far as Paul's own self-understanding, he knows

---

the prefix *syn*: *synklēronoma* (coheirs), *syssōma* (comembers of the body), *symmetocha* (coparticipants).

17. "Praying." This is inferred from Paul's reference to bowing to the Father.
18. Greek: *ton esō anthrōpon* ("the inside person").

CHAPTER 10

by experience the generosity of God, who chose him to carry this awesome commission, though he was formerly a violent persecutor of the church.

Paul's prayer for these Ephesian believers is that their church becomes a welcome home for Christ, as the community operates in a genuine spirit of love. In fact, the very *foundation* of this Christ-home should be the spirit of love (*en agapē errizōmenoi kai tethemeliōmenoi*; 3:17). No doubt the expectations for this communal love are set by God's own grace and love that Paul repeatedly points to in this letter.

Gifted for Oneness (4:1–16)

> So then, I, a prisoner in the Lord, urge you to live your lives in a manner worthy of the calling to which you were called, with true humility and gentleness, and with sincere patience,[19] to stay committed to one another out of love, enthusiastic about maintaining oneness[20] through the Spirit, bound like a chain[21] as a community for the sake of peace: one body, one Spirit, just as you were called into a one-hope calling; one Lord, one faith, one baptism, one God and Father of all, the one who is above everything, who reigns everywhere and transforms within everyone.
>
> Each and every one of us was given a special gift by grace measured out carefully by Christ. Thus, the saying:
>
> "When he ascended on high, he led as a prisoner captivity itself, and he gave gifts to the people."
>
> Now, this ascension—what does it mean if not also that he descended into the lower regions of the earth? The one who came down is the same one who went up into the highest of all heavens to fill all things with himself. And he gave these gifts: that there would be the apostles, the prophets, the gospel preachers, and shepherds and teachers, to equip the saints for the work of ministry service, with the goal of building up the social body of Christ, mov-

---

19. *makrothymia*. The language of patience here is not resignation or stoic indifference; quite the opposite, *makros* ("great") + *thymos* ("feeling"), akin to "with a big heart."
20. *henotēta*. Lit., "oneness" (from *hen*, "one").
21. *syndesmos*. Using the language "bonded like a chain," I wanted to capture the relationship between *syndesmos* ("bond") here and the term *desmios* ("prisoner," i.e., "chained/bound person"); note the same root *desm-*. I think Paul was making a wordplay connection between his chains and the bonds of unity.

ing toward the final vision that all become one by faith and knowledge of the Son of God, like a fully mature man,[22] measuring up to the full maturity of Christ. This maturity is important, so that we are no longer like immature children, tossed around like a boat in turbulent waters, and carried away by every strong wind of clever teachings of mortals—what seems clever can be a deceitful scheme. But as for us,[23] let us share the truth in love and let us grow up to become like him in every way, he who is the head, Christ. By him the whole body is interconnected and held together, every supportive ligament, every single part at work, supporting the growth of the body forming together its own building of a dwelling place through love.

Many scholars rightly see a move on Paul's part from mostly indicative expression in chapters 1–3 to more sustained and direct imperative discourse starting in chapter 4. The goal for Paul is that each believer's calling is to contribute humbly and passionately to the building up of the whole community through individualized gifts and strengths. These gifts were not meant to foster pride or jealousy but the opposite, to promote oneness, each unique individual making their special contribution to the vitality of the whole. This requires love (see vv. 2, 15–16), which is especially manifest in gentleness, deference, and patience (4:1–2).

This is the real test of maturity—not a theology quiz but the hard work of striving together graciously for the common good, setting aside wounded pride and petty point-scoring to build something together where the whole is greater than the sum of the parts. Sin divides and destroys; Christ knits together and fortifies.

Personally Transformed into the Likeness of Christ (4:17–24)

So then, I have this message and testimony in the Lord: do not live your lives any longer as the gentiles live, who lack clear purpose and direction[24]

---

22. *andra*. Here Paul uses "man" (versus *anthrōpos*, which is more generic, referring to "human"), perhaps imagining the church growing up to be like Christ (who became incarnate as a man).

23. My phrase "But as for us" has been added to break up a very long Greek sentence (vv. 11–16 is one sentence).

24. *mataiotēti*. This refers to emptiness (of mind, here), which I paraphrased as lack of purpose and direction.

in their minds; their thinking is clouded in darkness, as they are alienated from God's vitality, because of their ignorance and because of their hard hearts. In a state of numbness, they gave themselves over to lustful desires, practicing every kind of impure and hedonistic vice.

As for you, you were taught the opposite in relationship to Christ. If indeed you did hear about him and were taught real truth about Jesus. You were taught to cast away your former values and lifestyle, that old person who was corrupted by deluded desires, and to be made new by the Spirit who transforms your minds. And you were taught to put on the new person created to be like God by living truly righteous and holy lives.

This section runs parallel to similar before-and-after statements Paul made in chapter 2. Here the focus is on cognitive and moral transformation, which leads to new behaviors. Paul refers to the "old person" (*ton palaion anthrōpon*) within who is corrupted and affects the mental operation and lifestyle of the sinner. The Spirit transforms through the gospel of Jesus Christ by conforming them to the "new person" (*ton kainon anthrōpon*) within, resetting the internal operations of the heart and mind and producing healthy behaviors.

Walking in Love: From Harm to Kindness (4:25–32)

Therefore, throw away whatever is false and proclaim the truth, each person to their neighbor, because we belong to one another. It's okay to be angry,[25] but don't sin in your anger. Don't let the sun go down while you are still angry. Don't open space for the devil.

Takers[26] should give up taking; instead they must get to work doing good through honest labor.[27] Then they can share with anyone in need.

Don't let hurtful words leave your mouth—only whatever is good and constructive. Make it a goal to shower grace on those who hear your words.

---

25. *orgizesthe*. This imperative isn't *commanding* anger but assuming it.
26. *ho kleptōn*. While this is conventionally translated "thief," it is unlikely Paul means this in a criminal sense. The end of v. 28 emphasizes the opposite as giving (*metadidōmi*), thus my rendering of *kleptōn* as "takers."
27. *ergazomenos tais idiais chersin*. This is an idiomatic expression indicating honest and productive labor.

> And don't break the heart of God's Holy Spirit, by whom you were sealed for the day of redemption. If there is any resentment, anger, rage, temptation to shout, or verbal abuse, put all these things away—any hint of wrongdoing. Instead, be kind to one another, tenderhearted, generous with forgiveness[28] with one another, just as also God was generous with forgiveness toward you in Christ.

You would have to go all the way back to Ephesians 4:2 for the last time Paul mentioned *agapē*, and this passage (4:25–32) does not contain love language explicitly at all, and yet that is clearly the subject matter, specifically what the attitudes and actions of love look like within the Christian community: the dos and don'ts of loving your neighbor. This is reinforced by the beginning of chapter 5 (5:1–2), which in fact is a bridging text looking back to 4:25–32 and ahead to 5:3–20.

> So then, imitate the ways of God, as beloved children, and live your lives with love, just as Christ loved us and gave his own life up for your benefit. (Eph 5:1–2)

Theologians have long discussed Paul's call to imitate God, here focused on the character and lifestyle of God demonstrated in the loving attitude and self-offering of Jesus Christ. This is the model for Christian behavior. When it comes to the details of 4:25–32, I am struck by the gritty realism of Paul's advice. Members of the community will not always see things eye to eye and will sometimes be annoyed and offended by one another. Paul doesn't imagine a church without problems. He presumes they are a normal group of people who have natural disagreements and offenses but who are motivated by the gospel to treat one another fairly and to show patience, forbearance, and kindness to preserve the whole.

This passage climaxes with the phrase *charizomenoi heautois* ("generous with forgiveness with one another")—the verb *charizomai* verbalizing the key noun *charis* (grace) used frequently through Ephesians. Believers should be marked by grace in their community—a generosity of spirit in disagree-

---

28. *charizomai*. There are several Greek words for forgiveness (e.g., *aphesis*); this one is built on the root term *charis* (grace).

ment—"just as also God was generous with forgiveness toward you in Christ." There is an implied question here: *Who are you to harbor resentment toward one another when God forgave you and blessed you through Christ? Are you greater than God?*

The Resurrection Lifestyle (5:1–14)

So then, imitate the ways[29] of God, as beloved children, and live your lives with love, just as Christ loved us and gave his own life up for your benefit as an offering and sacrifice to God, a fragrant smell. As for any kind of sexual immorality, impurity, or lust, there shouldn't be a hint of it,[30] as you belong to the holy people. And the same goes for shameful conduct and foolish and crude conversation: these things have no place among you. Instead, be full of thanksgiving. Be certain of this, that any sexually immoral person, or anyone impure or driven by lust, who is also a worshiper of false gods, will not have an inheritance in the kingdom of Christ and of God.

Be careful not to let anyone trick you with deceptive and false arguments. For this very reason the condemnation of God is coming on the sons of disobedience. Don't become partners with them. Remember, back then you were darkness, but now you are light in the Lord. And so live your lives as children of light. And this light produces all kinds of good behavior as well as righteousness and truth, as you discern what is pleasing to the Lord. And you ought to refuse participating in any sort of meaningless activities that represent darkness; instead, expose that darkness. What these kinds of people do in secret is so shameful it shouldn't even be mentioned! Everything exposed to light becomes visible, and everything visible is in the light. Just as the saying goes:

"Rise, O sleeper, and get up from among the dead bodies, and Christ will shine on you."

The beginning of chapter 5 at the same time reinforces the messages of chapter 4 about personal and communal transformation and continues the same empha-

---

29. *mimētai tou theou*. The Greek simply has "imitate God," but the context clearly indicates a focus on love.

30. *mēde onomazesthō*. Lit., "let it be not named."

sis on lifestyle, particularly what it means to be people of the resurrection. This is made especially clear in the 5:14 liturgical verse: "Rise, O sleeper, and get up from among the dead bodies, and Christ will shine on you." Normally, Paul quotes Old Testament texts, but here this is clearly some sort of early Christian exhortation and affirmation of new life in Christ. The sleeper awakes in Christ to live in a brand-new day and a brand-new way, the way of God in Christ.

Ephesians 5:1–2 grounds that resurrection lifestyle in imitation of God, specifically the loving self-offering of Christ. Living a lifestyle of love ("walking in love") is the key indicator of knowing Christ and walking in the Spirit according to Paul, with the incarnation, life, and self-given death of Christ as the ultimate model. Paul's statement that Christ "gave his own life up" is framed in terms of a sacrifice that is pleasing to God, not unlike what Paul writes to the Romans: "present your bodies as a living sacrifice, holy and acceptable to God" (Rom 12:1). What's done for one another in love is also done as an offering to God, knowing that living a loving and generous life is what pleases God. Christ's love and his self-given death are not exactly equated, but they are related. To sacrifice his own life shows the extremity of his love, holding nothing back, because of his respect for God the Father and his compassion for weak human creatures.

Practicing Spiritual Vigilance (5:15–21)

> Therefore, examine carefully how you live your lives, not as fools but with wisdom, making the most[31] of the present season, because much evil is going on these days. So don't be foolish, but consider carefully what the Lord's will might be. And don't get drunk on wine, carried away in wasteful living; instead, be filled with the Spirit, uttering among yourselves psalms, hymns, and Spirit-inspired songs, singing and worshiping in hymns to the Lord with all your heart. In this, you ought to always be giving thanks to our God and Father for everything, praying in the name of our Lord Jesus Christ, as you defer to one another in reverence of Christ.

This section offers a brief warning not to be flippant and careless, because evil lurks everywhere and alertness is necessary. There is no time for frivolity; life

---

31. *exagorazomenoi ton kairon.* Lit., "buying back the season."

must be lived with intentionality, awareness, and proactive investment in the things of the Spirit. This sobriety is not meant to be somber; joy, thanksgiving, and jubilant worship are still important. But Paul wants the Ephesians to take seriously the urgency of the moment; every second counts for realizing the gospel's vision of Spirit-filled community.

When it comes to 5:21 ("as you defer to one another in reverence of Christ"), it is difficult to know whether this belongs more with what follows (the household community [5:22–33]) or with the material in this section (5:15–20). I have opted for the latter in terms of grammar, though it certainly sets the tone for what is to come in the letter. On the topic of spiritual vigilance, Paul wants the Ephesians to live in joyful worship and thanksgiving, which flows into generous communal life. And that means deference, each person to the other and vice versa.

Now, in my translation of *hypotassō*, I have opted not to render this "submit," though many English translations use this word. Paul is not really talking about a particular action, at least not in this verse. He is pointing to an attitude of humility and grace that puts the needs of the other person first and prioritizes the concerns of the other over focusing only on oneself. "Submitting to one another" makes it sound like no one is allowed to or supposed to lead. That is not Paul's point. It is about *love*. In contrast, a Romanized community creates a strict pecking order and tiers of power based on status and privilege. But a *Christian* community seeks blessing and benefit for all as equally as possible; and the leaders are not meant to bask in the spotlight but be quick to serve and foster the health of the community. This lifestyle statement about deference leads into his household commands.

Wives and Husbands (5:22–33)

> Wives, defer to your own husbands as you respect the Lord, because the husband is the head of the wife, just as Christ is the head of the church, just like a head looks after the body.[32] But as the church defers to Christ, so likewise wives ought to show respect for their husbands completely.

---

32. *autos sōtēr tou sōmatos*. Lit., "himself savior of the body." "Savior" here refers to giving life-sustaining protection and care.

Ephesians and Paul's Theology of Love

> Husbands, love your wives, as also Christ loved the church and gave himself for her, to make her holy, washing her with the water of preaching. The goal is to present to himself a radiantly glorious church, free of any spot, wrinkle, or flaw—instead, as holy and faultless. So husbands should love their own wives as they care for their own bodies. The husband who loves his own wife is also taking care of himself. After all, no one hates their own body. They nourish and care for it. And that is how it is with Christ and the church, as we are members of his body. "For this reason, a man leaves his father and mother and is bonded together with his wife, and so the two will become one flesh." There is a powerful mystery in this: I dare to discern and speak about the relationship between Christ and the church. Nevertheless, it is clear that each husband among you should take this as a model for how to love your wife as you naturally care for yourself, and likewise the wife knows her responsibility, that is, to respect her husband.

It is unclear why Paul transitions into extensive discussion of household relationships, besides the fact that these are the basic building blocks of society. Using a Greco-Roman household economy political structure, Paul addresses key relationship pairs in the family, beginning with wives and husbands (presuming here that all parties are believers in Christ). Wives are meant to respect and "defer to" their husbands. There is nothing here about women being less intelligent or needing to be disciplined or put in their place. Wives, in this patriarchal context, are meant to respectfully honor their husband's role as paterfamilias, the legal head of the household. Paul conceives of this like Christ's relationship to the church, not in terms of his absolute lordship but in terms of the role Christ plays in taking care of the church. Paul was not telling wives that they must always obey every command of the husband. Rather, submission (or my preferred term here "deference") is about allowing the family organization, as they received it from culture, to stay in place but to infuse it with the humility and grace of Christ.[33]

---

33. The academic scholarship on the household codes is too dense and complex to summarize here; I encourage interested readers to look at Lynn H. Cohick, *The Letter to the Ephesians*, NICNT (Grand Rapids: Eerdmans, 2020); and Nijay K. Gupta, *Tell Her Story: How Women Led, Taught, and Ministered in the Early Church* (Downers Grove, IL: InterVarsity Press, 2023).

CHAPTER 10

As for husbands, there is nothing here about firm-handed leadership or spiritual authority, and certainly nothing about control or discipline. The key command is *love* (*agapaō*; 5:25, 28). And to repeat what Paul said in 5:1–2, the expression of that love is self-giving to bless and care for the wife. The husband's role is meant to make her shine. Husbands should care for their wives like they care for their own bodies, invested in their wives' well-being as their own. Paul is probably imagining things we naturally do for our own well-being like eating, sleep, exercise, and going to the doctor. We humans naturally look after ourselves as a matter of instinct. Paul wanted men to treat their wives as extensions of themselves. Just as you wouldn't want to hurt yourself but rather strengthen yourself, so men should not hurt their wives but strengthen them. Again, the focus is on service, protection, and gentle cultivation. There is no hint here of domination or coercion. The husband bears responsibility for loving his wife, protecting her, and enriching her.

Children, Fathers, Slaves, and Masters (6:1–9)

> Children, obey your parents; this is the right thing for you to do. "Honor your father and mother"; this is the first commandment with a promise attached: "so you will be blessed and you will have a long life in the land."
>
> Fathers, don't provoke your children. Instead, help them grow up healthy through training and discipline guided by the Lord.
>
> Slaves, obey your earthly masters with fear and trembling; do so with true sincerity from the heart, as if serving Christ. Don't behave just for the optics, as a flatterer, but behave as slaves of Christ, as if carrying out the very will of God from your heart. Serve your master with a positive attitude;[34] do it for the Lord, not mere mortals, and know that whenever anyone—truly anyone[35]—does something good, it will be rewarded by the Lord, whether done by a slave or a free person.
>
> Now, you masters, practice the same good behavior toward your slaves: be very hesitant to threaten punishment. Just remember that you share in common with your slaves a Master in the heavens, and he won't treat you differently than he does them.

---

34. *met' eunoias*. Lit., "with goodwill."
35. *hekastos*. Paul's language is precise here; he emphasizes that anyone can be recognized by the Lord for their righteous behavior.

While Paul spends the most time on the relationship between husbands and wives, he also briefly addresses other household dynamics. The mention of children here does not *only* assume young children but could be adult children who live with their parents (which wasn't unusual at that time). Honoring one's parents, as Scripture teaches (Exod 20:12; Deut 5:16), is not absolute submission but respect and deference, recognizing the natural blessing of learning from an older generation. Fathers are also called to gentleness toward their children, with the wider aim of helping them to mature.

When it comes to slaves, Paul doesn't encourage sheer duty and blind obedience, but astonishingly he fixates on the condition of their hearts—genuine partnership with masters. Paul did not view the institution of slavery as evil, as much as we wish he did. He imagined that Christian slaves and Christian masters could operate in harmony toward the wise and fruitful operation of the home. The hope of these slaves is that *the Lord* would see their honest and good work and reward them, regardless of whether their human lord paid them any mind. I don't think Paul was trying to affirm slavery here as much as give a positive outlook to the many slaves who worked in difficult conditions and had little hope.

As for masters, Paul drives home the point that God will judge masters and slaves the same. That is a very different way of looking at the world compared to a Romanized social economics, where masters had absolute power and ultimate worth and slaves had nothing and meant nothing in Rome's eyes. Paul asserts firmly that God does not acknowledge social privilege, status, or titles. Masters carry a responsibility to treat their slaves kindly. Paul did not extend to masters the same kind of blank check Roman society often did that permitted harsh mistreatment of slaves.

It's important to keep in mind the bigger picture Paul has in mind when it comes to believers living a lifestyle of imitating God. It's all about *love*—respect, gentleness, kindness, deference, authenticity, and genuineness, and each one operating for the good of all and not just for oneself.

A Final Call to Stand Strong (6:10–20)

> Finally, be strong in the Lord and in the power of his might. Put on the armor of God so you can stand strong against the devil's strategy. The battle is not one of flesh and blood but against the rulers, authorities, cosmic powers of this dark age, against evil spirits in the heavenly realm. So equip

CHAPTER 10

yourselves with the armor of God to stand your ground on that evil day, so that, after it's all over, you are still standing strong. So stand at attention, gird up your loins with the belt of truth, put on the breastplate of righteousness, be ready by fastening up your sandals with the gospel message of peace. In addition to all of this, hold up the shield of faith. This shield will extinguish the flaming arrows of the evil one. Grab the helmet of salvation, and the sword of the Spirit, which is the Word of God.

And pray through the Spirit in every situation, uttering all kinds of prayers and petitions. Stay alert and don't ever give up as you pray for all the holy people. And pray for me, that a special message would be given to me whenever I open my mouth, so I can reveal the secret of the gospel boldly and powerfully. For this very mission I serve as an ambassador in prison shackles. I want to be bold in my preaching, as the gospel requires.

Paul ends the main section of his letter with a final appeal to stand strong, to stay in the fight, like the words of a dying general to his troops. Regardless of whether Paul thinks he might be in his last days, this passage expresses his ultimate hopes for the Ephesians. There are invisible powers at work, vying for control over their destinies. But the people of Christ are not powerless. They have potent weapons at their disposal in the forms of truth, righteousness, faith, and peace. And in an incredible moment of vulnerability and humility, Paul asks for prayers for himself, that he would stay strong in his imprisonment.

Last Words (6:21–24)

Now, I know you are eager to know more about my situation, how I am doing, so Tychicus will update you on everything; he is my beloved brother and a faithful servant in the Lord. I sent him to you for this very purpose, to inform you about our circumstances and to encourage your hearts.

Peace be to the brothers and sisters there, and faithful love[36] from God the Father and the Lord Jesus Christ. May grace be with all those who have an undying love for our Lord Jesus Christ.

---

36. *Agapē meta pisteōs*. Lit., "love with faith."

As with most of his letters, Paul concludes with business matters and a final blessing and benediction. These short fare-thee-wells from Paul often contain key reminders of his main messages. Here, he wishes upon them peace, just as he explains Christ himself is peace (Eph 2:4), as well as "faithful love" from God. In addition, Paul pronounces a blessing on those who have an undying love for Jesus Christ. This dual dynamic of love from God and love for Christ is (1) a very Deuteronomic way of thinking about religion and (2) a reinforcement of Paul's preaching about the gospel and the life of the church. In Ephesians, Paul does not dwell on the gospel as mere rescue from damnation. Rather, the heart of the gospel is the heart of God, God's love through Jesus Christ. These are the thoughts passing through Paul's mind as he languishes in a dingy, stifling prison cell. His physical situation is constricting, but his theological imagination is expansive. *If God is for us, who dares to stand against us?* With that kind of boldness, he preaches the good news of God's love, and the love that can bring down walls of hostility and separation between mortals. Love is the heart of Paul's gospel, through and through. Ephesians makes this clearer than any other letter.

11

Summary, Synthesis, and Implications

> You called, shouted, broke through my deafness; you flared, blazed, banished my blindness; you lavished your fragrance, I gasped, and now I pant for you; I tasted you, and I hunger and thirst; you touched me, and I burned for your peace.
>
> —Augustine, *Confessions* 10.27

In this chapter, our goal is to draw the threads of the previous chapters together toward key concepts and ideas we have emphasized throughout this book related to Paul's understanding of and language of love.

We are back again to try to answer an impossible question: What is love? We dare not give an official, master definition; it simply won't fully capture the grandeur and breadth of Paul's conception. But there are other ways to move in the direction of explaining what love is. While it is difficult to give a complete definition, we can paint a vivid picture of love by looking at other terms, expressions, actions, and ideas that tend to appear alongside love in Paul's letters.

> *Expressions and actions of love*: gift-giving, service, graciousness, sacrifice (self-sacrifice) (Rom 5:8; 2 Cor 8:24; 12:15; Gal 2:20; Eph 5:1, 25; 2 Thess 2:16), concern (2 Cor 2:4; 5:14), care (Eph 4:2; Eph 5:28), longing/desire for (Phil 4:1), labor for (1 Thess 1:3), sharing (1 Thess 2:8), goodwill (Phil 1:12–16), doing good (Rom 8:28), supporting/building up (1 Cor 8:1), showing mercy (Eph 2:4)

Summary, Synthesis, and Implications

Opposites of love: hatred, violence (Rom 9:13; 13:10; 14:15b), causing trouble/distress (Rom 14:15a), envy, animosity (1 Cor 13:4)
Products of love: unity/oneness (Rom 9:25; Col 2:2; 3:14), agreement (1 Cor 4:17), intimacy (1 Cor 8:3)
Related attributes and virtues: gentleness (1 Cor 4:21), patience, kindness, peace (2 Cor 13:11; Eph 6:23), faithfulness (Gal 5:6; 5:22–23; 1 Thess 3:6)

Again, this is a lot of information, too much to pinpoint love in a few words, but it truly is one of those things where you know it when you see it. If I was pressed to formulate a rough definition of love, I would (with fear and trembling) say something like this: *Love is a human dynamic of wrapping one's self around another person or thing and deeply investing in it with the core of one's being.* It is, at bottom, an attachment, sometimes chosen, sometimes instinctual, sometimes warm with affection, sometimes deeply passionate, but love is the human propensity toward bonding. And love is so deeply woven into the human experience and sense of purpose and fulfillment that anything that can be said about Paul's theology is really about love. To admit that is to say something that most Pauline theologies don't really say. Too many big studies on Paul either leave love out of the picture completely or reserve the topic for a small section on "church life" or "ethics." Of course, love is important to church life *and* ethics, but even more, it is at the living heart of all of Paul's theology. Paul's gospel is first and foremost about God's love for the world, and especially for people, and then the transformative work of redeeming those people to love God, people, and world rightly.

We began this book with Augustine, and it turns out, he was onto something with his preoccupation with love as the focus of Scripture and theology. Augustine argued that humans will find fulfillment (in Latin, *requies*, "rest") only when they have found love with God, which then leads to healthy relationships with others and the world around them. This is a good place to quote one of the most famous confessions of Augustine:

> Late have I loved you, Beauty so ancient and so new, late have I loved you! Lo, you were within, but I outside, seeking there for you, and upon the shapely things you have made I rushed headlong, I, misshapen. You were with me, but I was not with you. They held me back far from you, those things which would have no being were they not in you. You called, shouted, broke through my deafness; you flared, blazed, banished my

CHAPTER 11

blindness; you lavished your fragrance, I gasped, and now I pant for you; I tasted you, and I hunger and thirst; you touched me, and I burned for your peace. (*Confessions* 10.27; trans. Maria Boulding)

A few brief things can be said about this beautiful reflection praising the love of God. First, Augustine implies here (and states elsewhere) that love is the truest and greatest expression of faith in God, which is why through pangs of regret he confesses, "late have I loved you." Second, what Augustine finds in the person of God is commitment, from the beginning, from within, seeking and holding onto Augustine, even in the face of his rejection or disinterest. Finally, what Augustine makes clear about God's love is that it is persistent, focused, and passionate: God called, shouted, blazed, lavished. God did not save Augustine with cold indifference, the way many (then and now) view God. Augustine's God is full of emotion, full of deep longing and desire, and full of love. Augustine experiences wonder at God's relentless pursuit. Paul expressed the same: "But God proves his love for us in that while we still were sinners Christ died for us" (Rom 5:8). And a mark of love is left that is meant to catch fire, to inspire believers to love God and others deeply and well.

As we dwell on Paul's conception of love here in view of some kind of synthesis, I think it may be helpful to articulate this in terms of a series of theses.

Thesis 1: *Love is not a coldhearted action; in biblical discourse, it often involves and assumes a combination of heart, will, and action.*

In modern popular sentiment, love may appear like a fickle emotion, often fleeting and mercurial. Biblical writers did sometimes warn about desires that come on strong and disappear fast, but often they talked about and commanded love, knowing that it is the essential driver of the person. The Shema demands love because God covenants with the whole people of Israel and the whole of each person.

Throughout history there has been an unfortunate bifurcation between heart (the so-called seat of emotion) and the mind (the so-called seat of ration and logic). Building on that, there is a strong impression that the heart misleads, and only the mind can be trusted to do what's right. But the biblical writers didn't always make that distinction. For example, on a number of occasions, it makes sense to translate *kardia* (the Greek word for heart) as "mind."

Summary, Synthesis, and Implications

> So make up your minds [*kardia*] not to prepare your defense in advance. (Luke 21:14)

> For though they knew God, they did not honor him as God or give thanks to him, but they became futile in their thinking [*dialogismos*], and their senseless minds [*asynetos kardia*] were darkened. (Rom 1:21)

> But if someone stands firm in his resolve, being under no necessity but having his own desire under control, and has determined in his own mind [*kardia*] to keep her as his fiancée, he will do well. (1 Cor 7:37)

> Indeed, to this very day whenever Moses is read, a veil lies over their minds [*kardia*]. (2 Cor 3:15)

> Each of you must give as you have made up your mind [*kardia*], not reluctantly or under compulsion, for God loves a cheerful giver. (2 Cor 9:7)

All of the above are from the NRSV translation, and others might opt for "heart" in some of these cases; it is difficult to discern how Luke and Paul here would differentiate matters of the heart from matters of the mind, if at all. But I think the NRSV has chosen "mind" wisely in these cases, because both *nous* (mind) and *kardia* (heart) are terms that these authors tend to use to reflect the core or inner being of the person, the anthropological "control room," if you will. And in some of these cases, rationality and logic are involved (e.g., Rom 1:21; 2 Cor 3:15).

Paul understood that love comes from deep within (Rom 2:15; 6:17), and the human will behave properly if the desires of the inner person are properly focused on God. Likewise, God's saving actions are not the work of a robotic, heartless deity who must make things right out of sheer duty or obligation. If there is one thing we know about God from the Bible, it is that God *feels, expresses, and acts on love and concern for creation.* This is a good opportunity to expand on the title of this book, *The Affections of Christ Jesus*, and why I chose this phrase to encapsulate Paul's theology.

One of the most transformative insights I gained while researching for this book was the notion that Paul believed that God has a heart (whatever unique metaphysical way that works), and that the gospel comes out of the compassion of God that lives within that heart. The environment in which I was trained for academic study often treated Paul's gospel first and foremost as a theological system or framework that reflected the transcendent nature of the triune God. What I am struck by now, though, is the deeply *emotional* nature of Paul's gospel, which focuses on the love of God in Jesus Christ.

This comes out remarkably in a brief statement Paul makes in the introduction of his Letter to the Philippians. After the salutation, the imprisoned apostle expresses his joy at the thought of these cherished believers; though they are separated by a long distance, their hearts belong to one another. They experience a special bond through unity of mission and purpose, and a history of friendship and partnership in the gospel. Paul follows this with these striking words: "For God is my witness, how I long for all of you with the compassion of Christ Jesus" (Phil 1:8). There are a number of interesting things about this gushing self-expression. Paul is very transparent with his love and desire to have fellowship with these beloved friends. This longing (*epipotheō*) is a deep desire, a yearning, a hunger for something, a soul's wish.[1] And Paul connects that with *splanchnois Christou Iēsou*—the compassions or affections of Christ Jesus. This gives us profound insight into the way Paul thought about his relationship with others, as somehow enriched by living affections of Christ. *Splanchnon* is a reference to the bowels or gut, what many ancients understood as the seat of the emotions and the center of one's passions. When you feel dread in the pit of your stomach, that is your *splanchnon*. We find this well illustrated in the book of Sirach.

> When one cherishes a son,
> one will bind up his wounds,
> and with every cry one's *insides* will be troubled. (Sir 30:7 NETS)

The word here for "insides" is *splanchna* (plural of *splanchnon*). Love here is associated with attachment that affects one's insides, the gut (which corresponds to what moderns often refer to as the heart).[2] We see this reinforced in the Greek text of 4 Maccabees: "Observe how complex is a mother's love

---

1. See David E. Fredrickson, *Eros and the Christ: Longing and Envy in Paul's Christology* (Minneapolis: Fortress, 2013).
2. In Paul's Letter to Philemon, he refers to Onesimus as *ta ema splanchna*, often translated as "my own heart" but literally "my guts" or "my entrails" (v. 12).

for her children, which draws everything toward an emotion felt in her *inmost parts*" (4 Macc 14:13 NRSV).

Again, "inmost parts" is a form of *splanchnon*. Her compassion-oriented emotions (*sympatheia*) belong in the gut; this is what is troubled when someone cherished is in trouble or need. Israel held to the belief that the prophesied good news would come from this part of God, God's will and desire to take care of a beleaguered people. In the Gospel of Luke, Zechariah announces a prophecy in blessing of what God was about to do in remembering his covenant, raising up a Savior, bringing deliverance from enemies, forgiving sins, all because of "the affections of the mercy of our God" (*dia splanchna eleous theou hēmōn*; Luke 1:78). Jews did not believe in a distant, apathetic deity who controlled their fate. God was very much driven by the gut, full of mercy, compassion, and affection.

As we come back to Philippians 1:8 with this semantic context in mind for *splanchnon*, what did Paul mean when he wrote that he desired after the Philippians with the *affections* of Christ Jesus? It could mean that Paul's love and concern for the Philippians was inspired by Christ's own love and compassion for the world. Another possibility is that Paul's feelings of affection and love were somehow wrapped up in the wider love of God given to the world in the affections of Christ. I lean toward this second interpretation. Christ's affections could be viewed as a great storehouse of love and compassion, and when believers participate in the death and life of Christ, they draw from this bottomless treasury of affection. Paul knew his compassion for the Philippians was fueled by the love of Christ that binds all believers together.

This is a salutary reminder that Paul's gospel is not merely a divine solution to a pesky problem we call sin. God sent Jesus Christ with good news for the whole world because of God's love for the world, and Jesus Christ himself is the embodiment of the compassion and affections of God. It can only stand to reason, then, that the church is called to live out this same love reciprocally with God and with one another, and furthermore focus love outward in mission toward the world.

> **Thesis 2:** *The good news of God's love is not new with the New Testament; Jewish Scripture and tradition place love from and for God at the heart of covenantal life.*

There is a stubbornly persistent and insidious popular misconception that Judaism is about law and works and Christianity is about grace and love. For those who subscribe to this myth, I have to believe they have never read either the Old Testament or the New Testament carefully, because love and law are found throughout the entire Bible, beginning to end. And what I have come to be convinced of is that Paul would have been raised to meditate regularly on the Shema and both know the love of the covenantal God and strive to love God with his whole being, as was expected of all Jews. Furthermore, we have seen that the Septuagint translators' choice to render "love" using the Greek terms *agapē* and *agapaō* made a lasting impact on Hellenistic Jewish discourse, and also the vocabulary and theology of the early Christians. This was not the only love term that was used in the Septuagint, but it came to be distinctive of covenantal love. It is no coincidence that this became Paul's favored word for love, and terminology that appears throughout his whole collection of writings.

Whatever Paul taught about love owes a massive debt to the Old Testament's foundational attention to love as the heart of piety and religion. Law is the means of showing love, not its enemy; at least, that appears to be the intent of the Jewish law. Any good thing can be distorted and made into something it ought not to be. Paul may have found fresh ways of talking about love, especially in view of the coming of Jesus Christ, but one can easily and clearly detect a thread connecting Paul's love language to Deuteronomy and the expectation of trust, intimacy, and deep affection between God and his people.

> **Thesis 3:** *Jesus was remembered by the evangelists as a teacher of love of God and neighbor; and love of neighbor made a strong impact on the apostles, including Paul.*

This book is primarily about Paul, but when thinking about the key influences on Paul, I could not help but consider the teachings of Jesus. Now, there is a long-standing scholarly discussion and debate about whether, or to what degree, Paul knew the teachings of Jesus. I continue to be at a loss for why Paul (and the other New Testament letter writers, for that matter) did not quote from the words of Jesus very much. There are a few sayings here and there, certainly several allusions, but Jesus's life and death seemed to have been far more theologically important to Paul than the didactic words of Jesus. At least, that's the impression one gets from reading Romans or 1 Corinthians. And yet, twice Paul quotes the Scripture text "love your neighbor as yourself"

Summary, Synthesis, and Implications

(Gal 5:14; Rom 13:8–10; from Lev 19:18). Paul often quotes the Old Testament, so it is within the realm of possibility that he simply was inspired by this text, but given its importance in the Jesus tradition, one cannot help but think that love of neighbor caught on among early Christians precisely because of Jesus's emphasis on this in his teaching.

I think making this connection between Jesus and Paul is helpful for two reasons. First, there is a common sentiment today that Paul's concept of religion was nothing like that of Jesus. The latter preached the kingdom of God; the former preached justification by faith, so the stereotype goes. But scholars like James D. G. Dunn have made a strong case that there are some key similarities that often get downplayed or overlooked. That brings us to our second point. There is a high probability that Paul focused on love because Jesus focused on love. Now, there may have been a couple degrees of separation between them; after all, Paul was not a direct disciple of the earthly Jesus. So it could be that Jesus's teachings on love made its imprint on earliest Christian tradition, and *that* is where Paul got it when he came to faith in Christ. But even in that case, we can see a line of connection between Jesus's favoring of Leviticus 19:18 and Paul's.

Thesis 4: *Love is at the heart of Paul's theology conceived and gospel proclaimed, but he used a cluster of terms to talk about this love, including "grace," "faith," "compassion," "mercy," and "kindness."*

The term *agapē* became a kind of mascot word for early Christians, representing the essence of their gospel and religion. There were also other terms for love that were used by early Christians (including Paul), like *phileō*, and we can add to that affection language like *kardia* (heart) and *splanchnon* (gut/affection/compassion). But even beyond that, themes that pervade a writer's library go beyond just a few words; they tend to operate in terms of clusters. We have already mentioned this at the beginning of this chapter, but it is worth saying again; Paul's love language includes related terms of generosity, care, and desire. If we include *charis* (grace), *diakonos/diakonia* (service), *doulos/douleuō* (service as a slave), and *chrēstotēs* (kindness) to the wider picture, it is crystal clear that love was always on Paul's mind. And I have come to recognize Paul's language of faith (*pistis*) is intimately connected to his understanding of love. The Greek word *pistis* means more than mental belief. It was often used in relationship to commitment, loyalty, and friendship. And when Paul called for *pistis* in Christ, he was implicating love. This would have been Paul's version of affirming the commandment of the Shema to love God with one's whole self.

Thesis 5: *Whatever theory of atonement one finds most convincing for explaining Paul's theology, the foundation must be the love of the Father, Son, and Spirit.*

I get frustrated with most academic discussions of Paul's understanding of atonement or salvation, because they tend to be too mechanical or transactional, as if this is just business that God had to take care of. For example, sometimes justification-oriented discussions appeal to law court imagery with God as the judge. Or apocalyptic-focused conversations portray God at war with cosmic powers in a spiritual battle of epic proportions. I readily admit Paul uses these kinds of images to portray theological ideas throughout his letters, but what's often missing in the debate is the personal aspect of *why* God saves in the first place. The driving force is not simply to bring order, or justice, or peace; time and again Paul makes it clear that the motivation is the compassion and love of God that finds its fullest expression in the sending, ministry, sacrifice, death, resurrection, and reign of the Son of God, Jesus Christ.

Stating that is not meant just to magnify the fine print. It reshapes the whole discussion and underscores that pervasive importance of love as the heart of God and ethos of the way God made the world and how it should operate. That leads us to our final thesis.

Thesis 6: *Paul saw love as the distinguishing mark of a Christ-centered, Spirit-filled church, as the family of God.*

In a sense, this is probably the most obvious thesis statement we have proposed, and the one that needs the least defending. What makes a church a church is that it reflects the loving nature of God. It is a community of Spirit-filled believers, serving and caring for one another, and worshiping in love and unity with Christ at the center. Again, this should be clear from reading texts like 1 Corinthians 13:1–13, Romans 13:8–10, 2 Corinthians 8–9, and Ephesians. But the simple fact that Paul has to exhort his churches to grow in love and repudiate hostility, rivalry, envy, and bitterness means that it was a constant challenge. Michael Gorman puts it this way: "Love . . . is at the core of Paul's understanding of the experience of individuals and communities in Christ. It is the defining characteristic of the individual in relation to others and of the community as a whole; it is what 'counts' (Gal 5:6), as it puts faith, one's fundamental posture toward God, into action toward others."[3]

Paul wanted his churches to be full of truth and righteousness, wisdom and knowledge, self-control and self-discipline, but more than anything else, they best reflect the gospel as the body of Christ when they live in mutual love, care, and service. This is well demonstrated in Philippians 1:9–11: "And this is my prayer, that your love may overflow more and more with knowledge and full insight to help you determine what is best, so that in the day of Christ you may be pure and blameless, having produced the harvest of righteousness that comes through Jesus Christ for the glory and praise of God" (1:9–11). This was Paul's prayer for all of his churches. When churches kindle generous love (often amid complex differences and disagreements), they have the highest potential for fruitfulness.

The kind of love that Paul wanted to see in the church is a lot like a healthy family, full of care, unity, and mutuality. Jesus's generous sonship opens up a way for strangers and even enemies to come together as brothers and sisters who share Jesus's own status in the family of God. Families don't always agree; they bicker and fight, but in the end they are for one another, and that seems to be a point that Paul always returned to. The church is at its best when it is built up into a beautiful household of faith, strengthening bonds of unity as they share life, mission, work, worship, and burdens together. This is Paul's vision, his dream, his hope, the spiritual song of his apostolic heart: love as the center of a life of worship together.

---

3. Michael J. Gorman, *Cruciformity: Paul's Narrative Spirituality of the Cross*, 20th anniversary ed. (Grand Rapids: Eerdmans, 2021), 156.

Appendix: Early Christian References to Love of God, Love of Neighbor, or Both

GOSPELS: MATTHEW 19:19; 22:39; MARK 12:31, 33; LUKE 10:27[1]

Hiestermann observes that Leviticus 19:18 is the most often cited passage in the New Testament from the Pentateuch.[2]

Galatians	"For the whole law is summed up in a single commandment, 'You shall love your neighbor as yourself'" (5:14).
Romans	"The commandments . . . are summed up in this word, 'Love your neighbor as yourself'" (13:9).
James	"You do well if you really fulfill the royal law according to the scripture, 'You shall love your neighbor as yourself'" (2:8).
Didache	"Now this is the way of life: First, you shall love God, who made you. Second, you shall love your neighbor as yourself; but whatever you do not wish to happen to you, do not do to another" (1.2).[3]
Epistle of Barnabas	"You shall love the one who made you; you shall fear the one who created you; you shall glorify the one who redeemed you from death. You shall be sincere in heart and rich in spirit" (19.2). "You shall love your neighbor more than your own life" (19.5)

1. The Gospel of Thomas contains a saying, "Love your brother like your life" (25.1).
2. Heinz Hiestermann, *Paul and the Synoptic Jesus Tradition* (Leipzig: Evangelische Verlagsanstalt, 2017), 183.
3. Related teaching appears in Didache 2.1–7; especially important is 2.7: "You shall not hate any one; instead you shall reprove some, and pray for some, and some you shall love more than your own life."

APPENDIX

Origen	"However, now as he responds, he says, 'Love the Lord your God with your whole heart, your whole soul and your whole mind.' This is the greatest and the first commandment. His statement contains something necessary for us to know, since it is the greatest. The others—even to the least of them—are inferior to it."[4]
Cyril of Alexandria	"Therefore the first commandment teaches every kind of godliness. For to love God with the whole heart is the cause of every good. The second commandment includes the righteous acts we do toward other people. The first commandment prepares the way for the second and in turn is established by the second. For the person who is grounded in the love of God clearly also loves his neighbor in all things himself. The kind of person who fulfills these two commandments experiences all the commandments."[5]
John Chrysostom	"This is the summit of virtue, the foundation of all God's commandments: to the love of God is joined also love of neighbor. One who loves God does not neglect his brother, nor esteem money more than a limb of his own, but shows him great generosity, mindful of him who has said, 'Whoever did it to the least of my brothers did it to me.'"[6]
Bede	"Neither of these two kinds of love is expressed with full maturity without the other, because God cannot be loved apart from our neighbor, nor our neighbor apart from God."[7]
Ephrem the Syrian	"What is the greatest and first commandment of the law? He said to him, 'You shall love the Lord your God, and your neighbor as yourself.' . . . All this teaching is held high through the two commandments, as though by means of two wings, that is, through the love of God and of humanity."[8]

4. Manlio Simonetti, ed., *Matthew 14–28*, ACCS (Downers Grove, IL: InterVarsity Press, 2002), 157.

5. Simonetti, *Matthew 14–28*, 157–58.

6. Thomas C. Oden and Christopher A. Hall, eds., *Mark*, ACCS (Downers Grove, IL: InterVarsity Press, 2005), 174.

7. Oden and Hall, *Mark*, 174.

8. *Commentary on Tatian's Diatessaron* 16.23. See Arthur A. Just, ed., *Luke*, ACCS (Downers Grove, IL: InterVarsity Press, 2005), 178.

Bibliography

Aasgaard, Reidar. *My Beloved Brothers and Sisters! Christian Siblingship in Paul.* London: T&T Clark, 2004.

Ackerman, Susan. "The Personal Is Political: Covenantal and Affectionate Love in the Hebrew Bible." *Vetus Testamentum* 52 (2002): 437–58.

Akiyama, Kengo. *The Love of Neighbour in Ancient Judaism: The Reception of Leviticus 19:18 in the Hebrew Bible, the Septuagint, the Book of Jubilees, the Dead Sea Scrolls, and the New Testament.* Boston: Brill, 2018.

Anderson, Paul N. *The Fourth Gospel and the Quest for Jesus.* New York: T&T Clark, 2006.

Anderson, Paul N., Felix Just, and Tom Thatcher, eds. *Aspects of Historicity in the Fourth Gospel.* Vol. 2 of *John, Jesus, and History.* Atlanta: Society of Biblical Literature, 2009.

———. *Critical Appraisals of Critical Views.* Vol. 1 of *John, Jesus, and History.* Atlanta: Society of Biblical Literature, 2007.

Ando, Clifford. *The Matter of the Gods: Religion and the Roman Empire.* Los Angeles: University of California Press, 2008.

Andrews, C. F. *Mahatma Gandhi at Work: His Own Story Continued.* New York: Routledge, 1931.

Arnold, Bill T. "The Love-Fear Antimony in Deuteronomy 5–11." *Vetus Testamentum* 61 (2011): 551–69.

Ayres, Lewis. "Augustine on God as Love and Love as God." *Doctores Ecclesiae* 5 (1996): 470–87.

Barclay, John M. G. "ΚΟΙΝΩΝΙΑ and the Social Dynamics of the Letter to Philemon." Pages 151–69 in *La lettre à Philémon et l'ecclésiologie paulinienne.* Edited by D. Marguerat. Leuven: Peeters, 2016.

———. *Paul and the Gift.* Grand Rapids: Eerdmans, 2017.

BIBLIOGRAPHY

———. *Paul and the Power of Grace*. Grand Rapids: Eerdmans, 2020.

———. "2 Corinthians." Pages 1353–73 in *Eerdmans Commentary on the Bible*. Edited by James D. G. Dunn. Grand Rapids: Eerdmans, 2003.

Baron, Lori A. *The Shema in John's Gospel*. WUNT 2/574. Tübingen: Mohr Siebeck, 2022.

Barr, James. "Words for Love in Biblical Greek." Pages 3–18 in *The Glory of Christ in the New Testament*. Edited by N. T. Wright and L. D. Hurst. Oxford: Oxford University Press, 1990.

Barrett, Lisa Feldman. *How Emotions Are Made: The Secret Life of the Brain*. Boston: Mariner Books, 2018.

———. "Variety Is the Spice of Life: A Psychological Construction Approach to Understanding Variability in Emotion." *Cognitive Emotion* 23 (2009): 1284–1306.

Barth, Karl. *The Epistle to the Romans*. 6th ed. London: Oxford University Press, 1933.

Barth, Markus. *Colossians: A New Translation with Introduction and Commentary*. AB. New Haven: Yale University Press, 1994.

Barton, Stephen C. *Discipleship and Family Ties in Mark and Matthew*. SNTSMS. Cambridge: Cambridge University Press, 1994.

Bavel, Trasicius J. van. "The Double Face of Love in Augustine." *Augustinian Studies* 17 (1986): 169–81.

———. "Love." Pages 509–16 in *Augustine through the Ages*. Edited by A. D. Fitzgerald. Grand Rapids: Eerdmans, 1999.

Benko, Stephen. *Pagan Rome and Early Christians*. Bloomington: Indiana University Press, 1984.

Ben-Ze'ev, Aaron. *The Arc of Love: How Our Romantic Lives Change over Time*. Chicago: University of Chicago Press, 2019.

———. *The Subtlety of Emotions*. Boston: MIT Press, 2000.

Best, Ernest. *A Critical and Exegetical Commentary on Ephesians*. ICC. Edinburgh: T&T Clark, 1998.

Billings, Bradley S. "The *Apistoi* and *Idiotes* in 1 Corinthians 14:20–25: The Ancient Context and Missiological Meaning." *Expository Times* 127 (2016): 227–85.

Block, Daniel. *Deuteronomy*. NIVAC. Grand Rapids: Zondervan, 2012.

Bock, Darrell. *Luke 9:51–24:53*. BECNT. Grand Rapids: Baker, 1996.

Bray, Gerald, ed. *Romans*. ACCS. Downers Grove, IL: InterVarsity Press, 1998.

Brown, Jeannine K. *Philippians*. TNTC. Downers Grove, IL: IVP Academic, 2022.

Bruce, F. F. *The Book of the Acts*. NICNT. Grand Rapids: Eerdmans, 1988.

Bibliography

―――. *Paul: Apostle of the Heart Set Free*. Grand Rapids: Eerdmans, 1977.
Brueggemann, Walter. *Deuteronomy*. AOTC. Nashville: Abingdon, 2001.
―――. *Theology of the Old Testament*. Minneapolis: Fortress, 1997.
Brunn, Christopher, and Jonathan Edmonson, eds. *The Oxford Handbook of Roman Epigraphy*. Oxford: Oxford University Press, 2015.
Burns, J. Patout, Jr. *Romans: Interpreted by Early Christian Commentators*. Grand Rapids: Eerdmans, 2012.
Burridge, Richard A. *Imitating Jesus: An Inclusive Approach to New Testament Ethics*. Grand Rapids: Eerdmans, 2007.
Caird, George B. "Homocophony in the Septuagint." Pages 74–88 in *Jews, Greeks and Christians*. Leiden, Brill: 1976.
Campbell, Douglas A. *Pauline Dogmatics: The Triumph of God's Love*. Grand Rapids: Eerdmans, 2020.
Campbell, Will D. *Brother to a Dragonfly*. New York: Seabury, 1977.
Carroll, John T. *Luke: A Commentary*. NTL. Louisville: Westminster John Knox, 2012.
Carter, Warren. "Aquatic Display: Navigating the Roman Imperial World in Acts 27." *New Testament Studies* 62 (2016): 79–96.
Chandler, Christopher N. "'Love Your Neighbor as Yourself' (Lev. 19.18b) in Early Jewish-Christian Exegetical Practice and Missional Formulation." Pages 12–56 in *"What Does the Scripture Say?": Studies in the Function of Scripture in Early Judaism and Christianity*. Edited by Craig A. Evans and H. Daniel Zacharias. London: T&T Clark, 2013.
Christensen, Duane. *Deuteronomy 1–11*. WBC. Dallas: Word, 1991.
Ciampa, Roy E. "Composite Citations in 1–2 Corinthians and Galatians." Pages 159–89 in *Composite Citations in Antiquity*. Vol. 2. Edited by Sean A. Adams and Seth M. Ehorn. LNTS 593. London: T&T Clark, 2018.
Ciampa, Roy E., and Brian S Rosner. "1 Corinthians." Pages 696–752 in *Commentary on the New Testament Use of the Old Testament*. Edited by G. K. Beale and D. A. Carson. Grand Rapids: Baker, 2007.
Clements, Ronald E. "The Book of Deuteronomy." NIB 2:271–538.
Clifford, Richard J. *The Wisdom Literature: Interpreting Biblical Texts*. Nashville: Abingdon, 1998.
Cohick, Lynn H. *The Letter to the Ephesians*. NICNT. Grand Rapids: Eerdmans, 2020.
Collins, John J. "Love of Neighbor in Hellenistic-Era Judaism." *Studia Philonica Annual* 32 (2020): 97–111.
Collins, Raymond F. *2 Corinthians*. PCNT. Grand Rapids: Baker, 2013.

Craddock, Fred B. "The Poverty of Christ: An Investigation of II Corinthians 8:9." *Interpretation* 22 (1968): 158–70.

Craigie, Peter C. *The Book of Deuteronomy*. NICOT. Grand Rapids: Eerdmans, 1976.

Cranfield, Charles E. *A Critical and Exegetical Commentary on the Epistle to the Romans*. ICC. Edinburgh: T&T Clark, 1975.

Cross, Frank Moore. *From Epic to Canon*. Baltimore: Johns Hopkins University Press, 1998.

Das, A. Andrew. *Solving the Romans Debate*. Minneapolis: Fortress, 2007.

Davies, W. D., and Dale C. Allison. *Matthew 19–28*. ICC. Edinburgh: T&T Clark, 1997.

Denova, Rebecca I. *Greek and Roman Religions*. Hoboken, NJ: Wiley-Blackwell, 2019.

deSilva, David A. *The Letter to the Galatians*. NICNT. Grand Rapids: Eerdmans, 2018.

Downs, David J. *The Offering of the Gentiles: Paul's Collection for Jerusalem in Its Chronological, Cultural, and Cultic Contexts*. Grand Rapids: Eerdmans, 2016.

Driver, S. R. *A Critical and Exegetical Commentary on Deuteronomy*. 3rd ed. ICC. Edinburgh: T&T Clark, 1902.

Dunn, James D. G. *The Acts of the Apostles*. Grand Rapids: Eerdmans, 2016.

———. *The Epistles to the Colossians and to Philemon*. NIGTC. Grand Rapids: Eerdmans, 1996.

———. *The Epistle to the Galatians*. BNTC. Peabody, MA: Hendrickson, 1993.

———. *Jesus, Paul, and the Gospels*. Grand Rapids: Eerdmans, 2011.

———. *Romans 1–8*. WBC. Dallas: Word, 1988.

———. *The Theology of Paul the Apostle*. Grand Rapids: Eerdmans, 1998.

Eastman, Susan. "Christian Experience and Paul's Logic of Solidarity: The Spiral Structure of Romans 5–8." *Biblical Annals* 12 (2022): 233–53.

———. "Oneself in Another: Participation and the Spirit in Romans 8." Pages 103–25 in *"In Christ" in Paul: Explorations in Paul's Theology of Union and Participation*. Edited by Michael J. Thate, Kevin Vanhoozer, and Constantine R. Campbell. Tübingen: Mohr Siebeck, 2014.

———. *Recovering Paul's Mother Tongue: Language and Theology in Galatians*. 2nd ed. Eugene, OR: Cascade Books, 2021.

Eriksson, Anders. *Traditions as Rhetorical Proof: Pauline Argumentation in First Corinthians*. ConBNT. Stockholm: Almqvist & Wiksell, 1998.

Fee, Gordon D. *The First Epistle to the Corinthians*. NICNT. Grand Rapids: Eerdmans, 1987.

Bibliography

———. "Freedom and the Life of Obedience (Galatians 5:1–6:18)." *Review and Expositor* 91 (1994): 201–17.
———. *God's Empowering Presence*. Peabody, MA: Hendrickson, 1994.
Fitzmyer, Joseph. *First Corinthians*. AB. New Haven: Yale University Press, 2008.
———. *The Letter to Philemon: A New Translation with Introduction and Commentary*. AB. New Haven: Yale University Press, 2008.
Flemming, Dean. *Recovering the Full Mission of God: A Biblical Perspective on Being, Doing, and Telling*. Downers Grove, IL: IVP Academic, 2013.
———. *Why Mission?* Nashville: Abingdon, 2015.
Foster, Paul. "Who Wrote 2 Thessalonians? A Fresh Look at an Old Problem." *Journal for the Study of the New Testament* 35 (2012): 150–75.
Fotopoulos, John. "Paul's Curse of Corinthians: Restraining Rivals with Fear and Voces Mysticae (1 Cor 16:22)." *Novum Testamentum* 56 (2014): 275–309.
France, R. T. *The Gospel of Mark*. NIGTC. Grand Rapids: Eerdmans, 2002.
———. *The Gospel of Matthew*. NICNT. Grand Rapids: Eerdmans, 2007.
Fredrickson, David E. *Eros and the Christ: Longing and Envy in Paul's Christology*. Minneapolis: Fortress, 2013.
Furnish, Victor. *The Love Command in the New Testament*. Nashville: Abingdon, 1972.
———. *II Corinthians*. AB. New Haven: Yale University Press, 2021.
García Martínez, Florentino, and Eibert J. C. Tigchelaar. *The Dead Sea Scrolls Study Edition (Translations)*. Leiden: Brill, 1997–1998.
Garland, David E. *1 Corinthians*. BECNT. Grand Rapids: Baker, 2003.
———. *2 Corinthians*. NAC. Nashville: Broadman & Holman, 1999.
Gaventa, Beverly R. "Neither Height nor Depth: Discerning the Cosmology of Romans." *Scottish Journal of Theology* 64 (2011): 265–78.
———. *Romans*. NTL. Louisville: Westminster John Knox, 2024.
Gench, Frances Taylor. "Galatians 5:1, 13–25." *Interpretation* 46 (1992): 290–95.
Gendron, Maria, and Lisa Feldman Barrett. "Reconstructing the Past: A Century of Ideas about Emotion in Psychology." *Emotion Review* 1 (2009): 316–39.
Gloer, W. Hulitt. "Ambassadors of Reconciliation: Paul's Genius in Applying the Gospel in a Multi-cultural World; 2 Corinthians 5:14–21." *Review and Expositor* 104 (2007): 589–601.
Goldingay, John D. *Israel's Faith*. Vol. 2 of *Old Testament Theology*. Downers Grove, IL: IVP Academic, 2006.
Goodman, Martin. *Mission and Conversion*. Oxford: Clarendon, 1994.

Goodrich, John K. "According to the Riches of His Grace." Pages 105–28 in *The New Perspective on Grace: Paul and the Gospel after Paul and the Gift*. Edited by Edward Adams, Dorothea H. Bertschmann, Stephen J. Chester, Jonathan A. Linebaugh, and Todd D. Still. Grand Rapids: Eerdmans, 2023.

Gorman, Michael J. *Becoming the Gospel: Paul, Participation, Mission*. Grand Rapids: Eerdmans, 2015.

———. *Cruciformity: Paul's Narrative Spirituality of the Cross*. 20th anniversary ed. Grand Rapids: Eerdmans, 2021.

———. *The Death of the Messiah and the Birth of the New Covenant*. Eugene, OR: Cascade Books, 2014.

———. *Inhabiting the Cruciform God: Kenosis, Justification, and Theosis in Paul's Narrative Soteriology*. Grand Rapids: Eerdmans, 2009.

———. *Romans: A Theological and Pastoral Commentary*. Grand Rapids: Eerdmans, 2022.

Gottman, John Mordechai. *Principia Amoris: The New Science of Love*. New York: Routledge, 2015.

Grant, Frederick C. Review of *Agape and Eros*, by Anders Nygren. *Anglican Theological Review* 37 (1955): 67–73.

Grant, Robert M. *Paul in the Roman World: The Conflict at Corinth*. Louisville: Westminster John Knox, 2001.

Grieb, A. Katherine. *The Story of Romans: A Narrative Defense of God's Righteousness*. Louisville: Westminster John Knox, 2002.

Gupta, Nijay K. "The Babylonian Talmud and Mark 14:26–52: Abba, Father!" Pages 224–30 in *Reading Mark in Context: Jesus and Second Temple Judaism*. Edited by Ben C. Blackwell, John K. Goodrich, and Jason Maston. Grand Rapids: Zondervan, 2018.

———. *Galatians*. SGBC. Grand Rapids: Zondervan, 2023.

———. "Jesus and Paul." Pages 40–56 in *A Beginner's Guide to New Testament Studies*. Grand Rapids: Baker, 2020.

———. *Paul and the Language of Faith*. Grand Rapids: Eerdmans, 2020.

———. *Strange Religion: How the First Christians Were Weird, Dangerous, and Compelling*. Grand Rapids: Brazos, 2024.

———. *Tell Her Story: How Women Led, Taught, and Ministered in the Early Church*. Downers Grove, IL: InterVarsity Press, 2023.

———. *Worship That Makes Sense to Paul*. BZNW. New York: de Gruyter, 2010.

Guthrie, George. *2 Corinthians*. BECNT. Grand Rapids: Baker, 2015.

Bibliography

Hays, Richard B. "Christ Died for the Ungodly: Narrative Soteriology in Paul?" *Horizons in Biblical Theology* 26 (2004): 48–68.

———. *First Corinthians*. IBC. Louisville: Westminster John Knox, 1997.

———. *The Moral Vision of the New Testament: Community, Cross, New Creation*. San Francisco: HarperSanFrancisco, 1996.

Heim, David. "The Gospel in Seven Words." *Christian Century*. September 5, 2012. https://www.christiancentury.org/article/2012-08/gospel-seven-words.

Hengel, Martin. *Paul between Damascus and Antioch: The Unknown Years*. Louisville: Westminster John Knox, 1997.

———. *Studies in Early Christology*. Edinburgh: T&T Clark, 1995.

Henze, Matthias. *Mind the Gap: How the Jewish Writings between the Old and New Testament Help Us Understand Jesus*. Minneapolis: Fortress, 2017.

Hiestermann, Heinz. *Paul and the Synoptic Jesus Tradition*. Leipzig: Evangelische Verlagsanstalt, 2017.

Ho, Sin Pan. "Changes in the Centurion on Paul's Last Journey to Rome." *Biblical Theology Bulletin* 52 (2022): 99–110.

Hooker, Morna D. *From Adam to Christ*. Eugene, OR: Wipf & Stock, 2008.

hooks, bell. *All about Love: New Visions*. New York: HarperCollins, 2018.

Horrell, David G. *Solidarity and Difference: A Contemporary Reading of Paul's Ethics*. London: T&T Clark, 2016.

Hultgren, Arland. *Paul's Letter to the Romans: A Commentary*. Grand Rapids: Eerdmans, 2011.

Hurtado, Larry W. *Destroyer of the Gods: Early Christian Distinctiveness in the Roman World*. Waco, TX: Baylor University Press, 2017.

———. *God in the New Testament*. Nashville: Abingdon, 2010.

———. *One God, One Lord: Early Christian Devotion and Ancient Jewish Monotheism*. 2nd ed. London: T&T Clark, 1998.

Inselmann, Anke. "Emotions and Passions in the New Testament: Methodological Issues." *Biblical Interpretation* 24 (2016): 536–54.

Jervis, L. Ann. *Galatians*. NIBCNT. Peabody, MA: Hendrickson, 1999.

Jewett, Robert. *Romans*. Hermeneia. Minneapolis: Fortress, 2006.

Johnson, Luke Timothy. *The Acts of the Apostles*. SP 5. Collegeville, MN: Liturgical Press, 1992.

———. *Constructing Paul*. Grand Rapids: Eerdmans, 2020.

———. "Proselytism and Witness in Earliest Christianity." Pages 145–57 in *Sharing the Book*. Edited by John Witte Jr. and Richard C. Martin. Maryknoll, NY: Orbis Books, 1999.

———. *Reading Romans: A Literary and Theological Commentary*. Macon, GA: Smyth & Helwys, 2001.

Joly, R. *Le vocabulaire chrétien de l'amour est-il original?* Brussels: Brussels University Press, 1968.

Just, Arthur A., ed. *Luke*. ACCS. Downers Grove, IL: InterVarsity Press, 2005.

Kajava, Mika. "Religion in Rome and Italy." Pages 397–419 in *The Oxford Handbook of Roman Epigraphy*. Edited by Christopher Brunn and Jonathan Edmondson. Oxford: Oxford University Press, 2015.

Käsemann, Ernst. *Commentary on Romans*. Translated by Geoffrey W. Bromiley. Grand Rapids: Eerdmans, 1980.

Keener, Craig S. *Acts*. NCBC. Cambridge: Cambridge University Press, 2020.

———. *Acts: An Exegetical Commentary*. Vol. 3. Grand Rapids: Baker, 2014.

———. *Romans*. NCCS. Eugene, OR: Cascade Books, 2009.

Klassen, William. "'Love Your Enemies': Some Reflections on the Current Status of Research." Pages 1–31 in *The Love of Enemy and Nonretaliation in the New Testament*. Edited by W. M. Swartley. Louisville: Westminster John Knox, 1992.

———. "The Sacred Kiss in the New Testament: An Example of Social Boundary Lines." *New Testament Studies* 39 (1993): 132–35.

Koester, Craig R. *The Word of Life: A Theology of John's Gospel*. Grand Rapids: Eerdmans, 2008.

Konstan, David. *Friendship in the Classical World*. Cambridge: Cambridge University Press, 1997.

Lange, Armin, and Matthias Weigold. *Biblical Quotations and Allusions in Second Temple Jewish Literature*. JAJSup 5. Göttingen: Vandenhoeck & Ruprecht, 2011.

Lange, J. P. *The Gospel according to John*. Translated by P. Schaff. Bellingham, WA: Logos Bible Software, 2008.

Lapsley, Jaqueline. "Feeling Our Way: Love for God in Deuteronomy." *Catholic Biblical Quarterly* 65 (2003): 350–69.

LaSor, William Sanford, David Allan Hubbard, and Frederic William Bush. *Old Testament Survey*. Grand Rapids: Eerdmans, 1996.

Lazarus, Richard S. *Emotion and Adaptation*. Oxford: Oxford University Press, 1994.

Levenson, Jon D. *The Love of God*. Princeton: Princeton University Press, 2020.

Bibliography

Levering, Matthew. *Theology of Augustine*. Grand Rapids: Baker, 2013.
Lewis, C. S. *The Four Loves*. London: Bles, 1960.
Lincoln, Andrew T. *Ephesians*. WBC. Dallas: Word, 1990.
Louw, J. P., and Eugene A. Nida. *Greek-English Lexicon of the New Testament: Based on Semantic Domains*. New York: United Bible Societies, 1989.
Lundbom, Jack R. *Deuteronomy: A Commentary*. Grand Rapids: Eerdmans, 2013.
Marcus, Joel. *Mark: A New Translation with Introduction and Commentary*. AB. New York: Doubleday, 2000.
Martyn, J. Louis. *Galatians: A New Translation with Introduction and Commentary*. AB. New Haven: Yale University Press, 2008.
Matera, Frank. *God's Saving Grace: A Pauline Theology*. Grand Rapids: Eerdmans, 2012.
———. *New Testament Ethics*. Louisville: Westminster John Knox, 1996.
———. *Romans*. PCNT. Grand Rapids: Baker, 2010.
———. *II Corinthians*. NTL. Louisville: Westminster John Knox, 2013.
May, Simon. *Love: A History*. New Haven: Yale University Press, 2012.
———. *Love: A New Understanding of an Ancient Emotion*. Oxford: Oxford University Press, 2019.
McBride, S. Dean. "The Yoke of the Kingdom: An Exposition of Deuteronomy 6:4–5." *Interpretation* 27 (1973): 273–306.
McConville, Gordon. *Deuteronomy*. Apollos. Downers Grove, IL: IVP Academic, 2002.
McKnight, Scot. *Colossians*. NICNT. Grand Rapids: Eerdmans, 2018.
———. *Reading Romans Backwards: A Gospel of Peace in the Midst of Empire*. Waco, TX: Baylor University Press, 2019.
Meeks, Wayne. *The First Urban Christians: The Social World of the Apostle Paul*. 2nd ed. New Haven: Yale University Press, 2003.
Meier, John P. *A Marginal Jew*. Vol. 4, *Law and Love*. New Haven: Yale University Press, 2009.
Mesquita, Batja. *Between Us: How Cultures Create Emotions*. New York: Norton, 2022.
Metzger, Bruce M. *A Textual Commentary on the Greek New Testament*. 4th ed. New York: United Bible Societies, 1994.
Miller, Patrick. *Deuteronomy*. IBC. Louisville: Westminster John Knox, 2011.
———. *The Ten Commandments*. Louisville: Westminster John Knox, 2009.
Minns, Denis, and Paul Parvis. *Justin, Philosopher and Martyr: Apologies*. Oxford: Oxford University Press, 2009.
Mirguet, François. "What Is an 'Emotion' in the Hebrew Bible? An Experience

That Exceeds Most Contemporary Concepts." *Biblical Interpretation* 24 (2016): 442–65.

Moberly, R. W. L. *Old Testament Theology: Reading the Hebrew Bible as Christian Scripture.* Grand Rapids: Baker, 2015.

———. "Toward an Interpretation of the Shema." Pages 124–44 in *Theological Exegesis in Honor of Brevard S. Childs.* Edited by C. Seitz and K. Greene-McCreight. Grand Rapids: Eerdmans, 1999.

Moloney, Francis J. *Love in the Gospel of John: An Exegetical, Theological, and Literary Study.* Grand Rapids: Baker, 2013.

Moltmann, Jürgen. *Theology of Hope.* Minneapolis: Fortress, 1993.

Montefiore, Hugh. "Thou Shalt Love Thy Neighbor as Thyself." *Novum Testamentum* (1962): 157–70.

Moo, Douglas J. *The Epistle to the Romans.* NICNT. Grand Rapids: Eerdmans, 1996.

———. *A Theology of Paul and His Letters.* Grand Rapids: Zondervan Academic, 2021.

Moore, Agnes. *Demystifying Emotions: A Typology of Theories in Psychology and Philosophy.* Cambridge: Cambridge University Press, 2022.

Moran, William L. "The Ancient Near Eastern Background of the Love of God in Deuteronomy." *Catholic Biblical Quarterly* 25 (1963): 77–87.

Nygren, Anders. *Agape and Eros: A Study of the Christian Idea of Love.* Translated by A. G. Hebert and Philip S. Watson. London: SPCK, 1953.

O'Brien, Peter T. *Gospel and Mission in the Writings of Paul: An Exegetical and Theological Analysis.* Grand Rapids: Baker, 1995.

Oden, Thomas C., and Christopher A. Hall, eds. *Mark.* ACCS. Downers Grove, IL: InterVarsity Press, 2005.

Ogletree, Thomas W. "Love Command." Pages 490–94 in *Dictionary of Scripture and Ethics.* Edited by Joel B. Green. Grand Rapids: Baker, 2011.

Painter, John. "The Fruit of the Spirit Is Love." *Journal of Theology for Southern Africa* 5 (1973): 57–59.

Parsons, Mikeal. *Acts.* PCNT. Grand Rapids: Baker, 2008.

Peake, A. S. "The Quintessence of Paulinism." *Bulletin of the John Rylands University Library of Manchester* 4 (1917–1918): 285–311.

Perkins, Pheme. *First Corinthians.* PCNT. Grand Rapids: Baker, 2012.

———. *Love Commands in the New Testament.* New York: Paulist, 1982.

Peterson, Brian K. "Being the Church in Philippi." *Horizons in Biblical Theology* 30 (2008): 163–78.

Porter, Stanley. *The Paul of Acts.* Peabody, MA: Hendrickson, 2001.

Bibliography

Prothro, James B. *A Pauline Theology of Justification: Forgiveness, Friendship, and Life in Christ.* Eugene, OR: Cascade Books, 2023.

Riches, John. *Galatians through the Centuries.* New York: Wiley-Blackwell, 2012.

Rives, James B. "Religion in the Roman Provinces." Pages 420–44 in *The Oxford Handbook of Roman Epigraphy.* Edited by Christopher Brunn and Jonathan Edmondson. Oxford: Oxford University Press, 2015.

Rosner, Brian S. "Deuteronomy in 1 and 2 Corinthians." Pages 118–35 in *Deuteronomy in the New Testament: The New Testament and the Scriptures of Israel.* Edited by Maarten J. J. Menken and Steve Moyise. London: T&T Clark, 2007.

Sakenfeld, Katherine Doob. *The Meaning of* Hesed *in the Hebrew Bible.* Boston: Brill, 1978.

Sampley, J. Paul. *Walking in Love: Moral Progress and Spiritual Growth with the Apostle Paul.* Minneapolis: Fortress, 2016.

Scherer, Klaus R., Angela Schorr, and Tom Johnstone, eds. *Appraisal Processes in Emotion: Theory, Methods, Research.* Oxford: Oxford University Press, 2001.

Schreiner, Patrick. *Acts.* CSC. Nashville: Broadman & Holman, 2022.

Shore, Paul J. *Rest Lightly: An Anthology of Latin and Greek Tomb Inscriptions.* Wauconda, IL: Bolchazy-Carducci, 1997.

Silva, M., ed. *New International Dictionary of New Testament Theology and Exegesis.* Grand Rapids: Zondervan, 2014.

Simonetti, Manlio, ed. *Matthew 14–28.* ACCS. Downers Grove, IL: InterVarsity Press, 2002.

Smith, D. Moody. *The Theology of the Gospel of John.* NTTh. Cambridge: Cambridge University Press, 1995.

Smith, James K. A. *You Are What You Love: The Spiritual Power of Habit.* Grand Rapids: Brazos, 2016.

Spencer, F. Scott. "Getting a Feel for the 'Mixed' and 'Vexed' Study of Emotions in Biblical Literature." Pages 1–42 in *Mixed Feelings and Vexed Passions.* Edited by F. Scott Spencer. Atlanta: SBL Press, 2017.

Spicq, Ceslas. *Agape in the New Testament.* 3 vols. Saint Louis: Herder, 1966.

———. *Theological Lexicon of the New Testament.* Translated by James D. Ernest. Peabody, MA: Hendrickson, 1994.

Stegman, Thomas. *The Character of Jesus: The Linchpin to Paul's Argument in 2 Corinthians.* Rome: Pontifical Biblical Institute, 2005.

Still, Todd D., ed. *Jesus and Paul Reconnected: Fresh Pathways into an Old Debate.* Grand Rapids: Eerdmans, 2007.

Stuckenbruck, Loren T., and Wendy E. S. North, eds. *Early Jewish and Christian Monotheism*. London: T&T Clark, 2004.

Talbert, Charles H. *Matthew*. PCNT. Grand Rapids: Baker Academic, 2010.

Theodore of Mopsuestia. *Theodore of Mopsuestia: The Commentaries on the Minor Epistles of Paul*. Translated by Rowan A. Greer. Atlanta: Society of Biblical Literature, 2010.

Thiselton, Anthony C. *The First Epistle to the Corinthians*. NIGTC. Grand Rapids: Eerdmans, 2000.

———. *2 Corinthians: A Short Exegetical and Pastoral Commentary*. Eugene, OR: Cascade, 2019.

Thompson, James W. *Moral Formation according to Paul*. Grand Rapids: Eerdmans, 2011.

Thompson, Marianne Meye. *John*. NTL. Louisville: Westminster John Knox, 2015.

Thompson, Michael. *Clothed with Christ: The Example and Teaching of Jesus in Romans 12.1–15.13*. Sheffield: Sheffield Academic, 1991.

Thraede, Klaus. "Ursprünge und Formen des 'heiligen Kusses' im frühen Christentum." *Jahrbuch für Antike und Christentum* 11/12 (1967–1968): 124–80.

Thrall, Margaret E. *A Critical and Exegetical Commentary on the Second Epistle to the Corinthians*. 2 vols. ICC. Edinburgh: T&T Clark, 1994–2000.

Thurman, Howard. *Jesus and the Disinherited*. Richmond: Friends United Press, 1981.

Tigay, Jeffrey. *Deuteronomy*. JPS Torah Commentary. Philadelphia: Jewish Publication Society of America, 1989.

Trebilco, Paul. *Outsider Designations and Boundary Construction in the New Testament: Early Christian Communities and the Formation of Group Identity*. Cambridge: Cambridge University Press, 2017.

———. *Self-Designations and Group Identity in the New Testament*. Cambridge: Cambridge University Press, 2014.

Troftgruben, Troy M. "Slow Sailing in Acts: Suspense in the Final Sea Journey (Acts 27:1–28:15)." *Journal of Biblical Literature* 136 (2017): 949–68.

Villiers, Pieter G. R. de. "Transformation in Love in Paul's Letter to the Galatians." *Acta Theologica* (supplement) 19 (2014): 143–63.

Waaler, Erik. *The Shema and the First Commandment in First Corinthians: An Intertextual Approach to Paul's Re-reading of Deuteronomy*. WUNT 2/253. Tübingen: Mohr Siebeck, 2008.

Ware, James P. *Paul and the Mission of the Church: Philippians in Ancient Jewish Context*. Grand Rapids: Baker, 2011.

Bibliography

Weinfeld, Moshe. *Deuteronomy 1–11*. AB. New Haven: Yale University Press, 1991.
Wenham, David. *Paul, Follower of Jesus or Founder of Christianity?* Grand Rapids: Eerdmans, 1995.
Wilgaux, Jérôme. "Consubstantiality, Incest, and Kinship in Ancient Greece." Pages 217–30 in *A Companion to Families in the Greek and Roman Worlds*. Edited by Beryl Rawson. Malden, MA: Wiley-Blackwell, 2011.
Williams, H. H. Drake. *The Wisdom of the Wise: The Presence and Function of Scripture within 1 Cor. 1:18–3:23*. Leiden: Brill, 2001.
Williams, Margaret H. *Early Classical Authors on Jesus*. London: Bloomsbury, 2023.
Williams, Thomas. "Hermeneutics and Reading Scripture." Pages 311–30 in *The Cambridge Companion to Augustine*. Cambridge: Cambridge University Press, 2014.
Wischmeyer, Oda. *Love as* Agape: *The Early Christian Concept and Modern Discourse*. Waco, TX: Baylor University Press, 2021.
Witherington, Ben, III. *The Acts of the Apostles: A Socio-rhetorical Commentary*. Grand Rapids: Eerdmans, 1998.
Woltersdorff, Nicholas. *Justice: Rights and Wrongs*. Princeton: Princeton University Press, 2008.
Wright, N. T. *Into the Heart of Romans*. Grand Rapids: Zondervan, 2023.
———. "The Letter to the Romans." *NIB* 10:393–770.
———. "Monotheism, Christology, and Ethics: 1 Corinthians 8." Pages 120–36 in *The Climax of the Covenant*. London: T&T Clark, 1991.
———. *Paul and the Faithfulness of God*. 2 vols. Minneapolis: Fortress, 2016.
Yamauchi, Edwin M., and Marvin R. Wilson, eds. *Dictionary of Daily Life in Biblical and Post-biblical Antiquity*. Peabody, MA: Hendrickson, 2017.
Yinger, Kent L. *God and Human Wholeness: Perfection in Biblical and Theological Tradition*. Eugene, OR: Cascade Books, 2019.

Index of Authors

Ackerman, Susan, 44n16
Akiyama, Kengo, 82–84
Arnold, Bill T., 45–47

Barclay, John M. G., 119, 141, 163, 164
Barnes, M. Craig, 10
Barr, James, 69
Benko, Stephen, 109
Block, Daniel, 51
Brueggemann, Walter, 10
Burridge, Richard, 6

Campbell, Douglas A., 8–9
Charry, Ellen, 10
Ciardi, John, 13
Collins, Raymond, 181
Craddock, Fred B., 163

Driver, S. R., 48
Dunn, James D. G., 8, 76, 77, 117–18, 144, 213

Fee, Gordon D., 125, 135
Fitzmyer, Joseph, 144
Foster, Paul, xiin2
Furnish, Victor, 89, 93, 96, 180

Gandhi, Mahatma, 88
Garland, David, 162

Gaventa, Beverly, 10, 117n9, 165
Gench, Francis Taylor, 152
Goldingay, John, 54
Gorman, Michael J., 112, 114n7, 177, 215
Gottman, John, 22–24
Grant, Frederick, 35–36

Hays, Richard, 5, 6, 136, 157
Helm, David, 9
Hooker, Morna, 149
hooks, bell, 13, 20–22
Horrell, David, 6
Hurtado, Larry, 6, 7

Johnson, Luke Timothy, xii

Klassen, William, 89
Konstan, David, 63–64

Lange, Armin, 83
Lapsley, Jaqueline, 44, 47
Lazarus, Richard, 28–30
Levenson, Jon D., 42, 53
Lewis, C. S., 17–20
Louw, J. P., 33–34

Marcus, Joel, 82
Marty, Martin E., 10
Martyn, J. Louis, 142–43

INDEX OF AUTHORS

May, Simon, 15–17, 37
McBride, Dean, 42, 48, 51
McKibben, Bill, 10
McKnight, Scot, xii
Meier, John, 81, 93
Miller, Patrick, 104
Moberly, Walter, 41, 42, 50, 81
Moo, Douglas J., 8n16
Moran, William, 43–46

Nida, Eugene, 33–34
Nygren, Anders, 34–36

Painter, John, 150
Perkins, Pheme, 82, 88, 157–58
Peterson, Brian, 176

Sakenfeld, Katherine, 38–39
Sampley, Paul, 8
Schriver, Donald W., 10
Smith, Moody, 94

Thompson, Marianne Meye, 63
Thurman, Howard, 74
Tolstoy, Leo, 88

Villiers, Pieter de, 151

Ware, James, 178
Weigold, Matthias, 83
Wischmeyer, Oda, 184n2
Wright, N. T., xii, 8

Zaleski, Carol, 10

Index of Subjects

agape, agapaō, 33, 65–69, 98–100
ahavah, 40–41
authorship, xi–xiv

discipleship, 94–95

emotion theory, 24–30

faith, 142–46
freedom, 151–52, 153

Greco-Roman religion, 7–8, 10–11

hate, 146–48
healing, 171–73
hesed, 38–40
holiness, 141–42
Holy Spirit, 125–26
household code (Ephesians), 200–203

Jesus tradition and Paul, xiv–xv, 76–78, 212–13

law, 155–56
love
  affection, 18–19, 103–5
  charity, 20
  compassion, 162–64, 173–76
  desire, 57, 69–73, 103–5
  devotion, 59–61, 140–41, 142

double love command, 78–88
enemy love, 88–92, 118
familial, 46–47, 54–55, 105–8, 214–15
friendship, 19
generosity, 162–64
holy kiss, 108–10
reconciliation, 178–81, 191–92
romance, 19–20
sacrificial, 119–20
self-love, 21
unconditional, 15–16
unity, 156–57, 194–95
value affirmation, 57–59

Old Testament, Pauline use of the, xiv, 121–22, 154–55, 211–12

Pauline theology (general), 8–9
phileo, philia, philos, 33, 61–65, 100–103

Shema, 131–33
suffering, 117–18

trust, 22–24

zēlos, zēloō, 33

Index of Scripture and Other Ancient Sources

Old Testament

Genesis
25:28	40
26:5	49
27:14	40
29:18	40

Exodus
20:6	54
20:17	71
33:18	38
34:6–7	38
34:14	71

Leviticus
19:18	77, 82, 85, 91, 97, 173, 213, 217
19:18b	78n10, 82, 151, 153, 169

Numbers
14:18–19	38
25:11	71

Deuteronomy
1:30–31	47
5:1b–21	51
5:8–10	38
6–7	141
6:4	87
6:4–5	133
6:4–9	4, 31, 41, 42, 43, 80
6:5	131
6:7–9	51
6:10–15	41
7:7–8	47
7:8	41
7:9	39
8:5	47
10:12	45, 46
10:15	32
10:16	32
11:1	39, 45
11:13	45
11:13–15	49
11:22	45
14:1–2	47
26:17	49
30:6	32, 45
30:19–20	49
31:16–20	50
32:18	54

Joshua
1:8a	52
22:5	40, 130

Judges
5:31	40
16:4	40

1 Samuel
18:1	40
20:4	71

1 Kings
11:1	40

Nehemiah
1:4	41
1:5	130

Psalms
1:1–2	52
5:3	54
17:6	54
31:23	130
41:2 LXX	73
44	121–22
55:17	54
69:9 LXX	71

Index of Scripture and Other Ancient Sources

97:10	148	4:18	57	**Bel and the Dragon**	
105:13–14 LXX	72	6:1	54	37	130
118:97 LXX	57	6:6	130	**3 Maccabees**	
119	39	11:1–9	54	5:32	34
119:15	52	12:6	130		
119:48	52	13:13–14	60	**4 Maccabees**	
135	39	14:1–4	60	14:13	34, 210–11
145:18	133	**Amos**			
146:6–7	54	5:15	148	**PSEUDEPIGRAPHA**	

Proverbs

6:16–18	147	**Micah**		**Jubilees**	
7:18 LXX	70	3:2	58	7.20	84
8:17 LXX	62	6:8	58	**Psalms of Solomon**	
20:22	88	**Zechariah**		4.25	130
24:29	88	8:2	54	6.6	130
24:51 LXX	70			14.1	130

Song of Songs

6:9	42	**DEUTEROCANONICAL**		14.10	130
8:6–7	56, 60, 71, 123	**WORKS**		**Sibylline Oracles**	
		Tobit		5.360	130

Isaiah

		14:7	130	8.482	130
1:23	40	**Sirach**		**Testament of Benjamin**	
56:10	40	1:9	130	4.3	89
57:17	54	1:16	130	**Testament of Issachar**	
58:2	71	2:16	140	5.1–2	85
64:1–4	134–35	2:30	130		
65:17	135	6:37	52	**DEAD SEA SCROLLS**	

Jeremiah

		7:27–30	130		
14:10	40	17:26	147	**1QS**	
31:3	41	25:21	73	I, 9b–11a	89
33:6	54	27:17	34	**4Q269**	

Daniel

		29:5	109	4 II, 1–7	84
9:4	130	30:7	210	**CD**	

Hosea

		Susanna		IV, 14–21	83
3:1	40–41	35	73		

INDEX OF SCRIPTURE AND OTHER ANCIENT SOURCES

Ancient Jewish Writers

Josephus

Jewish Antiquities

1.259	14
2.66	65
4.208	70
5.558	70
6.30	64
7.66	64–65
7.107	65
7.111	64
8.304	65
12.393	65
13.45	65

Philo

On Drunkenness

159	70

Special Laws

2.63	85

New Testament

Matthew

5:43–48	90
5:45	92
6:24	30, 147
22:34–40	78, 86–87
22:37–39	1, 2
26:48	109

Mark

12:28–34	78–86
14:44	109

Luke

6:27–36	90
6:28	169–70
7:36–50	92
7:38	109
7:45	109
10:25–28	78, 87
10:29–37	87, 91–92
14:26	147
21:14	209
23:34	92
24:47	109

John

2:17	71
3:19	63
5:1	97
5:5	97
5:8	97
5:20	63, 101
8:28	97
8:35	98
8:39	98
10:11	63
11:3	63, 101
11:36	63
12:25	101
12:43	63
13:1–20	94
13:1–17:26	94
13:37	63
14–16	3
14:15	98
14:21	40
15:10	40
16:27	63, 101
19:12	101
20:21–23	109
21:15–17	40–41

Acts

14:8–18	171–72
19:11–20	172–73
27:1–28:10	173–76

Romans

1:7	100, 108
1:21	209
1:29	146
3:14	146
4:22–24	113
5:1–11	114–19
5:5	3, 125
5:6–10	139, 171
5:8	4, 8
5:10	128
8:8	140
8:17–18	116
8:28	139–40
8:29–30	139
8:31	128
8:31–39	119–24
8:38–39	4
9:3	127
10:2	71
12:1–2	140
12:9	147, 169
12:14	169
12:17	148, 170
13:8	4, 169
13:8–10	155–56
13:9	76–77, 97, 169
13:10	3, 169
14:15	97, 107, 149–50, 169
15:1	140
15:30	110

238

Index of Scripture and Other Ancient Sources

15:30–32	125	3:13	127	**Philippians**	
16:16	108	4:4–7	107	1:8	103, 210–11
1 Corinthians		5:1	151	1:9	5, 150, 169, 215
2:6–13	134	5:6	4. 142, 151, 215	2:1–2	126–27, 150
2:9	133–36	5:13	169	2:3–4	127
5:12	166	5:13–15	151, 153–55	2:6–11	127
6:11	140	5:14	3, 4, 77, 169	2:16	177
7:37	209	5:15	169	4:1	72, 100
8:1	169	5:17	72	4:4–5	170
8:1–13	131–32	5:22	169	**Colossians**	
12:3	137	5:24	72	1:3–4	143
12:31	159	6:2	154	3:8	146
13:1–13	156–62, 169	6:10	95, 108, 170	3:14	169
13:4	71	6:11	137	4:5	166
13:8	4	6:11–18	136	4:18	137
13:13	146	**Ephesians**		**1 Thessalonians**	
14:1	159, 169	1:1–14	186–87	1:2	144
14:13–16	167, 168	1:15–23	187–88	2:4	140
14:23–24	167, 168, 169	2:1–10	188–90	3:6	144
16:13	138	2:4–5	183	3:12	4
16:14	169	2:11–22	190–92	3:13	140
16:21–23	137	3:1–20	192–94	4:3–8	140–42
16:22	101, 110, 136–39	4:1–16	194–95	4:9–10	152
16:23	138	4:2	169	4:10–11	167
2 Corinthians		4:17–24	195–96	5:8	144
3:15	209	4:25–32	196–98	5:21–22	148
5:11–15	178–82	4:31	146	**2 Thessalonians**	
8–9	162–64	5:1–14	198–99	3:5	110
9:7	209	5:2	169	3:17	137
11:6	168	5:15–21	199–200	**Titus**	
13:11	110	5:22–33	200–202	3:15	110, 138
13:13	110	6:1–9	202–3	**Philemon**	
Galatians		6:10–20	203–4	4–5	143–44
1:8–9	137	6:21–24	204–5	15–16	100
2:19–20	4, 128, 150–51	6:23	110, 145	19	137
3:10	127	6:24	129		

INDEX OF SCRIPTURE AND OTHER ANCIENT SOURCES

James
1:14 — 72
2:23 — 61, 101
4:4 — 101

1 Peter
5:14 — 111

1 John
4:8 — 3
4:16 — 3
4:20–21 — 131
5:2 — 131
5:2–3 — 40

Jude
21 — 111

RABBINIC WORKS

b. Makkot
24a — 80

b. Shabbat
31a — 80

m. Avot
1:2 — 80

m. Berakhot
2:2 — 53

EARLY CHRISTIAN WRITINGS

Augustine

City of God
15.22 — 1

Confessions
9 — 2

10.27 — 206, 207–8
11.29.39 — 3–4

Enchiridion
31.117 — 1

Epistles
55.21.38 — 3

On Order
2.18.48 — 2

On the Spirit and the Letter — 3

1 Clement
49.5–6 — 161

Epistle of Diognetus
12.1 — 131

Ignatius

To the Magnesians
1.1 — 131

To Polycarp
5.1 — 131

Jerome

Commentary on Isaiah
64.4 — 135

Justin Martyr

First Apology
1.65 — 108

Tertullian

Apology
3 — 158–59

GRECO-ROMAN LITERATURE

Appian

Mithridates
47 — 67

Roman History
3.62 — 67

Aristotle

Magna moralia
1208 — 6

Nicomachean Ethics
1161b28–1162a2 — 106

Cato the Elder

On Agriculture
141 — 7

Cicero

On the Nature of the Gods — 10–11

Demosthenes

Against Aristocrates
23.56 — 64

Epictetus

Discourses
2.22.1 — 59
2.22.12 — 63
2.22.15–21 — 59
2.22.31a — 58–59
4.1.60 — 59

Index of Scripture and Other Ancient Sources

Plato

Lysis
215d — 63

Symposium
197d–e — 157

Plutarch

Advice to Bride and Groom
36 — 67

Alcibiades
4.4 — 67

Aristides
6.3–4 — 7, 67

Seneca

On Leisure
1.4 — 89

Sophocles

Ajax
678–79 — 89

Suetonius

Claudius
25.4 — 158

INSCRIPTIONS

CIL
1.2.1222 — 106